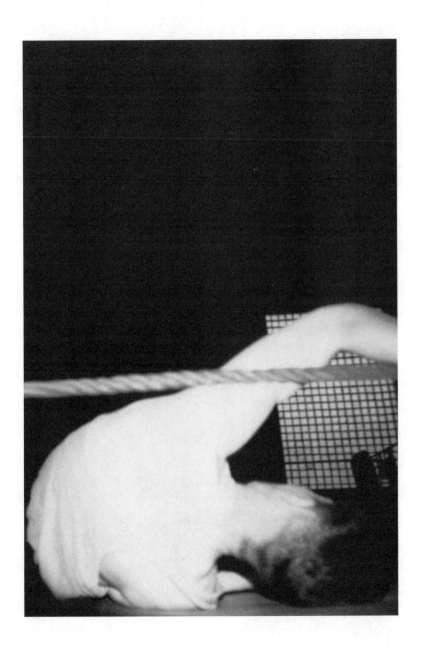

EVEN A DAUGHTER IS BETTER THAN NOTHING

MYKEL BOARD

GARRETT COUNTY PRESS

GARRETT COUNTY PRESS

www.gcpress.com

Garrett County Press Books are printed on acid free paper.

Garrett County Press thanks Robb Roemershauser for helping to get this book into print. You rock, Robb! Thanks also to Dade Darby.

GARRETT COUNTY PRESS FIRST EDITION 2005

DESIGNED BY KAREN OCKER

LIBRARY OF CONGRESS CATALOGING-IN-PUBLICATION DATA
Board, Mykel.
    Even a daughter is better than nothing / by Mykel Board.
            p. cm.
    ISBN 1-891053-00-0 (alk. paper)
    1. Board, Mykel—Travel—Mongolia. 2. Mongolia—Description and travel.
I. Title.
    DS798.2.B63 2005
    915.1'70459—dc22   2005000949

EVEN A DAUGHTER IS BETTER THAN NOTHING

INTRODUCTION

The formula: pick a weird title. About half way through the book, throw in a sentence with those words in it. The reader smiles, nods his head and thinks what an idiot the author is.

No formulas here. I'll tell you right up front, in the second paragraph. *Even a daughter is better than nothing* is a Mongolian proverb, something like "half a loaf is better than none."

As far as I can tell, it came from country living. The women stay inside to prepare meals, fetch water and make food. This activity doesn't change much no matter how big the family. On the other hand, the boys go out into the fields to tend the animals. The bigger the herd, the more boys are needed to tend it. If there aren't enough boys, then the girls have to help.

Things have changed since this expression came into the language. Today, Mongolian women rule the countryside. Since the fall of Communism, the government no longer buys the unsold meat. With no market, the need for huge flocks died. Big brother Russia sure wasn't buying. Newly impoverished men fled to the city, looking for work. Women took over the abandoned families, arranged *ger* life for survival, and took care of grandma, grandpa, and the flock of kids, grandkids, cousins, goats and sheep.

City men unused to the concrete jungle and its hostility, took to vodka and fighting. Women took to medicine and teaching. Today, half the doctors and most of the professors and teachers are women.

A fellow professor recently left her husband. They never bothered with an official divorce.

"Sometimes I wonder which is better," she said, "a Mongolian man, or nothing."

The expression "Even a daughter..." lives on, although the reality doesn't. That's not strange for Mongolia. Reality plays little part in the country. The title is an anachronism in the twenty first century. So is Mongolia.

◎ ◎ ◎

It's 1975. I've returned to New York from a moped tour of Eastern Europe. Right through Commieland, from the North Sea through Czechoslovakia. Ten months around the evil empire, where the red flag flies and people speak about Coca Cola only in whispers.

Back in America, the customs officer looks at the stamps in my passport. He squints at my long hair, beard and tattered knapsack.

"You have a nice trip?" he says.

"You sell any national secrets to the reds?" is the tone.

"I sure did," I answer.

Mom and dad wait at the other side of the gate. I run to them as I leave immigration.

"Our son the traveler," says Mom.

"Czechoslovakia?" says Dad, shaking his head, "It's like being in Outer Mongolia."

That's it! Outer Mongolia the farthest you can go. A place as distant and foreboding as the moon. Outer fuckin' Mongolia, yes! Yes! Prague is nothing compared to....Where? Name a city in Outer Mongolia? Yeah, right. Mongolia must be the furthest away you can go.

My fascination with the country begins then, at that moment. I read about Genghis Kahn, the commie takeover, the statue of Stalin in the center of the capital. I join the Mongolia Society, take books out of the library, call every travel agent in New York.

"Are you kidding?" says one, "They arrest foreigners in Mongolia. They peel your skin off. Did you know that?"

One company, Lindblad, has tours to the country. Two weeks for three thousand dollars—from Irkutsk in Siberia. You have to get to Siberia on your own. That wouldn't be so bad, except that it's group travel. All officially sanctioned by the party. You stay together and go where you're told.

No! No! No! I'm not a tourist. I want to live there. I want to see the *gers*, talk with the people, walk on Gobi sand, drink from the cleanest lake in the world. I want to lie next to a Mongol, wake up in the morning, gaze at the naked body next to me, and think Yes! Yes! Yes! I've drained my semen in the furthest place on earth. You don't do that on a two week tour.

As the years pass, the dream fades, but never dies. I keep my subscription to the *Mongolia Society Bulletin*. I go to grad school in linguistics and learn as much about the language as I can.

When I'm not thinking about Mongolia, I work as an English teacher, sing in *Artless*, a punk rock band, and write an opinion column for a San Francisco magazine. The column is called *You're Wrong*. I gain a reputation as "the bad guy." Conservatives call me a liberal. Liberals call me reactionary. I get "fascist!" "anarchist!" "male chauvinist!" "sexual terrorist!"

Once, in California, the audience attacks *Artless* with garbage. Trash cans empty. By the end of the show, I'm waist-deep in trash. It's there that I really see the joys of antagonizing. It's almost as much fun as nookie with attractive people of any gender.

Part of the reason for the hostility is my refusal to bend to linguistic faddism. In these days of hypersensitivity, accuracy in language has given way to fashion. Not for me. In this book, as in life, I use the traditional English word Oriental, rather than the fashionable word, *Asian*.

Indians and Semites are Asians, but they are not *Orientals*. When I write *Oriental*, that's what I mean. It often gets me in trouble. That's okay with me.

Writing, travel, bi-sex and trouble-making. That's my life until 1990, when I move to Japan.

◎ ◎ ◎

Tokyo 1990: Just out of the tub, I approach the TV with a rented porno video in one hand and guess what in the other. Flicking on the tube, broadcast TV shows an enormous public square. In the middle of the square is a statue of a man on a horse. His right arm is raised as if leading troops into battle.

The square itself is jam packed. Hundreds of young people, bundled up like Eskimos. They sit on the ground. Masses of them. Surrounded by cameramen, soldiers, official-looking Orientals. The camera zooms in for a close-up: a young man with a wide handsome face under his hooded parka. He waves at the photographer. Cords on his animal-skin mittens blow in the wind. As he speaks, his breath comes white from his mouth.

I know that place. It's *Sukhbaatar* Square. *Ulaanbaatar.* Outer fuckin' Mongolia!

Something's happening. Right there in the heart of the most obscure place on earth. Students, teens, workers. It's a hunger strike. A hunger strike in the capital of the world's second Communist country. My dreamland. Right there on Japanese TV. Yes! Yes! Yes!

Within a week the Japanese newspapers report the results. The Mongolian government gives in to the hunger strikers. They call elections, the first in Mongolia. Stalinism ends. The Mongolian People's Republic becomes MONGOLIA. They open the borders to foreigners.

1994: I've been back in New York for three years. I sing in my punk band, study Wing Chun kung fu, write sex, music, and travel articles, cause trouble, and finance it all by teaching English to Japanese businessmen.

At night, I waste my time on the computer, websurfing, emailing, usenetting. With all the stupid ads, hucksterism and banality on the net, I might as well be watching TV.

While scanning for information about bisexuality in Polynesia, I discover a group called soc.culture.mongolia. I check it out.

$10,000 IN CASH GUARANTEED

MAKE $50 AN HOUR, WHILE YOU SLEEP!

MONGOLIA FAQ

A FAQ, I find out, is Frequently Asked Questions, an information sheet in Q&A style. I read it, learning about the changes in Mongolia, the power shortages, the land roving. I learn about the hotels, the food rationing, life in the Gobi Desert. I post my own message.

"I'd like to teach English in Mongolia," I write. "Got any idea who I'd contact to find a job?"

Within days, the answers pour in.

"Are you kidding?" writes a college student in Indiana. "That's a place you study about, not one that you actually go to."

I tell him I'm not kidding.

A woman who was there with the Peace Corps writes: "Are you a Christian? There are tons there and the Mongols hate them. They're trying to destroy the culture."

I assure her that I'm a Jew and am not interested in converting anyone.

A professor from Germany sends me a message that changes my life.

"If you're serious about working in Mongolia, you can do it," he says. "You need to contact Dr. Alice Gaye at *The Joint American-Mongolian Business Advisory Group* (JAMBAG) in Maryland." He gives me an address in the northern suburbs of Washington. I write to her immediately.

In less than a week comes a reply:

"I can guarantee you a job in Mongolia," says the letter. "Just send me a resume, and $800."

The resume I have. The $800 I can invent.

I send the resume and a credit card cash advance check to the address. I know nothing about JAMBAG or Dr. Gaye except what came to me through the computer. Who cares? I'm this close to a twenty year dream. What's $800? Forty hours of teaching? I spend that on beer.

Time passes. The charge appears on my bill. I hear nothing from Maryland. Finally, I call.

"Mykel," says Dr. Gaye, "This is Mongolia you're talking about. They don't do things like other places."

"But three months?" I say, "that's hard to believe."

"Believe," she says, "believe."

A month later, I get a letter asking me for my passport and more money.

"Fees," says Dr. Gaye, "for a Mongolian visa and a Chinese transit visa." That means, of course, I got the job.

Yes! Yes! Yes! I'll be working for the School of Foreign Service at the National University in *Ulaanbaatar*. That's the most prestigious school in the country. They'll give me an apartment, electricity when they have it, and a $65 a month salary.

Immediately I start making Mongol contacts. I ask my friends, neighbors, Orientals on the street. A doctor-in-training introduces me to a Mongol med-school student. A friend who works in the local bookstore tells me some people from the Mongolian mission to the UN were in.

"Did you get any names or addresses?" I ask.

He shakes his head. "Mykel," he says, "they were scary. Real scary."

March 1994: Dr. Gaye tells me about a Mongolian-American group that meets annually in New Jersey. It's the Chinngis (you know him as Genghis) Khan ceremony, the largest American gathering of Mongols.

At the Rutgers University student center, things look normal. There's a front desk, a few Coke machines, some jocks trying to pick up girls. A hand-written sign, taped to the wall says MONGOLIAN CEREMONY, THIS WAY. An arrow points to a hallway. I follow it to a table with an *Admission $15* sign on it.

After paying, I enter an auditorium. In the rear section is a round white tent. A *ger*! My first one. Right there in New Jersey. I walk right up to it, reaching out my hand to touch it. It's rough and heavy. Large black cords hold the material to the frame. The top, trimmed in red, is folded back to make a skylight.

In one section of the white felt is a door, a yellow piece of wood, with a red chainlike decoration and red frame. I push against it. It opens. I walk in. Smash! My head bangs against the top of the frame. I'm five foot three. I've never hit my head on the top of a door. What an experience! It's heaven!

Inside the *ger* is a bed, a table, a few candles and a pitcher. The furniture is orange, decorated with intricate trim, mostly in the same chain-link design as the door.

Leaving the *ger*, I see that around it are ordinary tables and chairs. They're set up like at a bar mitzvah reception.

In the front of the room is a podium. Between the podium and the tables are another five dozen chairs. These are arranged in rows with a wide aisle in the middle. An altar stands to the right of the podium. The altar is a small easel surrounded by intertwining flowers. In front of that, a couple candles sit on a long piece of blue silk.

On the easel is a drawing I recognize from every picture book about Mongolia. It's Chinngis Khan, the object of this worship ceremony.

A short man with a mustache walks to the podium.

"Oh great Khan," he says, "we have gathered here to implore you to protect us as you protected the Mongols those many centuries ago. We thank you for giving us pride, for making us the greatest nation the earth has ever known. We worship you, knowing how long that worship has been forbidden."

From the back of the room comes the heavy beat of synchronized boot stomping. I turn to see four men marching up the wide center aisle. They're dressed in long kimono-like outfits: blue, red, burgundy, and black. Each wears a wide yellow sash around his waist. Each has his jaw set forward, and closed tight. All but the youngest has a mustache.

They carry long poles. From the top of each pole hang nine horse tails. At least that's what the program says they are.

When the group reaches the front, they turn and face the portrait. Solemn Mongolian words come from their lips. It's the first time I've heard the language, like Hebrew with a lisp. Beautiful.

After the speech, one of the men kneels in front of the portrait and lights a candle. Then, the four march out of the room.

Next comes a speech from the Mongolian Ambassador to the US, a square-shaped fellow dressed like a Japanese businessman.

"Mongolia has gone through difficult times," he says, "but we have survived."

The rest of the evening is speeches, a slide show about an orphanage, and dinner: choice of baked ham or lasagna. The only thing Mongolian about it is the tea, a salty white liquid more like soup than tea. Not bad. I wouldn't want to live on it, but I will.

I take my food to a table filled with Oriental teenagers.

"*Sain bain yy!*" I say.

"We don't speak Mongolian," says a thin boy, eating lasagna. "We're from New Jersey."

As it turns out, most people at the ceremony have never been to Mongolia. They're the children or grandchildren of Mongols. Of the rest, the majority are from Inner Mongolia, now part of China.

I tell the teens I'll be going to Mongolia myself.

"Good luck," says the boy who was eating lasagna. "I hear there's no food there."

◎　◎　◎

May 1995: I leave in August. My bags have been packed for a month. Dr. Gaye calls to say she'll be here in New York next week.

"We need to go over some final details," she tells me. "I want to make sure you know what you're in for."

"I've read the books," I tell her, "but if you want to meet, sure."

"The books don't tell you, Mykel." Her voice drops half an octave at my name. The last time I heard that tone was when my mother told me the family dog had died.

We meet in a deli around the corner from my kung fu gym. I'm there early.

Dr. Gaye is half an hour late. She's a large woman with a solicitous voice and a manner closer to a concerned mom than a doctor of Asian politics. She gives me a peck on the cheek.

"Thanks for waiting for me," she says, "I don't get this city. Northwest corner. South side of the street. East on 46th. West on 53rd. You have to be a boyscout to find your way around. I'll never figure it out."

She picks a salad from the refrigerator case, pays for it and rejoins me at the table.

"Well, it's only a couple months before the trip. You ready?" she asks.

"I've been ready for twenty years," I tell her.

She smiles sadly. "I hope it works out with you, Mykel. This university job might be my last chance as an agent there. Three strikes and we're both out. Did I tell you what happened to the others?"

"The others?"

She nods gravely.

"First there was Frank. He was a Ph.D. from Philadelphia. He'd traveled around the world and met his future wife in South America somewhere. He took the job to study Mongolian culture. He planned to stay two years. In three months, he was back."

"Why?" I ask.

"He couldn't take it. No heat in minus forty degree weather. No electricity for weeks. No hot water. Sometimes no water at all."

"What's the big deal?" I ask. "It's like camping."

Again, that sad smile crosses her face.

"Mykel," she says, "Mongolia is tough. Since 1990 people haven't had enough food to eat. For the first time in their lives, they have no jobs. They drink. And drink. Roaming bands of drunken, angry, unemployed thugs mug people at random. If they think you're Russian, they'll beat you up. Put you in the hospital."

I nod, swallowing hard.

"I heard about one case where they roamed with axes. Just going up to people's doors and hacking their way in. Smash! Smash! Smash!" she karate chops the table. "Once inside, they raped the Russian woman and stole the vodka."

"Rape and pillage," I say, "just like the old days."

Dr. Gaye is not amused.

"Even when it's not violent, it's unpleasant. Frank woke up every day to find a pool of vomit outside his apartment door. Just a local drunk....What am I saying? They're all local drunks."

"That can't be true," I say.

"No," she says, "you'll meet some of the greatest people in your life there. The Mongols are warm, friendly and more generous than anyone. But things are difficult now. And people are desperate."

"What happened to the OTHER American?" I ask. "You said I was going there with two strikes?"

"Ah Peter," she says, following the name with a wistful sigh. "I thought he was perfect. He was a quarter Mongolian, knew the language, and was prepared for everything. He wanted to be more Mongolian than the Mongols. He forgot he was supposed to be an American academic."

"How so?" I ask.

"Instead of making friends with other Americans...instead of keeping in touch with the embassy...he got himself in with the worst sort of people."

"What kind of people?" I want to know.

"Circus people. Can you imagine? You go to a country with so much trouble and you make friends with circus people? That is not a wise move."

"So he got in some kind of trouble?" I ask.

"He got kidnapped, that's what," she replies.

"Kidnapped?" I say, "by the circus?"

She nods. "They beat him up pretty badly. Then they hid him away in the countryside. They only asked for a thousand dollars so we got him back..."

"I guess they'll ask for more next time," I say.

She nods and continues, "but he was never the same after. He started drinking too much like a Mongol. A few weeks later, he didn't show up for work. After a few more days, the whole English department got worried. Dr. Sumiya went to his apartment. No answer. Eventually, they broke down the door."

I tense myself anticipating the grisly findings.

"Everything was gone," she says. "The place was cleaned out. Peter just upped and left, telling no one. I hear he's back in Seattle now, working with a

rehab organization."

I sit there in silence. Not knowing how to respond.

"Look Mykel," says Dr. Gaye, "I don't do this to scare you. You may not find it this bad. But I have to tell you everything. I don't want you coming back to me and saying you weren't warned."

I sit there in silence.

"Well," she says, "you still want to go? You can pull out, you know. Of course, my fee is non-refundable."

"I'm going," I say, pounding my fist on the table, "This is the most important adventure of my life. I'm not going to back out on account of some muggings, a kidnapping and vomit at the front door."

This time, the smile isn't a sad one.

"Okay Mykel," she says, "You've got your plane ticket to Beijing and your train ticket to *Ulaanbaatar*. Someone will meet you in *UB*. They'll take you to your apartment, and from there, you're on your own."

"Thanks for everything," I tell her.

"Good luck," she says.

It's my last night in New York. I've been packed for a month. Long johns, ski gloves, thermal everything. I bought a large metal lock-box. Dr. Gaye told me not to trust Mongolian banks. $1000 in cash, I split between a moneybelt and a "no-see" underarm wallet. Another two hundred lies conveniently in a pouch hung from my waist. As for the metal box, I packed that with 200 condoms. Wishful thinking, I guess. But my present quest for the Gobi doesn't lessen my eternal quest for nookie.

I buy a bottle of champagne and ask my girlfriend, Jean, to join me in a farewell evening at the Newark Radisson Hotel. It's good-bye for a year, so I'm going all out. The limo picks us up at 4:30.

The hotel directory calls it "the lap of airport luxury." It looks more like another piece of anatomy. Tall, thin, boring, it's not The Ritz I was hoping for.

As we walk in, it becomes obvious that the employees could use my English teaching skills.

"You want room two people?" asks the receptionist.

"Yes," I say, "I'm a member of the International Airline Passengers Association. I'm entitled to a discount."

"You airlines?" she says, "You no look airlines."

She thinks I'm a pilot or someone else entitled to a super cheap rate. I play along.

"I'll be glad to show you my airlines card," I say, reaching into my wallet.

"No," says the woman. "You say. I believe. You get minus fifty percent. You sign here."

Being unused to hotels, I'm not sure if the nineties still require a "Mr. and Mrs." in the guest book. But pilots don't fly with their wives. They fly with their stewardesses. I sign only "Mykel Board."

In the hallway, I consider carrying Jean across the threshold. Memories of a hernia operation in Japan stop me. We walk in together. I close the door. We kiss like newlyweds.

Out comes the champagne. A glass for each of us. Then another. Her eyes are wet with tears.

"Mykel," she says, "what are you going to be doing in Mongolia?"

"Teaching English," I tell her, "you know that."

"That's not what I mean," she says, "I mean what about us? What will that do to our relationship?"

"Nothing," I say. "You know me. I love you, but my freedom is first. I can't promise anything, except that our relationship won't change."

"But what exactly is our relationship? And how committed are you? Are you just going to fuck any man, woman or sheep that comes your way?"

Oy vey! My last night in New York and she wants to talk about the relationship! It's not what I have in mind. Besides, she knew from the beginning. Or she should have. Sex is my pick and shovel, my telescope, my metal detector, my sextant. I explore with it. Discover. Sex is a quest, an adventure. As important in my life as oxygen. Gender, age, race, none of that matters. But the act, the doing, the friction. Why travel if my semen stays in one place — inside me?

"I can't promise to leave the sheep alone," I tell her. "What if that's an insult in Mongolia? A guy might invite you to his place, offer you his sheep to screw, and kill you if you say no. So, no promises, ok?"

"But I thought you were allergic to wool." She whines.

"Yeah," I tell her, "But guys will put up with more than a little itch to get laid not to mention avoid getting killed."

"Okay Mykel," she says, "I'm glad you're honest with me. I don't know what else to say."

I kiss her again, figuring this is the best way to end the discussion. It works, so I don't sleep much that night. The next morning, we get up three hours early. Hung over, drained, I'm nervous about missing the flight. The hotel puts us on the "Airline Personnel" bus to the airport.

I'm travelling to Mongolia the cheapest way possible, through a maze of interconnecting transportation. I change planes once in Toronto, again in Vancouver. Then I fly to Beijing, stay there four days, and take the train to Ulaanbaatar.

I've booked a luxury hotel in China, and a "soft sleeper" on the train. I don't want the hardships to start until I get settled.

At the airport in New York, Jean walks with me to the gate. When I go to pick up my bags from the x-ray machine, a security guard comes over to me.

"Excuse me sir, is this your bag?" she says.

"Yes," I say, "is there some problem?"

"Would you open it please?"

"Sure," I say, fishing for the key.

The guard takes the bag from the conveyer belt to a table. Jean and I follow. I open the locks and flip the clasps.

The guard fishes around a bit and then comes to the locked money box.

"What's this?" she asks.

"It's a locked money box," I tell her.

"Could you open it please?" she says.

I feel my face reddening, but I say nothing. I take the key, open the box. Snug Fit Super Latex, says the package on top.

"Thank you, that's all," says the security guard.

Jean says nothing.

In the waiting room, Jean sits glum. I sit nervous about making the connections. The plane is already late.

Finally, I leave, we hug tearfully and kiss deeply. It's our last kiss ever, but that's another book.

GOOD-BYE NEW YORK, HELLO CHINA
GOOD-BYE CHINA...
AND THE WORLD AS I KNOW IT

Beijing is crowded, hot and sticky. It's August and the locals wisely wear shorts and sandals. That's fine for hairless Oriental legs, but not for my Jewish limbs. I'd rather suffer than discredit the race.

The city reminds me of Bangkok with the sex turned way down, the pollution turned slightly down and the BUY THIS NOW! scamming turned way up. Both the men and women are extremely good-looking, thin, delicate, with a touch of irony in their half-smiles.

I've checked into the hotel, taken a shower, relieved myself of the airline food, and am now ready to shop for my life in Mongolia. Things are cheap in Beijing, and Dr. Gaye has warned me that *UB*, expat talk for *Ulaanbaatar*, has nothing.

"And that nothing," she said, "is very expensive."

In New York, I'd tried to buy clothes.

"Where are the down coats and longjohns?" I asked the girl in Macys.

"This is August," she said, "we're not exactly stocked with those things. Where are you going?"

"Outer Mongolia," I told her.

"Yeah, but really..." she answered.

Now I'm in China, looking for those same things.

I'm happy to learn that many Chinese, can speak a little English, though they have an annoying habit of repeating things. At the hotel desk, I ask where I can buy one of those hideous sleeping bag coats. In my right mind, I make fun of that ugliness. But Mongolian temperatures drop to minus 40. I'll take ugly, thank you.

The clerk shakes his head. "Summertime now! Summertime now!" he says, "Too hot. Too hot."

I'm too hot to argue so I return to my room and the air conditioning. On the way, I pick up an English language paper. It tells what's on in the city: opera, a lecture, Mozart performed by a Chinese orchestra. Not exactly my cup of tea.

On the back page is a small ad for the HAO MEN RESTAURANT:

> **The dining hall, which can hold 60 guests together, is in the first floor. In the second floor, there are warmly KTV cabins equipped with modern projector. There, your best feeling will be double.**

Hmmmm, nothing like double best feeling. Far from the Times Square peep shows, maybe I can warm my KTV here. Somehow though, I can't imagine feeding quarters to a video booth in the capital of Red China.

Except for North Korea, China's sex reputation is the worst in Asia. Horror stories abound. *The Lonely Planet Guide* tells of a white man who was arrested for getting into the same taxi as a Chinese woman. Another section tells of a hotel reporting "prostitution" to the police:

In the middle of the night, the cops break into a couple's room. They roughly throw the naked man out of bed and begin questioning his Oriental bedmate. When she doesn't understand, it gradually dawns on the intruders that something is amiss. Finally, they allow the terrified man to show his passport. The Oriental in question is his Japanese wife. The cops leave without apologies. I'd better be careful.

Back in my hotel room, I take another shower to wash off the fresh sweat. Then, I head for the hotel bar.

I'm the only one sitting at the bar itself. A couple of Japanese businessmen sit at tables in the back. The pretty waitress hands me a drink menu. It's in Chinese on one side and English on the other. I look at the section called New Cocktails:

> **Chinese Love 35¥**
> **Beautiful Beijing 35¥**
> **Top Gun 35¥**
> **Romantic Seaside 15¥**
> **Prune Juice 12¥**

The barmaid has gone to a table to attend to the businessmen. Behind the bar now is a young man with a beautifully round scrubbed face. About seventeen, he's petite with brushed back hair, a wide nose, and thin but deep red lips. He smiles at me. I wink. Suddenly, he looks down. His lower lip trembles.

He leaves the bar and walks into an open pantry/storeroom. He faces the wall of the room. He studies it, moving his lips silently. From my position, I can't see if there is a poster or something he's reading.

The waitress returns. She takes the young man's disappearance in stride, as if it happens all the time. She asks me what I want. I order a beer. As I drink it, I stare at the guy in the pantry. He stares at the wall. Occasionally, he steals a glance my way. When he sees me looking at him, he returns his gaze to the wall.

I take a business card out of my wallet.

Mykel Board, writing, music, language.

On the back of the card, I write my room number. I leave it on the bar with a generous tip. As I get off the stool, visions of police breaking down doors come to me.

I pick up the card again, say "Good-bye," and head for my room. The bartender says nothing. He's still in the pantry.

The next day is much like the first. Hot, sticky, and commercial. Street vendors are everywhere. Dealing in cash dollars preferably. They bargain. You bargain. Mao would turn over in his mausoleum.

There are also street beggars: old men, little kids, moms, people who don't fare so well in the new free-market economy. Consumer goods sure, they're in abundance. All you've got to do is pay for them.

I go to Tiananmen Square, site of the bloody rebellion in 1989. Next to the square stands a huge electronic clock. I can't read the Chinese symbols, but there's something sinister in the way it ticks down, second by second. I later learn that it's a record of the time until "China is reunited." That is, until Hong Kong becomes part of The People's Republic.

A small Chinese man with a mustache approaches me.

"Can I practice with you?" he asks in English.

I look at the pudgy guy and wish that the bartender from last night had asked the same question.

"What do you mean?" I ask.

"I need English practice. You English, no? You English, no?"

"Not exactly," I tell him. "I'm American."

"Same same," he says. "I'm from Harbin. It's in the North. You know it?"

"No," I tell him.

"It's cold there," he says.

"I'm going to Outer Mongolia," I say, "so I don't worry about the cold."

"Outer Mongolia?" he says, "Why? You poor man. You poor man. There is nothing. Nothing."

From such a bleak introduction, we eventually establish a kind of friendship. He tells me his name is Wong and he teaches Chinese. His wife teaches English.

"Someday I'll go to the US to study linguistics," he says. "You help me, okay?"

He tells me of his past and what he suffered during Mao's "Cultural Revolution."

"They closed the universities," he says. "I speak Japanese and English so they say I was intellectual. They forced me to work in a factory. Five years. Five years. I learn to hate work, so now I'm in government. The water department. The government is bad, but it's better than work. Better than work."

Wong shows me around Beijing. He takes my picture under Mao's portrait and continues to write to me while I'm in *Ulaanbaatar*. I hope we meet again sometime.

The next day is leaving day. I'm supposed to meet my guide/interpreter, Mr. Lee, in the hotel lobby. I paid $60 to the local tour bureau for "the deluxe treatment." Lee is an expert, a near-perfect English speaker. He'll get me to the station, see me through customs, even carry my bags, all of them. The escort idea is so upper class, it gives me the creeps.

At 7:00AM I'm in the lobby, my luggage overflowing on a hotel cart. Instead of Mr. Lee, there's a taxi driver who has my name written on a little scrap of paper.

"I'm Mykel Board," I tell him, "you waiting for me?"

He speaks to me in Chinese. Rattling on.

The desk clerk helps.

"He says he's been waiting for you," says the desk clerk. "Waiting for you."

I point to my bags, "I was expecting Mr. Lee, but there's the luggage. Let's get going."

The driver's jaw drops when he sees my bags, packed for a year in Mongolia. He presses the heel of his palm to his forehead and rattles off another string of Chinese.

"He says, it's much," translates the desk clerk, "but both of you can manage it. Both of you."

I'm annoyed that this guy speaks no English. I'm doubly annoyed that he wants me to help load the bags into his cab. Does the upperclass really lift its own bags?

At the station, we struggle with the luggage. Together. Through the terminal into a waiting room. Then, he turns to leave.

"Yo!" I yell at him in my best Chinese, "That's not enough! I paid for help all the way onto the train."

"You no worry," he says, the first English he's spoken. "I go for water only. Water only."

That's the last I see of him.

I struggle with my too many bags, leaving and reentering the departure area, getting shoved around by the crowd. I'm pissed at my lack of help, and waste of sixty dollars.

Then I run into Mr. Lee, red-faced and out of breath.

"Why you no wait for me?" he asks.

"I went with the cab driver you sent."

"What cab driver?" he says, "I'm the driver."

As it turns out, the guy was a scam artist. Someone in the hotel tipped him off that I was leaving. He was going to try to hustle me for money. When he found out I already paid, he took off.

Mr. Lee helps me toward the train. At the scales, the customs guy looks at my bags and shakes his head. I know I have over seventy kilos more than my thirty allowance. A sign, in English, conveniently next to a cash register, says, "Extra Baggage Charge: $3 per kilo."

That's at least $200.

"Tell him I'll give him a hundred," I say to Mr. Lee.

He says something to the customs agent. The agent nods. I open my pouch, take out five twenty dollar bills and hand them to him. He lets us pass.

We head for the first class cars. A conductor stops us to look at the ticket. He speaks to Mr. Lee.

"He says you don't have first class," Mr. Lee tells me. "This is a second class ticket."

"I paid an extra hundred bucks for "soft-class," I tell him. "That means I get two people in a compartment with a toilet and shower inside."

"Sorry," says Mr. Lee, "your ticket is here."

He shows me the cabin. Four beds, a toilet in the hall, no sink or shower anywhere.

"Have a good journey," says Mr. Lee, taking off.

I share a compartment with two New Zealanders: a somewhat attractive girl with large breasts and short hair, and a long-haired chubby blond guy.

The meeting could have been in Europe, or in a Greyhound bus to Des Moines.

"Hi, where're you from? How long you been on the road? Why Mongolia?" Blah blah blah.

They're on a package tour, set up by a group called Monkey Business. The trans-Mongolian is part of the deal. China for a week, two days in Mongolia, then on to Irkutsk and Moscow.

"So how 'bout you?" asks the young man. "What're your plans?"

"Oh, I'm moving to Mongolia," I tell him. "I'm going to be working there."

"Yeah, but really..." he says.

We pass the Great Wall. I'm amazed. Not that it's so long, but that it looks so easy to climb over. It's only twenty feet high. No wonder the Mongols took over China. They could pole vault.

After the wall, there are hills and forests for awhile, then the desert starts.

Suddenly, in the middle of nothing but scrub, the train stops. The New Zealanders expect it. They read about it in their guidebook.

Evidently, we're still in China, in the border town of Erlian. We can get out and explore because they have to change the train wheels. The Mongols use a different track size than the Chinese. Of course, they don't have *machines* to change the wheels. Just a wrench and a hammer.

Outside the station, a few stands sell warm beer, soft apples and the Chinese equivalent of Cup'o'Noodles. Dinner. Back on the train, we're off again with only a cursory look by a Mongolian customs agent.

Ah Mongolia! Here I am. Twenty years in the making. Going through a surprisingly green desert. Yes!

Herds of camels, wild horses and goats, graze on the sparse grass. *Gers* appear like mushrooms over the land. A man rides his horse over the plains. He wears a *deel*, one of those Kimono-like outfits I saw in New Jersey.

During the trip, the New Zealanders and I joke about what we're going to do if no one meets us in *Ulaanbaatar*. Could you imagine being stranded in the middle of the capitol of Mongolia without a clue as to where you're going?

The train pulls in. After a 36 hour ride, I'm an hour and a half late. Already I've made a bad impression, keeping my greeters waiting.

The station is a big yellow building with five or six tracks behind it. A large cyclone fence is on either side. A tiny gate allows one person at a time to pass through.

The New Zealanders get out. They help me with my massive luggage. Along the platform, people greet, kiss and help each other with the baggage.

Soon the three of us and a couple people wearing *deels* are all that's left on that platform.

A skinny young Mongol with long hair and a head too big for his body, walks back and forth. He's chanting something.

As he approaches, I hear the words.

"Monkey Business," he says, "Monkey Business. Anyone for Monkey Business?"

I wave him over to our group. My compartment mates greet him and they go off together. Then, it's just me.

Half an hour passes. No one comes. I take my luggage and carry, drag and push it around to the front of the station. Welcome to Mongolia!

I stand, watching the traffic. All the warnings come back to me: the locals, the boredom, the danger. Don't talk to strangers. Don't get involved with 'The Wrong People.' Don't trust anyone. The guy whose job I'm taking was kidnapped.

I have no idea of where I'm supposed to go. I couldn't get there if I did know. I've got more than 200 pounds of baggage. I'm standing, the only Westerner, in front of the train station in *Ulaanbaatar*, Mongolia.

What the fuck? I begin to feel sorry for myself. Why am I out here in the middle of nowhere? Why do I put myself in these situations? Another hour passes.

A man, in his late thirties, sprouting gray cheek hair, speaks to me.

"You speak English?" he asks, in good English.

I nod.

"You need cheap guest house?" he asks, handing me a card with the name and address of a guesthouse on it. $5 is written in pen on the bottom.

"I don't know," I whine. "I'm supposed to meet someone here and they're not...Dr. Sumiya from...."

"The National University," the man says, finishing my sentence. "I know Dr. Sumiya."

"Come on," he continues, "my friend has a car."

Dr. Gaye told me Mongols are desperate since Russia pulled out. I shouldn't trust anyone. You never know what they're going to do. Taking a ride with strangers. My poor mother. If she only knew. But do I have a choice?

The guy signals to his pal in a tiny Flintstones car. The man gets out of the car and walks over to where we're standing.

There's no room for my luggage inside, so they throw it all on a dinky roof rack. Hanging over the edge, it threatens to topple before we even start our drive.

We go to the university, an old gray building with enormous yellow doors. We walk in and up worn wooden stairs. At the top, we make a right, then a left through another pair of doors. A thin young lady turns as we enter. Her glasses reflect the bright sun coming in through the windows.

"Hello," I say, "Is there a Dr. Sumiya here? I'm supposed to start teaching soon."

"Today?" she says, "We thought you come tomorrow. I'm supposed to meet you."

"Today," I say, "and you've met me."

The young woman apologizes, grabs a key, and talks to the driver. Together we pile into the car and go to my new home.

I live on the fifth floor of a five story walk up. The building, an old Russian-made apartment block, is at the top of the hill. It is one of two buildings with a fence around it. Just inside the fence is a little wooden guardhouse.

When we arrive, my new Mongol friends grab the two heaviest pieces of luggage. Step by agonizing step, they pull the bags upward. Finally there, we open the door. They set the bags down and sit hard on the couch. A dustcloud rises around them.

Though they never ask for money, I give them $10. They're surprised, but they take it, with plenty of *bayerlalaa's*. Then, everyone leaves.

Alone, I survey my apartment. It's three times the size of my New York City one. It's got rooms! You can actually leave one, open a door, and enter another one. That's the positive.

But, the toilet runs continually. It also doesn't flush very well. There's no hot water. One of the hotplate's two plates doesn't heat. An hour after I arrive, there's no water at all, no electricity either. This is going to be fun.

What are my first impressions of Mongols, other than they're cool enough to aid a helpless foreigner? They're not an attractive people. Their faces are too square. Their eyes are too far apart. In contrast to the delicate beauty of the Chinese, the Mongols are gross. They're more muscular, and more worn. In China, a 40 year old might look 20. In Mongolia, a 20 year old looks 40.

What do I have to look forward to except a visit from Yoko, my long-time friend and lust object from New York? She's Japanese, and they know how to look. But Mongolia? All-in-all it's not a boner-poppin' land of Oriental horniness. Again, it makes me ask myself what I'm doing here. I don't have to wait long for the answer.

My first Saturday: I'm on my way to The Hollywood Disco. It's in an old Youth Center that also houses a 'Quiet Bar' and a Korean restaurant. Someone told me that the club is open only from 6 to 10PM. Not very encouraging.

It's easy to tell the current in-club. It's the one with the $5.00 cover charge. That means DOLLARS, US hard cash. On a Mongolian salary, that's equivalent to $80. Could you imagine paying $80 to get into a club? Even in New York?

I get there at 7. I haven't eaten yet, so I hope they have food. The Korean Restaurant is supposed to be very expensive and not very good.

As I walk toward the entrance, I pass a couple of teenaged Mongols. One, slightly taller than me, wears a blue sports jacket over a t-shirt. He also wears fluorescent blue pants that look like they're made out of an old parachute. He's quite attractive, especially for a Mongol.

The other guy, slightly shorter and less good-looking, wears a flashy red blazer over a t-shirt and jeans. He also wears sunglasses, even though it's way past dusk. On their feet, they both wear the Chinese equivalent of Nikes.

They've set themselves on the stone fence outside the club's entrance. When I pass them, the shorter guy shouts to me. It sounds like, "Wanna be a go go?"

I look at them. The taller waves at me. Not a window-washing back and forth wave, but a limp-wristed fingers-pointing-down wave. Like brushing crumbs off a table.

I walk over to the pair. The taller one takes a pack of cigarettes from his pocket. "For Mongolians," he says pointing to the picture on the package. It's a Camel. He offers the pack to me. Although I don't smoke, I take one to be polite.

"Me, Artsenesneg," says the shorter one.

"Yo Art!" I say.

"Me, Bayarstineg," says the other one.

"Yo Barry!" I answer, slapping his open palm.

"I'm Mykel," I tell them. Of course, they hear it as *Michael*.

"Michael Jordan!" says Art.

"Michael Jackson!" says Barry, doing a little moonwalk on the ground.

They go through every Michael they can think of: Tyson, Douglas, Bolton, Rode-the-Boat-Ashore, and a few others I never heard of.

"Van Damme! You know Van Damme!" says Barry kicking high into the air.

"Me, Mongol," says Art, slamming the fist of his right hand into the palm of his left. "Mongol," he repeats.

I touch my palm to my chest. "American," I say.

"America!" he says, "San Francisco, Los Angeles, Hollywood."

"New York," I tell him.

"Nyork Nyork! OK!" he says, slapping me on the back.

I point to my non-existent wristwatch. "Hollywood?" I ask. "What time?"

He holds up nine fingers. "Yus!" he says.

"I go," I tell them. "I'm hungry." I rub my stomach.

"I'm hungry!" says Art.

"I'm hungry!" says Barry.

"I'm hungry! I'm hungry!" They start a sing-song chant, dancing around in a little circle. "I'm hungry. I'm hungry." About this time, I notice the boys are a little soused.

"Inside," says Art, "Korea!" He makes a motion like he's eating with chopsticks.

"Too expensive," I say, making a motion like I'm rubbing money between my fingers.

Both of them nod.

"I'm hungry! I'm hungry!" says Barry.

"I'm Mongol!" says Art, slamming his fist into his palm.

They both get up and motion for me to follow. Barry says, "Hamburger. Pizza. No much money."

I'm a bit scared of these guys. Drunken strangers, setting up a foreigner for the big take. But if I gave into every little anxiety or even common sense would I be in Outer Mongolia in the first place?

So off we scramble, over stone fences and piles of mud, through the middle of housing projects.

"Kiosk? Kiosk?" asks Barry.

I shrug.

On the bridge that leads downtown, we pass a row of shack-like kiosks. None of them sell anything like FOOD. They've got cigarettes, condoms, cup'o'noodles, milk powder, but nothing hot and filling. The three of us continue our trek into the center of town.

We pass a few more kiosks; all useless. When we come to the main cross street, Barry runs into the gutter to stop a car. Although there are official 'Taxis' in *Ulaanbaatar*, only tourists and rich folks use them. Normal people just hail any passing car. You pay the driver 100 *tugriks* (about 25 cents) a kilometer.

I may be bold enough to walk around with these guys, but I'm not about to let them convince a driver to dump us in a back alley. Instead, I point to the other side of *Sukhbaatar* Square. There's a cafe there. I hope it's open.

Barry and Art give up their car flagging. Instead, we walk toward where I pointed. On the way, we pass another kiosk, this one with tables and umbrellas outside. Barry talks to the guy inside and comes back with a can of California Cola, a bad Coke imitation. I thank him, but am really beginning to feel hunger pangs.

No sooner panged then done! Barry is at the kiosk, this time returning with three large hotdogs with mustard. I reach for my wallet. Art signals me to put it away. "*Tugrik*," he says. "Later, Hollywood, dollars."

"Yes, Hollywood!" says Barry, slamming his fist into his palm.

After the meal, we make our way back to The Hollywood. Barry has a heated conversation with the mountainous doorman. The teenager stalks off, pulling me and Art along. We go downstairs. Barry slams open another door, loudly walking into the room. We've entered THE QUIET BAR.

There are a dozen or so booths here, most of them empty. At one, sit a bunch of not-bad-looking girls. At another, is a Mongolian middle-aged couple dressed as a US middle-aged couple circa 1970. At a third booth, a man and a teenage boy sit over beer, deep in discussion. Soft disco music plays in the background.

I want to repay the hospitality of these guys, so I order beer for the three of us. "*Bakhgui!*" (No!) says Barry when I try to pay for them.

He stumbles loudly up to the bar. The girls giggle. Barry says something in Mongolian, pulling a wad of bills out of his pocket. They slip from his hand and float helter-skelter to the floor. He scrambles on his hands and knees to retrieve them. Eventually, some vodka comes. We drink it.

Art shouts something to the bartender. The music gets louder. Art gets up in the aisle between the booths and starts to disco dance. He's so drunk that he keeps bumping into the tables on all sides. The middle-age couple gets up and leaves. The man and teenager stop talking.

Barry gets up to dance with Art. They lurch back and forth between the Quiet Bar booths. Barry bumps into a table. Beer spills. The man and teen leave. The girls giggle louder and look at us. Is that a flirt? Barry grabs me under the arms and stands me on the floor. The two of them hold my hands and we spin in a mad ring-around-the-rosy. One of the waiters leaves and comes back with the very big doorman from upstairs.

Art says something, smashing his fist into his palm. We leave quickly.

The boys want to go upstairs to the disco. They need dollars. I pull out my wallet and empty it. Ten dollars. Though we need fifteen for the three of us, we go up anyway.

The doorman speaks some English. I explain that I only have ten dollars and there are three of us. He translates for Barry and Art. They discuss. The boys persuade the guy to let us in for my $10 and a bunch of *tugrik*. Art provides the *tugrik*.

Upstairs is fashion itself. Elegant tables with tablecloths. Elegant waiters and waitresses. Strobes and rainbow lights flash on an empty disco floor. Incredibly good-looking people sit at the tables. Dozens of them. Boys and girls who make you want to take their pictures and jerk off to them. Mongolians aren't ugly. They just hide the good ones.

We sit at a table on the far side of the dancefloor. Barry orders a bottle of vodka, Smirnoffs, in my honor. Mongols drink it straight. Soon a glass of apple juice comes for me. I'm foreign, so they think I need a chaser. Hah! I'll show them.

Near us, a tableful of cute Mongol girls stares in our direction. At other tables, a few Westerners cuddle or converse with their Mongol friends. Barry signals the cuties to come over. They shake their heads — and giggle.

He stumbles over to their table, unlit cigarette in hand. They look at the ceiling, each other, the other tables. He returns, pulls matches out of his own pocket and lights the cigarette. The girls giggle. He sticks his tongue out at them. We drink some more.

The music gets louder. Barry backs his chair on to the empty dancefloor. Like wheelchair disco without the wheels, he's hustling and bumping and doing whatever folks do in Mongolia. But he does it in a chair, by himself, in the middle of the dancefloor.

The big guy from the door approaches. Bang! Barry is back at the table. We drink some more vodka.

"You, American. We, Mongolian," says Art, smashing his fist into his palm. This time his elbow knocks over the applejuice.

The flood makes all three of us push back quickly. Pow! Pow! Pow! Each of our chairs knocks into a different person at a different table. Heads are turned. Curses are breathed. Apologies are mumbled.

By this time, I'm feeling pretty good. A few couples now disco among the strobelights. Art, Barry and I get up. Soon, we're in the middle of the dancefloor wiggin' out. The crowd parts around us, like passengers in a rush hour subway around an extremely smelly wino.

The music turns slow. I spread my arms to waltz with Barry. He laughs it off and we all sit down.

Then Barry throws up. Projectile, out, up, all over himself. All over the floor. All over the table.

A brilliant flash. YES! That's it! That's what the fuck I'm doing in Mongolia! I'm here to be at a 70s style disco with a bunch of drunken fuck-up teenagers, puking amongst the finely dressed beautiful people. I'm here to be laughing hysterically as the proper Mongols back farther and farther away in horror.

I didn't come here to go to museums or take pictures of national monuments. I didn't even come for the camels and yaks. I came for this. For the wild, the improbable, the unexpected adventure in everyday life. Life like I've never known it.

Vomit in New York is only vomit. But this? This is adventure. And sure as the return of the bouncer, I'm living it.

The door thug grabs Barry by the arm and hauls him up and away. When we next see the boy, he's on his hands and knees, cleaning the stairway where he evidently puked again while in the bouncer's custody. The rest of the night, I don't remember so well.

TWO

Sages, writing centuries before sponsors invaded TV-land, spoke of the Zen of Irritation. A constant barrage of trouble lets you appreciate a favor that might otherwise go unnoticed. When life usually goes wrong, you savor the few times it goes right. Even reaching neutrality is bliss.

In New York, I'd be angry when a train was late, or if a lightbulb burned out. Here, I'm ecstatic when I turn on the hot water tap and hot water actually comes out the faucet. My heart leaps when I make an appointment and the appointee is only an hour late. I'm in heaven when I jam myself on a bus and discover the fare is the same as it was yesterday.

I expect things not to work in Mongolia. Not only the electricity, hot water, banks and public transportation, but everything. When I crossed the border from China, my pen ran out of ink. My laptop crashed. My histamine became immune to my anti.

Two computer printers died on me, the first after two days in the country. The second lasted an hour. The snap on my only pair of dress pants snapped *its last snap after a week in Mongolia. My bed collapsed. My condoms sprung holes. That's just the way it is in Mongolia.*

It took me awhile to realize all this and to expect it. In the beginning, it was new to me. In this chapter, I've just arrived in the city and have to say:

HELLO MONGOLIA, GOOD-BYE PLUMBING

AUGUST 28

David is a Canadian-Israeli. He's in Mongolia as part of an UN-supported computer project. My first white friend in the country is a punk rock fan, a contrarian with a caustic sense of humor, and a Jew. My kind of guy.

He lives in the first section of my apartment complex. I live in the third. Visiting him is a pain, though. I can't walk from one building section directly to another. Instead, I have to go downstairs, out door number three, across the front of the building, back in through door number one and up another set of stairs. *Why* is a question I've learned not to ask here.

David's apartment is about the same size as mine, and his toilet also runs continually. Today he's visiting, helping me revive one of my dead computer printers.

"Looks bad," says David. "I think it's the motherboard."

"What's that?" I ask.

"It's the main circuit board...."

"I know what a motherboard is," I tell him. "What's that sound?"

It's a loud "sssssssssshhhhhhhhhhhhh" as if hundreds of movie-goers were trying to quiet the same noisy couple.

"Sounds like rushing water," he says.

I go into the bathroom to check.

Pow! Right in the face. A full blast of cold water from the long plastic tube that connects the toilet to the main pipe. It's dancing like a cobra. It attacks me. Blinds me as I grope, trying to strangle it. By touch alone, I find the cut-off valve and turn it. No change. Turn it again. The water shuts off. The ceiling, the walls, toilet paper, bathroom reading material — everything soaked.

Exhausted, I sit in the middle of an inch high puddle slowly draining into the apartment below. Water seeps into the seat of my pants while David laughs like it's a slapstick movie. I'm too tired to knock his bottom lip into his top teeth.

"Get out of here," I say, more in fatigue than anger.

He leaves. I consider toweling myself off, but all the towels are as soaked as I am. Dripping, I pad to the bedroom where I keep the plastic bag with my dirty clothes. Yesterday's t-shirt makes as good a towel as any.

With the hose back on, the toilet again runs continually. The sound has been driving me crazy. Now, I'm going to do something about it.

Using a vice-grip pliers, I clamp the hose shut and leave the pliers attached. It stops the sound, but every time I use the toilet I have to unclamp the hose, let the tank fill, flush, check for floaters, reflush, then reclamp the hose.

I've asked the superintendent to call a plumber. Three times, she's told me "He be there at one PM." Three times he never showed.

I'll ask again tomorrow.

AUGUST 29

The plumber shows up. At 4:30, he's only three and a half hours late.

About five feet tall, maybe fifty, he's got a scraggly beard and a nosefull of thick red veins. He carries a little leather pouch. In the bathroom, he dumps the contents on the floor: old pipe pieces, string, some hose and a wrench. He turns off the water flow, then takes apart the toilet. Everywhere two pipes meet, he detaches them, wraps string around the threads, spits on the string, and joins them together. By the time he's finished, the toilet neither leaks nor attacks. It does however, continually run.

SEPTEMBER 21

In a cost-cutting move worthy of governments everywhere, the early Mongolian communists decided it would be too expensive to put separate boilers in every building. After all, housing was free to tenants, so it had to be cheap to the government.

Instead of boilers, the Politburo set up three central heating plants. Their job was to fire up hot water and send it through understreet pipes. The pipes lead to all the buildings in the city. They never considered that one of the plants might break down — and if that happened, every building attached would suffer.

Besides that, utility plants make most of Mongolia's only pollution. For 365 days a year, the electric company spews coal smoke into the air. Starting today the heating plants add to it with their winter work. Winter is from September to June.

The *gers* have it better. Their wood or dung-burning stoves keep them toasty warm, although in the city, they don't help the pollution problem. Inside my apartment, however, the temperature only occasionally warms up to 50°. I've forgotten what my naked body looks like. Who knows what I've lost to the cold?

Although it's been freezing for almost three weeks now, the plants have not started yet. The rumor is that they haven't paid their coal bill. The Russian supplier cut them off. In this post-communist world, no money means no heat.

Furthermore, the rumor says that American foreign aid has just come through. The Americans want to keep democracy in Mongolia, so they'll pay for heat.

Who knows what the truth is? I even hear that Hillary Clinton is coming to Mongolia with news of a heating grant for the rest of the year. Hillary Clinton? The Mongols *already* have National Health Care. For now, I'd welcome the heat.

At 7AM, my radiators begin to clank. First there's a knock, like someone in another apartment hit a pipe with a sledge hammer. After the knock, comes nothing. Tubular silence for an hour, maybe two. Then another clank. A faint bubbling noise. A hiss. Things are beginning to work. Now all I need is heat.

I've prepared for this moment, asked advice from my fellow teachers, gotten the tools together. In this country, where everyone is a doctor, plumber, electrician, and veterinarian, I know exactly what to do.

The first step is to *bleed* the radiator. The theory is that during the summer, water drains from the pipes. Air replaces the water. When the winter hot water comes, it can't push the air out of the radiator. You have to turn a little screw. This allows the air out so the water can fill the pipes. Makes perfect sense.

There's more clanging now. I walk over to the china cabinet and grab my New York-bought, indestructible-screwdriver-with-a-handle-you-can-smash-with-a-hammer. I bring along the hammer too, just in case.

Walking to the livingroom radiator, I put the screwdriver tip against the radiator screw. It's large headed, embedded in the last coil of the radiator. Bleeding only takes a twist of the wrist. Yeah, right.

That screw hasn't been screwed since Mongolia was proclaimed the world's second Communist country. It's been painted, rusted, boiled, toasted. It's not going to yield to my single purpose wrist.

The Mongols say, "There's nothing wrong with a screw that a hammer won't fix."

Placing the screw driver off center, handle pointed up, I slam my hammer down on the end of it. Nothing happens. I try again. The screw turns a bit. Another whack. Another budge.

There's a hissing noise, a bubbling sound. Black liquid sprays from around the screw over me, over the wall. I turn the screw to close it off. Whew! Radiator bled.

Leaving to teach, I look forward to returning to a gloriously heated apartment. Maybe it'll get as high as 60°.

After school, a chemistry prof pal meets me in front of the university. His buck teeth and glasses remind me of Jerry Lewis in The Nutty Professor.

"Hey Mykel," he says, "You want see new bar? It authentic, like *ger*. It round. It new. I buy you beer."

I'm not so thrilled by the round and new part, but the rest is encouragement enough to join him. We go off to a big bar in a building, built to imitate a *ger*. This in a city where two-thirds of the population already live in *gers*. It's as if a bar in New York intentionally added cockroaches and car alarms to make it more authentic.

Still, it's a friendly place and we drink till midnight. When I finally stagger home, there is still no heat.

A churning rumbles in the pipes as though water is circulating, but the radiator doesn't warm up. I feel the pipes. The heat stops at a valve on the bottom, before the heavy coils. The radiator is warm up to there.

In another country, at another time, this valve might have had a knob on it. But this is Mongolia, 1995.

Freeing my vice-grips from the toilet, I let the water run as I return to vice-grip the valve. Logically, if I turn that valve, the hot water will rise to the coils.

Logic does not work in Mongolia.

Using both hands, I turn the valve and hear the water begin to flow. I also see the water begin to flow. Hot and inky black. Out the top of the valve, dribbling over my hand and on to the floor. Logically, if a right turn of the valve lets the water escape, a left turn will stop it.

Logic does not work in Mongolia.

Turning the valve to the left makes it worse. I've got a geyser now. Hissing like a viper, black liquid sprays straight up into the air. Spurting, shushing, pouring. Covering me, the wall, the carpet. Creeping toward the electrical outlet on the floor in the hallway.

Using my three towels, finally dry after the toilet attack, I dam the geyser. In five minutes, the water passes through the dam. Snatching up my one small cooking pot, I put it under where most of the spray sprays. In two and a half minutes, it fills to overflowing. I empty it and put it back under the spray.

Then I race down eighty seven steps and out the door to the little wooden guard station. I bang on the door. There's no answer.

I race back upstairs, empty the pot, then run to the super's office and bang on the door. No answer. Back up the stairs. Empty the pot. Squeeze out the towels. Empty the pot again. Race down the stairs over to door number one. Eighty-seven steps up to David's apartment. I touch the two wires together that ring his doorbell. It takes four or five rings before I rouse him.

"Do you know what time...," he starts, but the panicked look on my face stops him.

"It's an emergency," I tell him. "I need your biggest pot."

I explain the situation. He gives me the pot.

"Did you contact the guard?" he asks.

"I can't find the guard," I tell him, taking the pot and racing back up to my apartment.

My pot is overflowing. I mop up as best as I can. Then I switch to David's. It's 1:30AM. Two pair of feet thump up the steps.

David walks in the door.

"I found the guard," he says. "He was sleeping and not very happy about being woken up. Makes me feel secure."

Behind David walks a Mongolian. About thirty, puffy cheeks almost hide his eyes. His mouth hangs open with an upper lip curled into a snarl.

I show him the spraying radiator. He stares at it blankly, nods, then leaves. David leaves soon after.

David's big pot gives me an hour between emptyings. I set my alarm clock for two thirty. When it buzzes, I get up, empty the pot, set it for three thirty and go back to sleep. This continues until eight thirty the next morning. Then, I go downstairs to find out what the guard has done. He's not there.

At nine thirty, after emptying the pot, I try again. I can see him in his booth, leaning back against the wall, leisurely smoking a cigarette. Suddenly, he sees me. Opening the door, he leans out and starts talking very quickly, in Mongolian. He goes back into the booth and picks up the phone. Through the window, he motions for me to go back upstairs.

Within the hour, a plumber appears. It's the same guy who 'fixed' the toilet. He looks at the leak, shakes his head, then pulls out a large wrench. He tries to close the valve, just like I did. It spurts like Peter North in *Anal Rampage II*.

The plumber shakes his head, and clucks his tongue against the roof of his mouth. He points downward, then moves his hands as if he were a captain steering his ship. He's telling me that he's going to the basement to turn off the main valve. That'll stop the heat for the entire building. Then, I suppose, he'll come back with a new valve.

He leaves. The hissing, spraying and spewing soon stops. In a few minutes, he returns to my apartment. Settling himself on the floor, he unscrews the old valve. Then he takes some string from his black bag and wraps it around the threads. Ptui. He spits on the string and uses his index finger to smooth the saliva carefully over it. Then he reassembles the valve. Smiling, he nods to me, takes his tools and leaves.

Soon, the pipes start to make noise. The radiator does not heat up. The valve leak, however, is worse than before. I put David's pot underneath and race downstairs to find the plumber. He's gone. I look for the guard. He's gone. To the super's office. No super. Back to the guardhouse. There's the plumber.

He comes back up, looks at the leak and then at me. Shaking his head, he kicks the radiator. It doesn't help. Then, he goes back down to the basement to switch off everybody's heat.

Returning to my apartment, he unscrews the valve, and wraps more string around it. Resalivating, he carefully smoothes the string into an even mass, and reinserts the valve. This time when he goes to the basement, he leaves his tools. He doesn't have to.

The leak is gone. Fixed. Not a drop. There's no heat, of course, but I'll worry about that some other time. Then, I notice the slow drip from another radiator.

OCTOBER 5

This is another plumbing story but it's about INTERNAL plumbing. I'm my own plumber. In email, snailmail, and pleas to the embassy I've been trying to get METAMUCIL, X-LAX or a Mongolian equivalent. My system just doesn't work right.

Maybe it's the food. Next to British food, Mongolian has the worst reputation in the world. As with British food, I like it.

At least most of it. There is one dish in every culture that foreigners cannot stomach. Try springing a bottle of root beer on visiting Europeans. You'll understand in a minute what "can't stomach" means.

During my first week teaching, I asked my students what dish Mongolians love, but foreigners can't eat.

"Fat," said Bishbataar, a student I would come to know very well. "Nobody else likes fat."

"Most places have fat on their meat," I told him. "That's not so strange."

"I not talking about meat," he said, "I talking about fat, just fat. You know, fat."

He's right. Mongols love it. Plain pure lamb fat. Boiled, fried, any-which-way. Jews can do schmaltz on bread, but this is just a hunk'o'white jiggly fat yuck!

On the tasty side are two dishes I like in particular. One is called '*Buz*' (pronounced "boodz"). It's a boiled dumpling noodle outside, lamb inside. Delicious and not fatty.

The other is "*Hoosher*" (rhymes with "pusher"). It's like a Jamaican patty: a thin crust filled with chopped lamb, deep fried, sometimes served with cabbage on top. Delicious, but it's a bit hard on the stomach, especially given the native habit of eating six or seven at a time.

I'm discussing these foods with my fellow teachers. As natives everywhere love to do, they warn me against the local dangers.

"Beware the *hoosher* from street stands," says Namjil, one of my favorite teachers, and a good friend. "The meat is often bad. If you buy from a restaurant or someplace inside, there's no worry. They're hot and fresh. But if you buy from someone on the street, you should make sure you see lots of Mongolians eating there. If no one buys, that means something is wrong with the food. It's bad and you could get diarrhea."

Diarrhea! That's just what I need after a week of nothing more than an occasional hamster grain.

I look for the most out-of-the way, grubby, empty-of-customers *hoosher* stand. I find one on a hill, near the local monastery. There, a small row of kiosks stands across the bridge from a run-down shopping center. In the shopping center are the remnants of a state-run grocery store, a combination dry-cleaners bootleg cassette shop, and a softcore porn cinema.

Among the kiosks, one with peeling paint sells soggy carrots and potatoes. Another one sells packets of *Coffee King*: 50% sugar, 40% non-dairy creamer and "10% real coffee!"

Between the two kiosks stands an old woman. She's wearing a dirty red *deel*. A babushka is loosely tied over her head. In front of her are two big metal bins. Although the shops and kiosks on either side are crowded, not a soul is buying from her.

"*Hoosherarree*! *Hoosherarree*!" she shouts.

I reach for my *tugrik*.

"Gurav (3) *Hoosher*," I say, handing her the money.

She opens the bins, scoops out three sopping-with-grease patties, barely warm. I gobble 'em down. They taste ok.

Three hours later, nothing happens.

Four hours later, I'm home, working at the computer. Suddenly, I feel very tired. No stomach ache, just extreme sleepiness. I go to bed. An hour later, I wake up, not feeling so good.

It's not until a few minutes later that I actually realize how bad I feel. I have the chills. I'm nauseous. My stomach aches. I can't think straight. Can't move. Move? I gotta move, unless I want to puke in bed.

I just about make it to the bathroom. Sitting on the floor in front of the toilet, I return my essence to the great water. I'm barely able to keep my head up enough to get over the rim. Then the stomach pains start. Biting, rolling pains. Banging pains, like water in a radiator pipe.

Quickly, I de-dress and switch position. On the john, I got the pain, but no production. Then nausea, fast and hard, I swivel to switch ends. In my delirium, I forget how close the toilet is to the wall. Smash! My forehead goes into the door frame. Bang! I'm knocked off the seat, nearly unconscious on the floor. My stomach won't let me nurse my head. Blaargh! and double blaargh!

Then pain turns into production. Almost on the floor. Just in time, I twist to sit on the throne. I explode. Kerpow! Brown attack! Then, the nausea returns.

I keep switching, not knowing which end is in worse trouble. That includes my now-throbbing head...My body is pain. Head, stomach, bowels. I want to die! Come on, right now — put me out of my misery! I've been to Mongolia, what's left to live for?

After twenty or thirty years, I'm completely empty. Nothing to come out of anywhere. Even the dry heaves have heaved their last. I crawl back into bed and shake a bit. Somehow, I fall asleep.

The next morning I'm alright. A bit tired, very thirsty, but without pain. Right now I need to eat some plain white rice, that's all. Unzipping the sleeping bag, I head for the kitchen.

Aaargh! I'm going to die. Frost covers the windows — on the inside. It's freezing! Looks like I'm going to have to call a plumber.

THREE

THE BONES

I had gotten used to the bones. In fact I rather liked them. They're scattered all over *Ulaanbaatar*. Cows, sheep, horses, and goats. Their freshly slaughtered carcasses are on sale daily. The bones end up everywhere.

Also, unlike in more civilized countries, the Mongols — like the Mexicans and Thais — don't kill their stray dogs. They're left alone, like stray people, to either be adopted, fend for themselves or die of causes other than the specicide in developed countries. People here love dogs. Families leave their after-dinner bones outside for the strays, who pick 'em clean. Add to that the hawks, vultures, and other meat-eating birds, and you get lots of bones.

I use a scapula as a spatula. (Say THAT ten times fast!) It's easy to clean, effective, and looks cool in the kitchen. That said, there was one day when the city bones gave me the creeps.

First, a word about the Mongolian sky. Outside *UB*, it's like one of those astronomy charts from high school. Stars on stars, with the Milky Way, like a white scar through the sky. Except for a few mountains blocking the Western view, I saw stars horizon to horizon. Later, when the moon rose, there were fewer, but it was still an awe-bringing sight. The lack of industry, cars and people make Mongolia one of the least polluted countries in the world. I saw it in the sky.

In *Ulaanbaatar*, it's not quite as good. Compared to the air in the cities of our dog-killing country, *Ulaanbaatar* air is clean, especially in the summer, but it's not like the countryside. In the city, you can see only fifty or sixty stars — not hundreds.

On Wednesday, however, either the factories are working overtime, or it's a cloudy night, because the sky is black. I sit at my desk, typing. In the day, when I look out my bedroom window, I see the mountains rising up behind the hill I live on. At night, if I turn off the room light, I can see the Mongolian sky — usually starry, sometimes moonlit.

But tonight I look and see nothing. It's as if someone pasted black paper on the outside of my window.

The bedroom door is closed. The wind whistles over the balcony, rattling that door. There's a persistent banging. BLAM! BLAM! BLAM! A piece of wood must've blown loose. It knocks against the railing. BLAM! BLAM! BLAM!

There's another pounding. It must be the neighbors. They have the rudest visitors. Hammering at the door, coming in at all times. Sometimes, it sounds like they're right in my apartment. I don't answer my own door unless I'm expecting someone. Too many late-night drunks prowl around, looking for trouble.

Tonight, after the pounding, there's a strange scraping sound, as if someone were brushing branches against the outside of my door. The sound stops.

It's time to leave for the movie at the embassy. I put on my coat and go to my apartment door, sliding back the bolt and turning the knob. The door won't open.

I try again. pressing against it with my shoulder. It won't budge. I look through the cracks to see if something is wedged outside. Nothing. Then I realize the door is locked — and it's been locked from the outside.

I have one of those locks where you need a key to lock or unlock it from BOTH the inside and the outside. There's also a sliding bolt on the inside. When I'm home, I use the bolt. I never fasten the main lock. I might have to get out fast.

The only way for that lock to be locked now is from the outside. Someone with a key to my apartment has tried to get in. He turned that key in the lock.

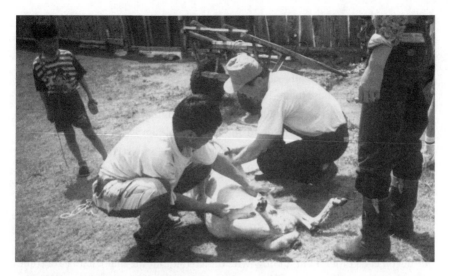

When he couldn't get in, he turned the key the other way, locking the door. I use my key to open it. The hall is pitch dark.

The bulb on the landing is burned out. So is the one on the landing below. The one below that has been stolen. That's not so strange. I usually climb the stairs with a flashlight.

But tonight, that darkness is frightening. I listen, straining against the lack of light. There is only silence as I leave my apartment. This guy with another key is somewhere close. I stumble down the dark stairs and walk to the embassy.

It's cold, so I take the shortest route, climbing over the fence that surrounds this building. Then I walk through a few housing projects, cross the street, climb over another fence. I pick my way through an open dirt field with the skeletons of a few trees and bushes between it and the river. Often, in this space, cows and horses wander, scratching at the last few shreds of dried grass or tree bark. There are always bones here, thrown by passers by, some gnawed clean by their animal murderers.

Tonight, it's darker than usual. The blackness outside my window at home now surrounds me. The flashlight barely penetrates the dark, like headlights in a thick fog. Only the white bones reflect the pale light. They make me shiver worse than the cold. Seeing them — especially the skulls — is like listening to fingers scrape a blackboard or a key scrape a metal lock.

They were horses, cows, goats, dogs. Now, they're white, hollow shells, with two black nose slits and two black circles staring at me through the flashlight rays. They lie flat, the lower jaw torn away by the same animal who tore away the flesh that covered them.

I'd like to hurry past them, but I have to pick my way through. Step-by-step, I try not to outpace the weak light in my hand. Eventually, I get to the riverbank. I jump from the top of the levee to the river bed, then walk across a concrete dam that's collapsed in the middle. On the other side, I hoist myself up and walk the few yards to the embassy guardhouse. I enter, saying hello to my friend who works there.

"Mykel," he says, "you don't look so good. Are you sick?"

"No," I tell him, not wanting to explain, "I'm just a bit cold, that's all."

The movie tonight is *SCAM*, a light switcheroo about people trying to out-hustle each other. I don't know who directed it, but the main actors are some girl with a body and skull-faced Christopher Walken.

The action takes place on a Caribbean island. Jamaica, I think. It's a series of breaking and enterings. Him into her place, her into his place, both of them into an old accomplice's place. There are a couple of big black native islanders. They break into someone's country home, cut his head off and put it in the pantry. Just what I need tonight. As soon as the movie finishes, I run back to my apartment to make sure everything is still there.

"Oh please God," I beg. "Please could he only take the money! Not the computer! Anything but the computer!"

In order to avoid the bones, I take the long way, along the river to the road. I cross by bridge, and make the long trek up the hill.

Before I get home I need to make two important phonecalls, appointments for the next day. I have no phone in my apartment.

The desk crew in the lobby of a nearby hotel is nice enough to let me use their phone. Usually I stop to talk with them too, but tonight I'm in a hurry.

While on the phone, the main hotel door creaks open behind me. The cold air from outside hits me on the back of the neck. I turn around to see a large man walk purposefully toward the front desk. He's a typical square-shaped Mongolian: leather jacket, big fur hat. His temples bulge with his jaw bones, when he clenches his teeth.

When he gets to the desk, he unzips his jacket and reaches inside. He pulls out a small plastic wallet, flips it open, and shows the contents to the young woman and bellhops sitting at the desk. Their jaws drop. It's the law!

The policeman asks some questions. Heads shake. Shoulders shrug. Nobody knows nothing. I can feel the cop's quiet anger, but he doesn't raise his voice. He just leaves.

I quickly hang up the phone and race back to my apartment. Up the hill, through the gate, into the door of my building. It's pitch dark in the hall as I run up the 87 steps. Forgetting to use the flashlight, I trip. I go down, banging my shin on the steps, scraping my palms. Groping for the bannister I pull myself up. Blood softly trickles under my pants, down the front of my leg.

From the bottom of the last flight, I see light shining through the cracks in my doorframe. Did I leave a light on when I left? I can't remember.

The door is locked. A good sign, I think. I unlock it and walk in.

The place is in total chaos. Papers everywhere, blankets on the floor. Books strewn about.

Just like I left it. Everything there, perfectly out of place. I kiss my computer and bolt the door. Tomorrow, I'll change the lock.

FOUR

The closest I've come to Ivory Tower employment has been working as a cashier at the NYU bookstore. I've heard about the mortarboard bureaucracy, but so far never experienced it. Now I'm a visiting professor, in the School of Foreign Service, at the most prestigious university in the weirdest country in the world.

The school year starts normally enough. My few classes meet in the same rooms every week. The conditions are a bit primitive: BYOC (Bring Your Own Chalk), and rooms with no lights or heat. You'd expect that in a third world country, though I'm not sure WHAT world Mongolia's in.

My office is a desk in the English Department. It's pushed up against a number of other desks in the large open room in the front.

Next to me is Erdenbataar, a big man in his fifties, who looks more like a wrestler than an academic. He's one of three other males in this department.

In back, Dr. Sumiya, the department head, has the only private office. That office houses a small xerox machine, one of two in the university. Sometimes it makes extremely poor copies. Most of the time it doesn't work at all. For copy paper, Toila, the department secretary, uses old exams and radio-news transcripts. There's a paper shortage. Even if there weren't, Mongols use nothing only once.

My students are all in second year English. One class, 2D, is more urban and sophisticated, mostly sons and daughters of the former party elite, or the new capitalists. They're lazy, smart, and always on the make.

2C, the other class, has only two boys among twenty country girls. These girls have less English background than those in 2D. But, they're more earnest and study harder than the others.

The classes run normally for the first week or two. I'm getting used to the system, and my fellow teachers, mostly married middle-aged women. They're friendly, bold and a joy to be with. The three male teachers are quiet--at least while working. Maggie, a sexy young woman from Northern Ireland, is the only other foreigner in the department. She'll be leaving soon, though, so she concentrates more on packing than on classes. Then there's Sainamdrar, a skinny young grad assistant with a beautifully bold face and an erotic innocence that warms my loins.

They say a good teacher learns more than he teaches. I must be good. Lesson number one: Nothing is what it seems.

You know how in Kafka's The Trial, Joseph K is continually stymied by the system? He can never discover the exact nature of his crime or how to appeal when he's falsely accused. That's how I feel teaching at the university and that's why I call this chapter:

LIFE AT KAFKA U

It's the third week of classes. I'm teaching 2D. Tsegtsetseg, a pretty girl, about nineteen, raises her hand before I begin the lesson.

"Mykel-*baksh*," she says, "I ask you a favor, ok?"

"OK," I answer, "if I can do it, I will."

For some reason this gets a laugh from the class. Tsegtsetseg blushes, but continues. "For me and some other, this only class today. We need free day. Can we change?"

"Fine," I say, "Any time I'm not teaching is ok. You make all the arrangements and find a classroom. No Saturdays though. I need my weekends."

"We do," says Tsegtsetseg, "we find and tell you."

By the next week, they've taken care of the changes. We move to room 161 on the ground floor. It's a shabby room, right in front of the constantly opening, constantly cold, front door. The desks are long yellow tables with benches built into the front of them. The lights never work and the chalkboard is a warped piece of brown slate that won't hold chalkmarks. But it's a room, and I'll manage.

I ask Dr. Sumiya how I should report the room change.

"You just go to Ichibat," he says, "he'll copy it down so there won't be any trouble."

Ichibat is in charge of most everything for The School of Foreign Services. An older man with a gray crewcut, he looks like a toughguy. You soon learn he's got a good heart.

Neither Ichibat nor his heart is in the office when I report the change. Instead, I see a male secretary, officious, with round glasses and hair slicked back like a mobster. He understands no English. Fortunately, I've brought Sainamdrar to help translate.

In quicker time than it would take in The States, everything is straightened out, approved and recorded.

As the term progresses, I learn to save the brown paper wrapping on my CARE packages from home. These I tape to the blackboard slate. I write on them with a black marker. It almost works.

Because my teaching schedule is rather light, I offer to give a morphology course for the other teachers. Morphology, the structure of words, has been a favorite topic of mine since college. It fascinates me that words like snot, sneeze, snort, snout — all those sn words — have to do with the nose. It's the stuff of good lectures.

Dr. Sumiya smiles when I approach him with the plan.

"Excellent," he says, "it'll really help the teachers handle vocabulary. Tell me when you're free and I'll schedule it. You can teach right in the English Department."

I spend a week preparing four lectures on the structure of English words. The lecture series is to start at 10AM on October 10.

I arrive at 9:45. Namjil and Sainamdrar are there. Neither is interested in my handout...or the lecture. At 10:30 Namjil asks me to go to another room.

"You see, Mykel," she says, "Doytseg is absent today and her students have nothing to do. Maybe you could lecture them."

So lecture them I do. Namjil politely sits in. Some students smile at appropriate points. One or two take notes. It's not quite what I expect.

When I arrive for the next lecture, I expect the worst. It's worse than that. The department door is locked. Closed tight. A couple of cleaning ladies, mopping up yesterday's mud tracks, scowl at me. I try to shoulder the door open. It doesn't budge. Besides, the school halls are empty. Deserted.

Giving up, I leave and go to the expensive *Ulaanbataar* hotel, one of the few places in town that serves breakfast. At about eleven, I return to the school for my regular class. The classroom's empty. Not one student. Not only have my fellow teachers rejected me, but the students as well.

Ten minutes later, the room fills with students. I don't recognize one of them. Three months teaching the same people and not one familiar face.

"Are you here for an English class?" I ask a young man wearing jeans and a black turtleneck shirt.

"*Bid olgakhgui*" (I don't understand) he says.

"Does anyone here speak English?" I ask.

A woman in her mid-twenties with a bad complexion half raises her hand. When I look at her she says, "I...a little."

"What class is this?" I ask.

"This Russian class," she answers.

"Russian?" I ask. "Have you always had a Russian class here?"

"Always," she says.

A big guy, with a round face and fleshy hands, smiles slowly, like he's just figured something out. He speaks to the young woman.

"What time you think?" says the woman.

I look at my watch. "Ten after eleven." I say.

She laughs. "You mistake. It ten after ten. No more summer time. It finish on Sunday." She looks at her watch. "It ten after ten."

I race upstairs bursting into the English Department. Behind every table sits a teacher. My sudden entrance catches them off guard. A look of disappointment flickers across their faces. Erdenbataar steals a glance at his watch. Gutalmaa, a small woman with piercing eyes, pierces those eyes toward the ceiling. Somehow, I have the feeling they are not here by choice.

Gutalmaa looks at Dr. Sumiya then at me.

"Where were you?" she asks. "We want to hear your lecture about inter and intra. It sounds so thrilling."

I explain my mistake and apologize. "How come no one told me of the time change?" I ask.

"We thought you knew," says Namjil. "Everybody else knew."

Since it's late, we reschedule the second lecture for next week. No one comes to that one, though, so I scrap the course.

For the next month, life goes as normally as possible in Mongolia. Then, on Monday, I arrive at the English Department to prepare for my classes. Toila greets me at the door with a frown on her usually happy face.

"Mykel," she says, "We have to change one of your classes. There's going to be a lecture on American History during that time. It will be in the room you use now."

"When is the new time?" I ask.

"Saturday morning," she says.

"No way!" I say, "I need my Saturdays. It's the weekend. WEEK END!"

"I'm sorry," she says, "I tried change the day, but it's impossible."

"Who can I speak to about it?" I ask.

"You can talk to Ichibat," she says, "but I don't think it will help."

I go to see Ichibat. Again, I bring Sainamdrar to translate. This time he's in. He sits at his desk, looking stern and administrative.

Sainamdrar explains my problem. Ichibat pushes himself up from the desk and walks to the wall. He unhooks a huge chart and lays it on the desk.

"It's a plan of all the classes," Sainamdrar explains to me. "That way we can see everything."

Ichibat points to the time period where I HAD my 2D class — before we changed the time and place. He speaks to me in slow Mongolian. Sainamdrar translates.

"You teach at this time," she says, "and now we need that space for the history lectures."

"But I don't teach at that time anymore," I tell her. "I changed the time."

She translates. Ichibat looks puzzled. He no longer speaks to me, but to Sainamdrar. He asks when the class now meets. I explain the time and room change. Ichibat looks at the chart.

"There are no classrooms available at that time," he says. "You cannot be teaching then."

"But I've been meeting in that class," I tell him. "Every week since the change, I've been in Room 161."

He looks at the chart again. "Were you in room 161a or 161b?"

"I don't know," I answer.

"It doesn't matter," he says. "Both those classes have something else."

"It can't be," I say, "I've been teaching a class there for two and a half months."

"You have not," he says. He then tells me that room 161a has ANOTHER English class in it. 161b has a French class.

Knowing this is wrong, I ask him if we can find out the problem. He nods and we go out to check.

Asking around, we discover that Siirtbat, a young heavy-drinking teacher, teaches in Room 161a, when he can make it. That means I've been teaching in 161b.

It's on to the French department, just down the hall. The door is closed. Locked up tight. No one around. No one to ask. Just gone, vanished. We return to Ichibat to report our findings.

"There's no way of checking," says Ichibat, "but it doesn't matter. It's all here on the chart. You have to change your teaching time because there are no classrooms."

My having actually taught in this non-existent classroom makes no impression. I try a different tact.

"Isn't there some other time you could change it to?" I ask.

He shakes his head and begins pouring over the chart again.

"Well," he says, "there is one room available at 8:40 in the morning on Wednesday."

"I'll take it," I tell him. "At least I'll have my weekends."

The next class, I explain the forthcoming change to my students.

"There's going to be an American History lecture in our original classroom at the original time we met," I say. "According to school records, the time and place we've actually been meeting does not exist. We cannot continue to meet there because a French class has been meeting there, not us. We only thought we were meeting in that class, but we weren't because it's impossible. So now we have to change to a time where there are classrooms."

Although the words come out of my mouth, they make no sense to me. The students, however, understand perfectly and agree, without comment, to the new time and place.

At the new time, the students show up for class no later than usual. I'm resigned to getting up before the sun rises. It's not so bad, though, because after class, I can go home and nap.

The next day, I leave the English Department for home. On the way out, a third year student stops me in the large atrium at the top of the stairs. A petite girl with a constant frown, I recognize her from the times we've passed in the hallway.

"Where were you?" she asks. "We waited a half hour for you and then went home?"

"Where was I when?" I ask.

"Yesterday, at the lecture," she says, clucking her tongue in annoyance.

"What lecture?" I ask, annoying her further.

She sighs and sends both hands out in a gesture of pure exasperation.

"At the American History lecture, of course," she breathes. "You were supposed to give a lecture on American History."

"I was supposed to lecture on American history? I don't know American history."

She walks over to the wall. On it, now hangs the chart that Ichibat used to prove there was no classroom for the class I'd been teaching.

"Look," she says, pointing to a large white block with some Cyrillic writing, "It's right here in plain Mongolian. Can't you read?"

"Nobody told me about this," I say.

"I'm sure someone told you," she says. "Didn't you have to change your classroom?"

"Yes, but..." I start.

"Well, that proves it," she says, still annoyed at my stupidity.

Having learned the uselessness of protest in a situation like this, I apologize.

"You're absolutely right," I tell her. "How stupid of me. I have a master's degree in Linguistics. So naturally people want to hear what I have to say about American History. And I should know this because the American History lecture is in a classroom I used to teach in. Although my class changed rooms and times, it really didn't. A French class has been using that room so I couldn't have been. I was assigned a different class time to make space for the lecture, even though the lecture was not held at the time I was having my class. Since my classroom changed, I must have known that I was the one giving the lecture in the first place. Right? It all makes perfect sense."

"Of course it does," says the young woman. "What is it with Americans? The most obvious things just go bye bye for you."

I nod, shrug my shoulders and say, "You're right. It's just a different way of thinking, I guess."

She nods and stomps off. Me? I have to get to bed. Tomorrow's my early class...I think.

FIVE

HILLARY

The American Embassy in *Ulaanbaatar* is not like embassies elsewhere. There's no pillared mansion, no marines with guns, no winding staircases with chandeliers. The main 'road' is the concrete top of the river levee. Parallel to it runs a dirt path that, in September, is more mud than dirt. The building itself is a white hut with peeling paint and occasional electrical fires. A small wooden guardhouse in front is the checkpoint. Anyone with a Western face passes without problem.

Dorj, a local student, is one of the guards. We help each other with our native tongues. We often sit together in the guardhouse, his English book open at the desk. Sometimes people ask me permission to enter, showing me their passport or the inside of their bags. They think I'm some sort of official. We laugh at their mistake.

Dorj's main job is opening and closing the gate when anybody says the word "Gate" into a radio that transmits to an intercom inside. That intercom also picks up any 2-way radio conversations in the neighborhood. Near Dorj's seat are two buttons. They're labeled in Russian. One says START. It opens the gate. The STOP button closes it.

For Americans in *Ulaanbaatar*, the embassy is a hangout. A bulletin board offers apartments for rent, see-the-country helicopter trips and counter-top water purifiers. Wednesdays and Saturdays, they show movies in the library. Wednesdays bring a more adult crowd. The movies have Tommy Lee Jones, Jessica Tandy and Robert DeNiro. Saturdays, the crowd is mostly missionaries and their kids. Then, the movies have animals in them. There's also a tiny bar with free snacks and buck-and-a-half beers. It's low key, unassuming and unromantic. As far away from the world of real diplomacy as Mongolia is from the world of real events. Could you imagine the status of the Mongolian Ambassador?

"Ah, you're the guy who sold us that Whitewater Property. You're right, I did promise you an Ambassadorship..."

It must be the bottom of the totempole. The dumping ground of promises just barely kept. It's forgotten, backwater, third world, without the romance of famine or war. The embassy holds quarterly "meet the ambassador" get-togethers with the Americans in town. Ambassador Ford missed the last one. He had taken a helicopter trip to the countryside. The pilot forgot to bring enough fuel for the return. At the meeting, the ambassador's wife explained the situation; only newcomers were surprised.

Mongolia is not like other countries. It's a land where most people live in *gers* and wear *deels*. Here, "Welcome to Mongolia" is not a greeting, but closer to "Ah, you're beginning to understand!"

"I haven't had hot water for a week!"

"Welcome to Mongolia!"

"I made an appointment to meet the labor minister at 10AM. I waited until 1PM. Then someone told me he was visiting his family in the countryside for the week."

"Welcome to Mongolia!"

"Today I paid twice as much for busfare as I did yesterday! In the meantime, a loaf a bread is almost as expensive as in New York. In two days, it went up fifty percent! And bananas! I paid five bucks for two of them!"

"Welcome to Mongolia!"

There is a quaintness to the town. Cows graze on the lawn in front of government buildings. Herdsmen, just in from the countryside, wearing their bright red or brown *deels*, ride on horseback past the urban luxury hotel. In the summer, kids swim naked in the river that runs outside the embassy. You begin to look at the breakdowns and inefficiencies as a way for the city to rebel against the nine-to-five workaday world.

BUT, Hillary Clinton is coming to town! She's in China for the international women's conference and she's making a side trip to *Ulaanbaatar*. The Secret Service will be all over the place. The town should be wild with all these guys in dark suits with little pins and sunglasses with earplugs. The papers will talk about it for months — just like they did when Richard Gere visited with the Dalai Lama.

The man behind the embassy bar tells us, "She's supposed to be here a week from Monday. I hope she doesn't come, though. It'll be a pain in the ass."

His hopes are not to be fulfilled. The movies are canceled for a week. There is new activity at the embassy. The smell of tar hangs over the tiny compound. Mongolians, wearing an approximation of white coveralls, roll rainproof paper on the roof. Next to the building, a new fence is slowly rising around a pile of rubble they've been calling "the new extension."

On Saturday, I'm at the Flower Hotel waiting in the lobby to use the phone. I need to make last minute arrangements for Yoko's visit. She's coming next week and who knows, maybe in this exotic land I'll get farther with her than I did in New York.

While I wait, I hear English voices. To my right, David talks with a bearded blond man wearing a down vest. After I finish my call, I ask them what they're discussing. The American is in town to prepare for Hillary's visit. He needs to get to the embassy. One of the receptionists at the hotel is on the OTHER phone trying to call him a taxi. She shakes her head.

"I'm sorry," she says, "there are no taxis now."

"Welcome to Mongolia!" I say.

He tells me his name is Larry. I offer to walk him to the embassy, not far from the hotel. He agrees. As we walk, we talk.

"What exactly do you DO?" I ask.

"I'm an advance weasel," He answers, "I set things up."

"How do you become an advance weasel?" I ask.

"Go to New Hampshire at the right time and pick a winner," he says.

I nod.

We come to the turn-off onto the levee. There is no light here, just a path through broken stone next to the bridge.

"Where are we going?" asks Larry.

"This is the road to the embassy," I explain.

"???????" he says.

The only sound is Larry's boots kicking an occasional pebble into the river. Slowly, in the dark, we pick our way over the stones that lead to the path along the levee. When we get on level ground again, the conversation continues.

"So when exactly is Hillary coming?" I ask.

"I don't know," he says. "I'm leaving next Sunday. It's gotta be before that. I think she'll be here Tuesday."

About this time we reach the embassy. Dorj is not on duty, but I know all the guards and greet Sanbat, the night worker. Larry takes his leave and enters the embassy. I go back to my unheated apartment.

The next day, Dorj and I work together on our mutual language deficiencies. We also talk about the upcoming visit and presidents in general.

Dorj tells me he likes George Bush, but not Clinton. Why?

"George Bush was in the army and fought against the Japanese in an airplane." He continues, "Clinton was never in the army. He was skipping the army in Vietnam. You have to know hardships to be president. You have to know war."

I ask him about Orchibat, the current Mongolian president.

"I don't like him," says Dorj. "He is not a strong man."

"Which leader did you like?" I ask. I assume he'll answer Choibalsan, Mongolia's Stalin, or *Sukhbaatar*, the founder of Socialist Mongolia. His name means "axe-hero." I assume wrong.

"I like Chinngis Khan," he says. "That was a real man."

Dorj still doesn't know when the first lady is due. Only that it's "sometime next week."

Monday morning a fellow teacher tells me, "Hillary's coming on Wednesday. One of my students told me. She heard it on the news."

That afternoon, I visit Dorj to check. A small brown and white cow grazes on the grass in front of the embassy. I pet it as I walk past into the guardhouse.

The familiar face of another guard greets me.

"Dorj no here," he says, "Margash, margash."

I know enough Mongolian to understand 'tomorrow.'

"Hillary Clinton?" I ask.

The guard shrugs.

On Tuesday, the sky is dark. A cold wind chills the city air. At the embassy, a slew of cars have parked on the dirt path in front of the little building. Instead of tight-lipped forty year olds in black suits and sunglasses, there are smiley-faced twenty year olds in jeans and denim jackets — at least as many women as men. Not my image of secret service.

Dorj and I are inside the little guardhouse. Suddenly, the intercom crackles with English as it picks up transmissions between members of the advance crew. Words like COPY, ROGER and OVER find their way, probably for the first time, through the air to our intercom.

The brown and white cow is back. Again, grazing on the front lawn. The clouds grow increasingly ominous.

"Lots of action, huh?" I say to Dorj.

"We hear today," he says. "She comes on Thursday. I don't know what time."

"Are you working on Thursday?" I ask.

"Eight in the morning till three in the afternoon," he tells me. I ask what time the honored guest arrives. He shrugs.

Above the intercom static, we hear a conversation between an advance-man making a test drive to the airport and an advance-woman at the embassy.

Suddenly the clouds burst without a pre-drizzle. Thunder crashes, very close. The cow in front of the embassy vainly looks for shelter. It winds up huddling next to a metal storage bin across the now mud path. We hear the advance-pair over the intercom.

A: Radiocheck one two three three two one.

B: Jones? James. Have you loud and clear. Over.

A: James? Jones. We're transmitting from the gate. Have some lightning here. Over.

B: Jones? James. I can see it. Over.

A: James? Jones. Looks like quite a storm. Over.

B: Jones? James. Welcome to Mongolia. Over.

A: James? Jones. Was there a reply? Over.

B: Jones? James. Did you copy? Over.

A: James? Jones. Can you copy? Over.

B: Jones? James. Had you broke and unreadable if that was an attempt to contact. Over.

A: James? Jones. Can you copy? Over.

B: Jones? James. Can you copy? Over.

A: James? Jones. Negative contact scan one, switching to scan two. Over.

B: Jones? James. How copy me now? Over.

A: James? Jones. Roger, have you loud and clear. Volume has to be all the way up. Over.

B: Jones? James. You're starting to break up. Over.

A: James? Jones. One two three, three two one, do you copy? Over.

There's a pause. Some voices come on in Mongolian. I ask Dorj what they're talking about.

"That's a lady who works here calling her husband — one of the drivers. She's telling him to get some lamb meat at the store if he has enough money."

Thursday I finish my teaching duties by noon. Dorj waits for me at the embassy. Tsenga, one of the other guards, is also there. He, however, is not dressed in his usual cotton shirt and jeans. Today, he wears a white shirt, brown suit — at least two sizes too big — and a wide green tie. He looks uncomfortable.

"She will come at 3PM," says Dorj.

"How do you know?" I ask. "Was there some kind of official announcement?"

"It says here."

He points to a little post-it note, written in Mongolian. It's stuck on the reception window, next to another sign announcing the name of next Saturday's movie: GLORY.

"I leave at 3PM," Dorj says. "I see Hillary and then leave."

"You think she'll REALLY be here at 3PM?" I ask.

"It says here."

"But this is Mongolia!" I tell him.

He doesn't get it.

At 2 o'clock the action begins: A green army bus sputters through the mud path. It turns off onto the patch of grass across from the embassy. Out pile a dozen Mongol military men. Half-dressed, in red, white and green, they tuck in their shirts, pull up their suspenders, and brush off their hats when they leave the bus. The soldiers line up along the mud path. After the soldiers come the police, dressed in blue. They station themselves behind the soldiers in the muddy grass. Then there is a Russian jeep followed by a local black jalopy.

It turns onto the embassy driveway. Dorj opens the gate. They enter the compound. A middle-aged man comes out of the jeep. With gray hair and somewhat of a pot belly, he seems to be the coordinator. There is also the required pair of square headed, blond crew-cut young men with dark suits. They are not wearing sunglasses. There's a young woman, dressed in a black skirt with a bright red blazer. She has a walkie talkie.

The middle-aged man carries an old fashioned black radiophone. He sets it down and then comes to meet Dorj and me.

"William Anderson, Secret Service," he says, sticking his hand through the little hole in the window.

I take his hand.

"Mykel Board," I say. "This is Dorj."

"I'm just trying to set this up," he tells us, indicating the radio phone. He detaches an antenna from the set. Holding the receiver to his ear, he moves the antenna to the desk in the guardhouse.

At about this time, the Peace Corps coordinator walks in. We know each other from the Wednesday movies. She waves to me and I ask her how she is. After she walks through, into the embassy, William Anderson speaks to me.

"I know security is usually somewhat lax here," he tells me. "But as it gets later, you're going to have to ask for ID — even from people you know."

He returns to fiddling with the radiophone antenna. He tries setting the phone on top of the broken metal detector. Then the floor near the door. Finally, he carries it outside and sets it up just behind the gate.

He speaks into it, "testing one two three three two one." The voice comes through our walkie talkie. He then speaks into his lapel.

"Testing one two three three two one," he says. His voice booms onto the street through a speaker somewhere outside the building. Satisfied, he smiles.

A young American with a brown crewcut and a blue denim jacket enters the guardhouse. Dorj gets up to talk with him. The gray-haired man waves him off.

"He's ok. He's Secret...He's ok."

I see the pin on his lapel. Dorj looks at me, wrinkling his forehead. I smile and wave the guy through.

"Security," says the American, "I like that."

A large white van comes to the gate. With a TV memory of self-destructing

Beirut Arabs, I turn to William Anderson.

"It's ok," he says. "That's the caterer."

Dorj opens the gate and the truck pulls in. The driver opens the van and takes out tray after tray of what looks like potato salad, cold-cuts, soft French cheese, coleslaw, French bread, cookies, cake. The works. Dorj who's been there since eight in the morning, hasn't eaten all day. I had a slice of bread with Russian jam for breakfast — six hours earlier.

"You think we could get some of that food in here?" I ask William Anderson.

He laughs. "I haven't eaten yet myself. That food's for the bigshots. We don't eat. We never do."

Then he notices the cars parked on the street and on the grass near the soldiers.

"No vehicles parked on the street," he says into his lapel. His voice echoes across the river. "Move those cars!"

One of the blond crewcuts trots into the embassy. A few minutes later, Mongol embassy workers trickle out of the building. They get in their cars and move them across the grass to the river bank. After half an hour, two cars are still unclaimed. The Mongol police try the doors. Unable to open them, they push the cars on locked tires, through the mud, toward the riverbank.

Two of the more casual Secret Service men station themselves in front of the moved cars. They wear jeans, brown leather jackets and hiking boots. They're more than conspicuous in the midst of the uniformed Mongols.

The woman in the red blazer comes to talk with Dorj. I figure she must be James (or Jones) from the walkie talkie.

"We need to keep tight control here," she says, "the gate should be opened only for the motorcade and the wife of the president of parliament. You know the president's wife, don't you?"

Dorj and I both shrug. James or Jones looks skyward.

"Also," she continues, "you'll be able to tell the official vehicles because they each have an identifying sign on them. They're the only ones who pass."

"Excuse me," I say, "but the guard is supposed to change at 3PM."

The woman looks at me like I had proposed assassination.

"Does the next guard speak English?" she asks.

"No, he doesn't," answers Dorj.

"Great!" she says, looking skyward. "Will somebody be here who speaks English?"

"I can stay if you want me to," Dorj says.

She looks at me. "Could you stay too?" she asks, "We'd like to have an official native speaker here."

"Sure, I'll stay," I tell her.

"You know the motorcade won't arrive at three, don't you?" I asked James or Jones.

"Don't you have a schedule?" she says.

Dorj takes a small piece of paper out of a desk drawer. It's the itinerary written in Mongolian.

"Three o'clock: American Embassy," he translates.

James or Jones smiles a see-I-told-you-so smile and says, "We have this carefully timed," she says, "She'll be here at three o'clock. We'll have the Official Greeter ready."

She nods to Tsenga, looking more uncomfortable than ever in his suit. Then, she notices a crowd of Mongols in front of the guard house.

"Who are these people?" she asks.

I tell her I don't know.

"Don't you think you'd better check their invitations?" she tells me. "We only want prominent Mongols waiting here."

She looks at me like I've been derelict in my duty. Then, she walks off.

"Should I look at their invitations?" I ask Dorj.

"I will do it," he says and walks out to check them.

By this time, Dorj and I are really starving. It's three fifteen with no word on the arrival time. The official greeter has left his official greeting post to do some shopping. He comes back with some hard Mongolian cookies and four bottles of Good™ Cola.

At three thirty, an English-speaking voice crackles through the walkie talkie. I can make out the words "delay" and "wants to stop to shop for presents."

At four o'clock, the walkie talkie hisses again. It's hard to hear what comes through on this side, but William Anderson replies.

"Gate secure: One greeter. No press. No public."

William Anderson turns to me.

"Tell the Mongol to open the gate," he shouts from outside the closed window. Not knowing the words in Mongolian, I say "Open the gate," to Dorj.

He presses the START button. Distant sirens gradually get louder. Police cars pass the embassy as a large black car turns and enters. In the window of the car, we see a small piece of paper with CONTROL written on it in black marker. Then there is a Cadillac limo, flown in by the air force just for the occasion. I can see the back of the first lady's head inside. Her hair is longer than I expected.

Next comes an old jeep with a paper STAFF sign on it. Then two mini-buses with JUULCHIN, the official tourist bureau, painted on the side. The next paper signs say PRESS 1 and PRESS 2. Then a few more cars, including an old Russian Lada with the sign STRAGGLER on it. I'm about to tell Dorj to close the gate when one more car follows. It's a putt putt of a car. The driver, the only occupant, is a middle age Mongol. There is no official paper — just a sticker on the back that says MGL.

After that car goes through the gate, William Anderson calls to me.

"Tell the Mongolian guard to close the gate," he says.

"Close the gate," I say to Dorj. He pushes the STOP button.

Right after Dorj closes the gate, a shy Mongolian woman, maybe sixty-five comes into the guardhouse. She holds up a small white envelope.

"I've been invited," she tells me.

I smile and nod. Dorj goes out, looks at the envelope, and waves her past. Behind her follow a stream of visitors — mostly women — each carrying a little white envelope. I stay in the office. Dorj goes out and looks at every invitation. He then sends the guests onward.

William Anderson stands between the guardhouse and the embassy. He reviews each invitation. He also checks cameras, bags, gift parcels. I know many of the entering people. They say hello to me. Some hand me their invitations. I send them to William Anderson.

Bianca, a large woman with gray hair, works with the United Nations. I know her from the expat pizza hours she organizes at The Green Club, the only "Indian" restaurant in town.

"I didn't know you worked here," she says.

"I'm on special duty," I tell her.

A Mongolian man approaches me. He says, "I, no invitation. Lose.

l newspaper," He shows me a laminated card with his picture and Mongol text.

"See him," I say, pointing to William Anderson. The man smiles and nods. William Anderson turns to me.

"Ask the Mongolian guard to tell him that we can't let him in without an invitation," he says.

I turn to Dorj. "Tell him, he can't come in without an invitation," I say.

Dorj talks to the man. Reluctantly, he leaves.

From our position, we can see into the embassy reception room. As we sip our Good™ Cola, we watch the reception. The invited guests down the salad, cold cuts and the rest. They seem to enjoy themselves.

Turning away from the action inside, I watch the plain clothes Secret Service agents by the river. A car pulls up alongside them. An older Mongolian man and woman get out. They open the trunk. The Secret Service men walk over to them.

The couple begins to pull paintings out of the trunk, displaying them to the agents. The Americans shake their heads, and make shooing motions with their hands. The couple doesn't understand. The Mongolian man moves his hands toward the ground, showing he's willing to lower the price. Our nation's guardians are not interested.

Eventually, a Mongolian soldier comes over to talk with the couple. They, reluctantly load up their paintings and drive away. By this time, the First Lady is finished with her visit. People slowly leave the building.

"Should we open the gate?" I ask William Anderson.

"Not yet," he says. "Leaving always takes awhile."

A tall bald Westerner in his early fifties, dressed in a conservative gray suit, walks from the embassy building to our guardhouse. With him is a younger, shorter westerner and a Mongolian. Cradled in the arms of the tall man is a small white dog.

In the guardhouse, the tall man nods hello to Dorj and me. He speaks to the Mongol — in Mongolian. Then, he speaks to the Westerner.

"I've asked the driver to take you wherever you need to go," he says. "He's very trustworthy. You can be sure you'll get your..." His voice lowers at this point. I can't make out the rest.

The shorter, younger, man and the Mongol leave the guardhouse. The tall man with the dog turns to us.

"Lots of excitement, today," he says.

"There sure is," I reply. Dorj smiles.

"We're not used to so much security," the bald man tells me. Then he smiles, shrugs and walks off, back to the crowd at the embassy.

Dorj anticipates my question. "That was the ambassador," he says. "His Mongolian is very good. He doesn't know a lot of words. But he can pronounce them very well."

We hear a tap on the window. It's William Anderson. "Tell the Mongol to open the gate!" he says.

"Open the gate," I say to Dorj.

He pushes the START button.

The motley motorcade leaves the compound. This time Hillary looks out of the Cadillac, waving to the few people standing around.

"Great," I say to Dorj, "we can leave now."

He shakes his head. "No. She will come back at six o'clock."

"Six o'clock?" I ask.

He shrugs.

When 7PM rolls around, the cookies and cola have lost their effect. Our stomachs growl in counterpoint, occasionally reaching a juicy crescendo.

William Anderson stands inside the gate. His thumbs are tucked into his belt. His head tilts downward. His eyes are closed. Then, the radio crackles. He taps on the window. Sirens ring in the distance. Dorj opens the gate and the motorcade enters again. An hour later they leave. We can go home.

William Anderson packs up his radiophone. The Secret Service guards have left. The army men and police pile into a trio of old buses. Dorj and I go to the closest bar for some food and a couple beers.

I ask Dorj to order some *buz* and a beer for me. He talks to the waitress. She answers him, shrugging her shoulders.

"They are out of beer," he tells me. "Do you want vodka?"

"This is a bar and there's no beer?" I ask him.

"Welcome to Mongolia," he says.

SIX

A HORSE IS A HORSE, OF COURSE

Imagine ten thousand fraternities, each with ten thousand wooden fraternity paddles. Now bend over...

Yoko is finally here from NY. We've hired a jeep and driver through a local tourist bureau. I got a deal because I teach them English. We're spending a few days in the countryside, about 350 miles West of *Ulaanbaatar*. There, we ride our first horses, trial by fire — or at least splinter. Mongolians use wooden saddles.

Yesterday we went to the remains of a huge Monastery. The commies destroyed most of it during "the bad times." Now, they're rebuilding.

We're staying in a *ger* hostel; big white *gers*, specially cleaned and protected for the tourists. Being off-season, they set up only three, plus the head *ger* where the caretakers live and prepare our meals.

Today, we have three objectives. First, get on horses and take pictures of each other. Second, visit a local monastery and ruins. Third, visit some sand dunes.

Morning is horse time. We wait for the driver to introduce us to the local herdsman who is supposed to rent us the horses. After an hour we give up and walk there ourselves. There's a little kid, about eight years old, on a horse. We use sign language and my very bad Mongolian to tell him we want to ride. He gets off his horse, a quiet little thing. I get on.

He leads the horse around in a big circle. This isn't bad. It's like a pony ride. I ask him to give me the reigns. He does, and we gallop a couple of feet. Lots of fun! Then Yoko takes a turn. La de da — it's a snap.

In the distance, we see our guide on horseback. The young man is dragging three other horses. One is brown and placid, another, a somewhat sad looking gray stallion. The third seems half-horse, half-mule, and is jet black with dread-locks. He pulls at the bit and rises in the air, hoofs flaying. That one is mine.

"Now we visit the monastery," says our guide.

"We're going by horse?" I ask.

He looks at me as if I had asked whether the heat was out in *Ulaanbaatar*.

"Of course," he says.

All this "saying" is actually his very bad English, my worse Mongolian, an awful dictionary, and a lot of sign language. I translate here for simplicity.

"You want horse riding. You got horse riding."

Neither Yoko nor I have ever ridden before. The wooden Mongolian saddles are covered with a cloth as thin as the hair on my balding head. The metal trim seems especially designed to cut into both thighs simultaneously. The short stirrups are tied to the sides of the saddle. Your toes go pigeon. Your knees cramp in a position similar to the most painful part of a deep kneebend.

"Where's the monastery?" I ask.

"Just over there," says the guide, pointing vaguely at some very rocky mountains.

In Mongolian: "*Chyoo!*" means "giddyup!" You usually say it while striking your horse on the rump with your palm or a stick.

"*Chyoo!*" says the guide. And we're off. At each step the saddle smacks our ever-increasingly tender parts. I try standing up, like the Brits do in horse races, but there's nothing to hold on to. I grip the front of the saddle with one hand, hold the reins in the other, but the pain in my thighs is too much. I sit down again. The pain shifts.

Our guide thinks it's cute to constantly say "*Chyoo!*" to get our horses running. He's in a hurry. Hurry means our sitting parts get twenty whacks for every one we'd get at a slow walk. And twice as hard. I try screaming, "Enough fuckin' *Chyoo*, already!" But it doesn't help.

An hour later, we've gone around the mountain to the *hiid*, a Mongolian temple. Few things have felt as good as getting off that horse.

Actually, there are three *hiids*. One is a small building on ground level. Colorful inside, but not very active. The second is the ruins of a much larger temple destroyed during the purges of the 1930s. The third one is way up on the side of the mountain. To get there, you have to climb over boulders and up loose rocks. Leaving the horses behind, we climb up, over and through the rocky mountain to reach the colorful building. It's closed.

During the communist times, the government closed the temples. They also murdered thousands of monks, Pol Pot style. The temples returned after the fall of communism. Some were rebuilt in old locations, some completely new. Mongols take pride in the return of Buddhism. The Dalai Lama's picture is as ubiquitous as Chinngis Khan's. Although they have the buildings, they don't always have enough people who know what to do with them.

After enjoying the view and resting a bit, Yoko and I climb, slide, skid our way back to the bottom of the mountain. We're heading toward our horses for the return trip. NOT something I look forward to.

"Oy! Oy!" comes a voice from above.

They've opened the *hiid*. A young man wearing purple robes and a yellow hat stands at the balcony watching us. Yoko and I look at each other.

"They're open now," says our guide. "We can go in."

Well, we figure, if they opened for us, it would be rude not to pay our respects. So we clamber back up the rocks to the monastery.

They had not opened for us, but for regular prayers. Inside, a monk unwraps the cloth cover of his prayer tablets and lays them in a stack on the table. It's a thick stack. He starts chanting, going through one tablet at a time. Sitting in the small room are three men who look like local herdsmen. There's also a boy, about 6 year old, who's dressed like a monk. The boy sits near the main monk and occasionally leaves on errands.

We sit, very gently, on the floor. I rest on the side of my foot relieving, as much as possible, pressure on my tender areas. After a long time, the prayers stop and the herdsmen get up to drink something with the monk and give him some money. Our guide says, "lets go." We quietly walk out, climb down the mountainside and (ugh!) get back on our horses.

We do not return the same way we came, however. Mongolian horses are famous for being able to go anywhere — like pack mules. Our guide is going to show us. So, instead of going around the mountains like we did on our arrival, we are going to go over them.

"*Chyoo!*" We're off! Toward the mountain. The wooden saddle turns the butt bruises a deeper shade of purple. Yoko's horse holds back. Our guide grabs the reins and pulls. They ride as one. My horse gallops to keep up. At the foot of the mountain is a path between two boulders, almost as wide as an open hand.

The guide eases the two horses in his charge up to the opening. They slip their sure-footed hooves through the cracks and enter. My horse gets to the opening. He balks. He turns. Walks around. I pull on the reigns, slapping his rump, inflicting nowhere near the pain he's inflicting on me.

Gingerly, he puts out a hoof, slipping it through the opening. Then another. Twice more, and we're on the mountain.

Yoko and the guide are two horselengths ahead, slowly following a narrow path with bare branches that spring against our faces and beat our legs as we pass. Up, up, we go, completely losing sight of the land below.

We go through a narrow pass into a dead end cave. A spring flows from the side. Water drips down the wall. The guide motions for us to get off our horses.

He shows us how to tie the horses' legs together so they can't run away. Then we climb some boulders to get closer to the dripping. The guide says this is special water. Good for our health. We see a little *ovoo* in front of the wet rock wall. Someone placed a few small *tugrik* notes on it.

Pronounced like "oboe," the instrument, but with a 'V' and the accent on the second syllable, it's a Mongolian animist figure. Made from a pile of stones, bones and whatever else is in the area, it's usually topped with a makeshift flag. *Ovoos* come in all sizes, from six inches tall like this one, to six feet tall. We've already seen a few on the side of the "road" on our way here. Yoko and I both add a few *tugriks* to the pile, hoping it might salve our aching asses and bring us good luck.

The guide kneels by a little puddle formed in the cave floor. It's covered with

a still green muck. Parting the stagnant muck, he sucks the water into his mouth. He invites us to do the same. As I lean to drink, my supporting arm finds its way into a mudpile — up to the elbow. So much for good luck. I manage to slurp a few drops before letting Yoko try her luck. She's better at it than I am.

After the drink: back on the horses and back up the mountain. Once we reach the top, we have to go down. The guide, again taking control of his and Yoko's horse, slowly leads them down the hill.

My horse trips. He doesn't fall, just sort of skids on the right foreleg. He's had enough, though. Let those two go down if they want. He's staying right here.

"*Chyoo!*" I yell, slapping hard enough to hurt my hand.

"*Chyoo* you!" says my horse or that's what he's thinking.

"*Chyoo!*" I yell again, slapping the same spot.

The horse moves, but horizontally, not downward. To a place where the step down is steeper and more dangerous. The guide, now somewhat below me, looks up and laughs. He makes a swatting sign with his hand. I try again.

Slowly the horse, one leg at a time, bouncing like a camel, climbs down the precipice to the next level. The bouncing continues until we're at the foot of the mountain. The other two have kindly waited for me.

Once the three of us are together, the guide circles around in back of us.

"*Chyoo!*" he says with a loud clicking noise. All three horses are off at a gallop. I try easing the pain by standing in the stirrups, but the pain of the metal saddle rim against my thighs again is worse than the slapping pain against my bottom. I sit again.

Finally, somehow, we're back at the hostel. I climb off my horse and waddle to our *ger*. It's after one and time for lunch. I'm glad to see our jeep parked in front. I was afraid they'd forgotten about our trip to the sand dunes.

Inside the *ger*, Yoko flops down on her bed — on her stomach. Just as exhausted, I prefer to stand. While waiting for lunch, both of us discretely check our new bruises and blisters. I let my gaze wander to Yoko's bed as she inspects her wounds. Somehow, though, it's just not sexy.

"Wouldn't it be funny," says Yoko, "if they expect us to take the horses to the sand dunes?"

"Don't even joke," I say. "I'm never getting on a horse again. I'm probably never sitting down again."

Then a couple of young boys approach. I'd guess they're about nine or ten years old, maybe younger. One of them is the boy who first put us on a horse, back when we thought it was easy — like a pony ride.

As is typical in Mongolia, the boys just open the *ger* door, walk in and sit down on a bed. Luckily, both of us have already examined our saddle bruises and are presentable, if not exactly "fit." Yoko is rolling herself a cigarette when the boys come in.

She has somehow managed to sit, while I continue to stand near the table. I can see the boy's curiosity. Although they must live in a *ger*, I doubt they've seen one with backpacks, flashlights, English books, a ready-to-go coffee filter, imported coffee, an American guy and a Japanese gal. Their eyes dart around and settle on Yoko's tobacco and rolling paper.

"Roll 'em a cigarette," I suggest.

"They're just little kids," says Yoko.

"This is Mongolia," I reply. The final answer to all questions.

Yoko gestures with the tobacco, a questioning look on her face. Both boys smile and nod. She rolls them each a cigarette. The older one reaches out his grimy hand and takes them. He passes one to his younger friend. Before long, they're puffing away like pros.

While the boys smoke, I walk over to the boiling water on top of the small wood stove that heats the *ger*. Yoko sets up the filter and pours the water through the coffee. We feel the boy's eyes on us.

"Make 'em a cup of coffee," I suggest.

This time Yoko says nothing, but just pours an extra cup that I hand to our guests. They take it gratefully and share it between puffs on their cigarettes.

There is a rustling outside. Our door opens again. It's lunch. There's cabbage salad, lamb soup, bread, a nice meal. There's also the two boys. Our host sees them and scoots them out like a pair of stray dogs. Still, giving two little kids cigarettes and coffee had its thrill. I wish we had some vodka.

Yoko was able to sit down for most of lunch. I try, but can't last more than a minute.

"I've got to go to the bathroom," Yoko tells me.

"Fine," I say, "you don't need permission."

"It's not that," she says, "I'm scared."

"Huh?"

"There are wolves in the desert," she says.

"Wolves don't attack people," I tell her. "Unless there's the smell of blood. Besides, wolves only come out at night."

"Er...Mykel," says Yoko, "It's...er...that time of month for me. Blood. Smell. Smell of blood, get it?"

"Well, it's the daytime," I tell her. "I'm sure you'll be safe. I'll just stay inside and rest up while you go out."

Fortunately, she is soon back, without toothmarks.

After lunch, it's time to go to the sand dunes. We bring our dishes to the main *ger* and go to the jeep. There is no jeep.

"Sand dunes!" we say to our guide, pointing to the word in the Mongolian-English dictionary.

"Yes, yes!" he says pointing to the horses.

"I can't do it!" I cry to Yoko. "I'll die! I'll just die."

She shrugs, walks over to her horse and gets on.

Well, if SHE can do it, I can. I get on the horse, grinding my teeth against the pain. Our guide gets on his horse, and with a *"Chyoo!"* we're off.

I stay behind as much a possible. My horse occasionally slips in a hole or otherwise stumbles. He isn't much in a hurry anyway. The guide breaks off a stick with which I'm to hit the horse's rear to speed him up. As much as I can, though, I try to save BOTH of our rumps.

The guide again leads Yoko's horse. She has no choice but to *Chyoo*! when he wants to *Chyoo*! I hold back, still going slow until forced to speed up when I'm in danger of losing sight of the pair.

We come to a big river. The guide steers his horse into the middle of it. The water comes almost to the animal's belly. He pulls on the reins of Yoko's horse until it, too, enters the river. The two of them ride through. My horse heads right to the bank and stops short, almost throwing me.

He looks back at me.

"You crazy?" His eyes say. "This is a river. Water! Wet! Get it? You think I'm a fish?"

I take the stick and bring it across his rear. "*Chyoo!*" I say.

The horse moves — but not into the river. Instead, he does a little dance to move further down the bank, toward a deeper part of the river.

"*Chyoo!*" I say, striking again.

The horse whinnies.

Yoko and our guide wait on the other side, smiling at my rebellious charge. The guide makes a striking motion with his hand.

I again hit the horse. "*Chyoo*! You mangy mule. You'd better *Chyoo*! if you don't wanna end up at the glue factory!"

I don't know if he understands, but he goes into the river. So do I — up to my knees.

A few yards after the river, the desert starts. First, there's flat sand, then sand hills, and finally dunes. These aren't the Lawrence of Arabia kind. They're not pure white with nothing but sand as far as a horse can *Chyoo*! These are dirty dunes, covered with what looks like seaweed and driftwood. The sand is loose. It constantly shifts under the hooves of my unsteady steed.

Fortunately, the going is slow. I'm in such pain that one more gallop would make me get off and walk. The slow camel lumber to the top of the dune keeps me just below the point of intolerable agony.

Once on top of the dune, we get off the horses and trudge around in the knee deep sand. What a relief! It could be knee deep elephant feces and I'd still be in heaven! We take some pictures, gaze over the desert, try to figure out how to use our legs again. Then it's back on the horses.

Are we returning to our *ger* to nurse our wounds? Nope. Our guide has something else in store. He wants to introduce us to his family. It's only a short ride. Maybe two miles. Maybe three. In the opposite direction from our *ger*.

"*Chyoo!*" off we go again. When I started this trip, I tried to switch between the butt pain of the saddle (sitting) and the thigh pain of the metal saddle rim (standing in the stirrups). Now that is no longer an option. My knees have cramped into an L-shape and there's no way in hell I can stand.

The guide and Yoko are off in the distance, winding their way through a scraggly mess of tall thin weeds, higher than they are. I have to *Chyoo!* more than I want for fear of losing them in the brush. When we came out the other side, there's only one *ger* in sight. It's clear sailing. I let those two run ahead, while me and his old grayness mosey on in — about 1/4 hour later.

Our guide has a small fenced-in area with some horses. There is a wooden tool shed and a medium-sized white *ger*. The *ger's* round inside is about 15 feet across. There are three or four beds. There is also our guide's family: his wife, his mother and father, his brother, his brother-in-law, his two year old son and ten year old daughter and his brother-in-law's daughter, also about ten years old.

The family offers us *airag*. This fermented mare's milk tastes kind of like cow's milk with a lemon squeezed in it. It's better than it sounds. They also offer us vodka. Exactly as good as it sounds.

When we're sufficiently sloshed, it's dinner time. We're the hot topic of conversation during the whole visit. After dinner, the vodka makes a second round. Grandma wrinkles her nose in obvious disapproval. She speaks in Mongolian, of course, but it's easy to figure out.

"Vodka!" she says, making a 'pshaw' gesture. "This is what's good!"

She unbuttons her *deel*. Reaching a wrinkled hand inside, she pries open the garment and whips out her breast. Grinning, she shakes it around, pointing it toward each of us, as if offering a suck. She jabbers away, smiling, nodding, standing tall over the vodka bottle. She leans over my glass and squeezes her tit. Nothing seeps out to dilute the vodka.

Yoko and I sit quietly, listening to each other's skin redden. The others in the *ger* laugh.

We drink more vodka, as Grandma suckles our guide's two year old son. Between my twenty words of Mongolian, Yoko's dictionary, their twenty words of English, we say a few things.

"No, we're not married," I tell them.

"Don't you want a boy to take care of you when you're old?" asks our guide. He nods to his suckling two year old.

"Boy?" says Grandma. "This is a man!"

She puts down the little boy sucking at her breast. Standing him up, she pulls down his cotton shorts. Using her free hand she rubs lightly on the little penis getting it to rise ever so slightly.

"A man! See a man!" she says.

After the sex show, we make our way outside. The family follows. Yoko takes out her camera. The family disappears. A few seconds later, they return, dressed in their finest clothes. Everyone is spruced up. They bring out their prize horse, a big white one. They put the little boy on the horse and pose around him. We take pictures. They thank us. Then they bring out our damned horses. As the sun starts to set, we get on and wave good-bye.

"*Chyoo!*" says the guide.

Enough! I'm sitting on raw hamburger meat. I'd rather spend the night in the desert than *CHYOO* another inch.

"No *Chyoo*!" I say.

The guide shrugs and rides ahead, pulling Yoko and her horse with him. As it grows darker, it gets harder to keep them in view — but I won't race. I strain my eyes to follow them. More than once, the guide comes back to me with a worried look on his face.

"*Chyoo*! *Chyoo*!" he says.

I shake my head no and continue to waltz my horse forward. I've had it! I don't care when I get back. NO MORE *CHYOO*!

By now, it's hard to see. I can barely make out the silhouette of the two riders ahead, now stopped. The guide talks to Yoko. He gestures, putting his hands on his head, acting like he's swinging a club, holding his arms in a "big fish" pose. Then he gallops off, ahead of Yoko, toward our camp.

By the time I catch up with her, the guide's returning outline appears in the distance.

"What's up?" I ask.

"Wolves," she says. "He saw wolves up there. He's ridden ahead to scare them off. There were four of them. If we don't hurry and get back to the *ger*, there will be more. Lots more. He won't be able to scare them all off."

The guide returns. He looks even more worried.

"*Chyoo*!" he says.

"*Chyoo*!" I say, deciding the half hour of intense pain is worth avoiding a Little Red Riding Hood end to this story.

We're off. Teeth gritting doesn't work anymore, I just scream in pain. My horse stumbles. Ride, scream, stumble. Ride, scream, stumble. Maybe I scare the wolves off. When we're finally back, I'm unable to dismount, frozen in the saddle. Yoko and the guide lift me out. Inch by inch I straighten my legs.

The guide tells me that if I don't get back on a horse immediately, I'll lose the "pain benefit" of my riding experience. I have to keep riding and each time it'll hurt less and less.

"I can tell you where to ride in Ulaanbataar," he says. "My friend has a horse."

"That's okay," I tell him. "That's okay."

He shakes his head and slowly walks away, back toward the main *ger*.

SEVEN

WHERE'S HAMISH

The trans-Siberian railroad passes through *Ulaanbataar* on its way between Beijing and Irkutsk in Russia. The only other train in Mongolia is a tiny branch off that. That branch goes to a city called Baganuur.

Why does Baganuur deserve this privilege? It doesn't. But it did at one time. The Russians lived there. They maintained large army barracks. It was also the coal center of the country, the lifeblood of Mongolian electricity and, in winter, heat.

The Russians have abandoned the town. The coalmines still function, sort of. The train still goes there, and it's a place to explore. Yoko and I plan to go there by "bus" and return by train.

Our *Lonely Planet Guidebook* tells us the city has two hotels, each with a restaurant, plus "an especially good restaurant" called the Urgo Bar, suspiciously near a hospital complex.

Actually, there are two reasons we go to this city. First, we can take the train back. It might be a nice trip. Also, Hamish, lives there.

Hamish is a Scottish friend of Maggie's. She's the other "native speaker" at the university, sexy as a chipped front tooth and the object of my increasing lust. Her friend Hamish is the only foreigner in Baganuur. Everyone knows him, she says. He's starved for company and would welcome us with open food cans and a warm place to unroll our sleeping bags.

In *Ulaanbaatar*, there are a very few public buses, a few more private buses, and lots more private jeeps, vans and trucks. If you want to go to another city, you head for the long distance bus station and walk around repeating the city name. Eventually someone nods his head. You ask the price, agree and get it, or disagree and continue your quest.

Finding a van to Baganuur is as easy as skinning a lamb. For 1500 *tugriks* each, we're off on the hundred kilometer trip. It takes three hours. About twenty kilometers is poorly paved. The rest isn't paved at all. Most of it's little more than dirt tracks left by the car ahead. As we enter the city, we see that it's cold and gray and falling apart. It's also raining.

The van lets us off in front of the local department store. We go in and look around. There are some Mongolian cookies, some homemade fur hats, some Vietnamese sugar-coated raisins. Not much else.

It's about 3 o'clock and we're hungry. We walk the few blocks to the Urgo. Closed for remodeling. By the yellowing "closed" sign, it's been remodeling for the past half dozen years. So we look for the City Hotel. No hotel. We ask a few passing strangers for a restaurant. One girl, about 12, offers to walk us to one. We follow. She leads us back to the department store. There, on the second floor, we discover a restaurant. We also discover that it is closed — dinner break. In what other country would a restaurant close for a dinner break?

Soaked and starving, we decide it's time to find Hamish and figure out what to do with the rest of our time in the city. Like everywhere else in Mongolia, people in Baganuur have no addresses. Mail stops at the post office. In town, people simply know where everyone lives. Why have addresses if you already know where people live?

We stop someone on the street.

"Hamish?" we ask.

"I no English," comes the answer.

"Hamish? Hamish?" we say to anyone who passes.

A thin man with a thinner mustache stops. "You want to change money?" he asks. Other people just shake their heads or scurry past, pretending not to see us. We figure if anyone will know the only foreigner in town, it'll be the cops. There is a cop box just up the street near where the City Hotel isn't.

Inside the box are two cops. One is skinny with a long face and huge chin. The other is plump with a neck that folds several times before it reaches his chest. He's got a wide mustache that bristles over his lips. In another life, they were Laurel and Hardy.

"Hamish?" Yoko asks.

"Hamish?" I translate into Mongolian.

Both cops shrug. Obviously not understanding.

"*Anglikhun*" (Englishman), I say, not knowing the Mongolian word for "Scott."

They don't understand my Mongolian either.

"*Bid Amerikhun*. Ter Yaponkhun. Hamish *Anglikhun*," (I'm American. She's Japanese. Hamish is English.)

This time they understand. They don't know any Englishman. Have never seen an Englishman. Have no idea where we might find an Englishman. But they're willing to help.

They invite us into their little hut to get out of the rain. The fat one with the mustache runs into the street, blowing his whistle to stop a passing car. The driver sheepishly gets out, carrying his license, wondering what law he's violated. Then the cop asks him about Hamish. He shakes his head and smiles. The cop waves him on.

They take turns, stopping cars, asking about Hamish. We watch the drivers shake their heads. Occasionally, one makes a vague pointing gesture — over there somewhere, as if he once saw a foreigner in that direction.

After eight cars, Laurel comes to us with a driver. He's about 23 years old, driving a Japanese Jeep. He's got a large hairy birthmark on his chin, sort of like an off-kilter goatee. No he doesn't know Hamish either, but he does have a friend who speaks Japanese and he'll take us to her.

We pile in the jeep, wave good-bye to the friendly cops, and wind up in a very large house on the outskirts of town. The driver leads us in. There is a houseful of young Mongols and one young Japanese guy who looks familiar to me.

Everyone except our driver speaks Japanese. I immediately learn how bad mine has become. I struggle to keep up with their conversation, often asking Yoko to translate into English.

The woman who owns the house is an attractive, slightly butch Mongol who speaks decent Japanese. There is another girl there; she studies Japanese in *Ulaanbaatar*. They're planning to drive back the next day. Wow, what luck! Yeah, right.

We're treated to a nice lunch, soup, bread, the works. Most of the conversation is in Japanese. I ask Takuya, the REAL Japanese guy, where he's from.

"Odawara" he says.

"Do you know a school called Logos?" I ask.

"I went there a short time."

I knew it! He was my student! I thought I recognized him, though he didn't recognize me. I don't get exactly why he's here, but somehow he's the one responsible for the expensive jeep.

During lunch, we talk about what we plan to do in Baganuur and how we came to find Hamish. They never heard of Hamish, but did know a Canadian who lived there once — a few years ago. He went back to Canada.

We tell them of our plans to go to the coal mine, the local monastery, the abandoned Russian Army base. They tell us they'd like to take us on a tour and go to those places themselves, but they can't afford the gas. We offer to pay for the gas.

Then, they ask where we plan to stay for the night.

"With Hamish," I tell them.

They laugh.

"Don't worry," says the attractive butch girl, "we'll find something for you."

They invite us to accompany them for the rest of the evening.

"We're going for fun," explains Takuya, "we're playing basketball."

To me, playing basketball has all the thrill and excitement of shopping at K-mart, but we don't have much choice. So off we go to the local gym. They change into their shorts and throw a ball around for awhile. Yoko and I sit along the side and catch balls accidentally thrown at our heads.

I notice that one by one the people we came with sneak off into the locker-room. Occasionally, one comes back, smiling, and then disappears again. Eventually, only Yoko and I are left on the bench, watching a couple of complete strangers play ball. I go to the back room to investigate. I meet Takuya.

"What do you want?" he says, not in a very friendly way.

"I just wanted to see what's back here." (There wasn't much that I could see. Just a room with a couple of padded benches.)

"You saw," he says and motions toward the door.

I go back out and sit on the bench. Our host crew comes out, plays ball a bit, then leaves.

"We found a place for you to stay," says the short Mongol girl from *Ulaanbaatar*.

"Yes," says the taller more athletic one, "but you must pay."

"Don't worry," she continues, "we know how expensive hotels are in *Ulaanbaatar*. But here, you only have to pay $20."

The guidebook says there's a hotel in the city for 100 *tugriks* (about 20 cents) a night. However, we don't know where it is and these folks don't seem to be anxious to help us to find it.

"We can't pay $20," I tell her.

Yoko and I discuss the situation in very fast English. We decide on a $10 upper limit.

"We can pay $10," says Yoko. Not exactly the best way to bargain, but it's cold, windy, wet, and getting late. Hamish is looking more and more like a mythological creature or a practical joke.

We walk with the crew to an apartment block on the edge of town. There are no lights in the stairwell. It smells of piss. We climb to the sixth floor and knock.

A muscular young woman who still has most of her teeth answers the door. She's obviously friends with the crew that brings us. The basketball gang starts to converse with her. After a few minutes, the smaller one who speaks better Japanese says in Japanese: "She says she's sorry but there's no place to cook here."

"We don't need to cook," says Yoko.

They talk some more.

The smaller basketball player returns to us.

"She says, she's sorry, but there are no beds or bedding here."

"We have sleeping bags," says Yoko.

They talk some more.

The basketball player says in Japanese, "She says you can stay here. You need to pay only $10...each."

"No fuckin' way!" I say to Yoko — in English.

She cleans it up for our Mongolian friends. "I'm sorry, we're not so rich." she says. "We can pay $10 for both of us together. Five," she points to herself, "and five," She points to me.

They talk again.

"Ok," says the basketball player who has done most of our communicating, "$10 for both."

We smile, shake hands on it, making plans to see the crew the next morning. Yoko says something in Japanese to them that I don't understand. They seem to think it's fine and say goodbye.

Butch girl #2 shows us to our room. A bedroom with one bed and a couch even shorter than I am.

The following posters are on two of the four walls: Bono from U2, two unidentified people, one pretty Anglo-looking female with short blond hair and one ugly Italian-looking male with a comedic smile, Michael Jackson wearing a bright red Chinese robe, New Kids on the Block, Marky Mark, and some sexy barefoot guy in a black leather jacket sitting in the dirt in front of a car.

On another wall is a rug used as a wall hanging. On it is a picture of a pair of Mongolian rams with ironic smiles on their faces. Opposite the rug is a dresser. Behind the dresser, the wallpaper hangs loose, as if there were a flood above and the dripping water swept it away.

Oh yeah, next to the Marky Mark poster is a window. Under the window is a shelf. On the shelf is a six piece set of barbells — 20 pounders, and a chest flexor.

In the time it takes to take this all in, our hostess comes with two cups of *Coffee King*. She speaks neither English nor Japanese, but she smiles.

"You know Hamish?" I ask her.

Yoko subtly kicks me in the shin.

Butch girl #2 also likes to talk on the phone. The only phone, however, is in "our" room. That's OK, we don't disturb her.

We eventually get to sleep. Waking a few hours later with leg cramps, I abandon the couch for the floor, it's cold, but at least I can stretch out.

At 8:30AM on Sunday morning we wake up. Why? A phonecall for the weight-lifter! After an hour, she hangs up and we're treated to more *Coffee King*. Then we dress. Yoko puts on her coat.

"Aren't they meeting us here?" I ask Yoko.

"I said we would meet them downstairs," she says.

"Are you kidding???" I reply, "This is Mongolia! You said you'd meet them at 10:30 and you're going down at 10:25? It's freezing out! By the time they get here they'll have to microwave us before we can bend enough to get into the jeep."

As it turns out, they're only half an hour late. I even have some feeling left in my right foot, though not a lot.

"We promised to pay for the gasoline," I remind the crew.

"Look at the odometer," says the guy with the huge mole on his chin, "remember 312."

We get in and we're off. First we go to the abandoned Russian base. It's a huge complex with rusting red stars, barely readable quotes from Lenin, murals about "the everlasting friendship between Mongolia and The Soviet Union," a commie ghost town.

We take lots of pictures. A squatter family, living in the abandoned building comes out to talk with us. The man, in his late twenties, has tied his horse to one of the old fences on the property. Takuya asks if he can ride it. The man nods.

The Japanese boy climbs on and rides back and forth among the buildings. When he returns I ask if I can take a picture of the crew. One of the Mongols translates. Suddenly they all disappear. I figure they're camera shy. Maybe the squat is illegal. I figure wrong.

In a few minutes they've returned, spruced up in clean clothes, with freshly combed hair. I take their picture and they thank me. We then say our good-byes.

Then its off to the coal mine. It's a strip mine, just a huge ravine cut into a mountainside. There are coal truck tracks in the bottom and on them are cranes and deep railroad cars, looking empty and abandoned. Since Yoko lived in West Virginia during her college years, it isn't particularly interesting to her, so we only stay a short time. Then, we head for the local *hiid*.

When we get there, a service is in progress. A bunch of very young monks are praying away, pretending to ignore us. With the recent decline in the economy, parents often drop off their youngsters at the local monastery. Let the church take care of them.

These kiddie monks dress in smaller versions of the same robes as the old monks, yellow hats and turned-up-toe, leprechaun-looking boots. They watch me like they've never seen a whiteman before. What about Hamish? Don't they know Hamish? Everybody knows Hamish!

The Orientals in the group make the circle around the *hiid*, stopping to pray at the Buddha image. They also get a pocketful of souvenir seeds that are supposed to bring good luck if you take them home. Neither Yoko nor I are quite sure whether you should eat them, plant them, burn them like incense, or just put them in a jar and contemplate them. I feel funny doing the pray-to-Buddha bit, so I just hang by the doorway.

"You're Christian?" asks the car driver.

"No," I say, "I'm a Jew."

"Isn't that a kind of Christian?" he asks.

I smile and walk out of the *hiid*. It has gotten very cold. The small puddles around the temple are ice. A freezing wind blows in from somewhere even colder.

After the temple tour, the crew tells us they're heading to *Ulaanbaatar*. I smile. But, there is no room for us. I frown. But, they will take us back to Baganuur, where we can easily get a ride to *Ulaanbaatar*. Well, it's better than a smack on the rump.

We pile into the jeep. During the ride, there is some discussion. The various members constantly look back at Yoko and I. My former student pretends he doesn't know what's going on. At a gas station, we stop to fill up.

"You can wait here," says butch girl #1 in Japanese. "The gas station owners will ask people who stop for gas to take you to *Ulaanbaatar*."

We take our bags out of the jeep and walk into the gas station office. Inside the office are the gas jockeys. Two old ladies wear matching babushkas. They look at us, wide-eyed in fear. There is more talk. After a bit, the butch girl talks to Yoko in Japanese.

"They don't know you," she says, "so they don't want you to stay here. But they did tell us where there is a bus stop, so you can get a bus back to Baganuur. We will take you there."

"We want to take the train back," I tell her.

"Train? The train came already this week," she says. "You're too late."

So we move our bags back in the jeep. Off we go, a few miles to the bus stop. During this ride, the driver with the huge mole seems upset. He talks with the girls.

When we get to the bus stop, the fem girl speaks to us — to Yoko, actually — in Japanese.

"Remember you promised to pay," she says. "We need to ask you for some money."

"Sure," I say, "how far did we go?"

They check the odometer and see that we went 55 kilometers. From somewhere appears a calculator. After some quick figuring, they point to the calculator 7500 *tugriks* — about $16.

"Huh?" we say simultaneously. "We only paid 1500 *tugriks* to get all the way from *Ulaanbaatar* to Baganuur. How can it be 7500?"

We check the mileage, the number of kilometers per liter of gas, the whole bit. We figure it cost 1700 in gas. We offer two thousand. Moleman shakes his head, stomps his foot and sits back with his arms folded.

He speaks to the fem girl who translates into Japanese. I can't get all of this, so Yoko then translates for me. Moleman wants to charge us 150 *tugriks* per Kilometer. Like a taxi. If we had taken a taxi, he says, that's what we would have paid.

"But we said we'd pay for gasoline!" I say to Yoko. She repeats it, in Japanese, to the fem girl who says it to moleman, in Mongolian.

There's some more bickering in Mongolian and finally moleman grabs the calculator. He punches in the 7500 number and then divides it in half.

"But for you: 3700 *tugriks*!" His final offer.

We're stuck. We're in his jeep, between nowhere and *Ulaanbaatar*. We have to get out. We pay.

About this time, the bus comes. We unload our stuff from the jeep. Yoko says goodbye. I don't talk to them. We get on the bus, buy a ticket for Baganuur and head back to town. The bus lets us off where we came in, in front of the department store. There's Hamish, waiting for us. Yeah, right.

It's late afternoon by then, and VERY cold. We haven't eaten all day, so we go to the restaurant inside. It's open and even has hot noodles and lamb. We eat, then go outside and wait for a car to take us to *Ulaanbaatar*. There are no cars.

We wait. We jump around to keep warm. Put our hands in our pockets and rub them. I felt like a sperm in a spermbank, waiting for the ecstasy of thaw, only there isn't going to be a thaw — not for hours. Two of those hours we wait.

A little Russian Lada pulls into the lot. Yoko and I run over to the tiny car. So do the dozen other people waiting for rides. The elderly man and woman inside roll down the window and shout something. The Mongols back off, shaking their heads and mumbling. The couple parks the car in the lot and goes into the store to shop.

Finally, through the frost covering my eyeballs, I make out a van, driving towards us through the empty street. I ask Yoko to grab her seeds and do something religious with them. I say every Hebrew word I can think of. The van stops. Yes, indeed, it's going to *Ulaanbaatar*. We get in...saved.

Back in *UB*, Maggie tells me Hamish will be in town this weekend. It's his birthday. I'd like to give him a present, but I'm not a violent person. If I were, I'd know where to find him. It's easy. Just ask anyone. Everyone knows Hamish, don't they?

EIGHT

In 1995, presidential wannabe Bob Dole attacked the entertainment business. Specifically targeting movies, he said they were responsible for a breakdown in public morals and family values. When he spoke about Hollywood, he was referring to the one in California, the city of sin. He could, however, have been talking about the Hollywood Disco in Ulaanbaatar. That's why this chapter's called:

BOB DOLE WAS RIGHT:
HOLLYWOOD BREEDS SEX AND VIOLENCE

I'm returning to The Hollywood for the first time since my adventure with Art and Barry. Yoko has gone. With her my hopes of easy nighttime nookitude. The same human colossus as before guards the disco entrance: doorwidth shoulders, no neck, mouth perpetually hung in the Mongolian equivalent of 'duh.' He takes my $5 and ignores me as I walk upstairs to the bar. Even in Mongolia, a disco must be where people go to pick up other people. Why else come here? To dance?

It's ten o'clock and the dance floor is empty. A few Mongols sit at the black and silver tables along the sides. I sit at the bar.

I try to order a Tiger beer. The third time I ask, the bartender slams it down on the bartop. I thank him.

Coolly, I pop open the can and pour it into a glass. To relieve the boredom and provide a conversation starter, I brought a black plastic folder. On the outside of the folder is a MEAN PEOPLE KICK ASS sticker, inside is an English language newspaper. I take out that paper and pretend to read it.

An electric fan at the far end of the bar blows gently across the few of us sitting there. Next to the fan is a young woman, about 25. She turns her head back and forth, as if she's drying her hair. Each time she faces me our eyes catch. I look away. I don't want to make a commitment before I can check her out. I need to watch without being watched. Doesn't she know you can't just stare? You've got to send a signal, then look away. You take turns. You check her out. She checks you out. Then you look back and she looks away. That's how it works. What's the matter with her? Hasn't she ever picked someone up in a bar before?

I go back to the paper, occasionally glancing to my left. She's still staring, smiling whenever our eyes meet. OK, if she's going to violate the rules, she deserves the worst. I stare back. Up to down. Right to left. She's chubby, with thighs like Virginia hams (I prefer them like Virginia Slims). She's got high cheekbones and almond-shaped eyes. But her face is too round. Her eyes are too far apart. She's definitely a NO — at least at this pre-intoxicated stage of the evening.

Two beers later, there is a tableful of girls in front of the one sitting at the bar. One is petite, youngish, narrow hips, high cheekbones, beautiful skin, small in all the right places. Two others are non-descript — neither beautiful nor ugly. The last is a bit older than the others — maybe 26 or 27. She's got a sexy oval face and short hair. She wears a man-cut suit jacket and ugly checked pants. A tough girl...and she's looking at me.

Suddenly aware that the pick-up rules in Outer Mongolia might be different from those in the inner world, I look back at her. She lifts her beer glass and toasts me. I toast her back. She makes the circle-and-3-finger OK sign and motions for me to come sit next to her. I do.

She asks me, in German, if I speak German. I do. Her name's Oyuntseseg, she says. Her brother studies in Germany. She's at The Hollywood with her fellow workers, all female. I ask her if she'd like a beer. She would. I buy one for each of us. The music suddenly gets louder. They're playing a song called "The Skatman." It's a hit across the restaurant/bar scene in Mongolia. It's disco, jazz and rap — all the worst. I've heard it so many times I love it.

She asks me to dance. I get up. Her fellow workers join us in a big circle.

Like Westerners, Mongols don't touch when they disco. Unlike Westerners, however, they also don't like to move their feet when they dance. They just shift from side to side raising first the right heel, then the left.

Me? I can't dance. My lack of coordination precisely matches my lack of rhythm. I try to move one foot off the ground every time the bass drum hits. My unusual timing amuses the Mongols.

As we dance, Oyuntseseg moves forward. I back up. She retreats. I advance. I step to the side. She steps to the side. I step to the side again. Mmmmm, disco!

Our circle has grown. Some of Oyuntseseg's fellow workers have found male partners. The small, most attractive female is with a big tough-looking guy. About six foot tall, he has a stocky body, a square head and even less of a neck than the door thug. He also has a big black eye, at the stage where the blue begins to fade into red and yellow.

After Skatman, we dance to one more and then go back to our table.

"Can I see you tonight?" I ask my new date. (I speak in German. I write in translation.)

"Tomorrow," she says. "Now, no good."

She makes a sign with her thumb as if she's drawing a mustache on her upper lip. Then she changes that to an index-finger-across-the-throat. I'm not sure what it means. When I ask, she just does it again.

Eventually, it dawns on me that her husband, "the man with a mustache," would kill her, "slit her throat," if he found her playing around. He expects her home tonight.

"I'll come to your place tomorrow," she says, "at 3AM."

I give her my address. She says she knows where it is.

We get up to dance again. I see a wiry young man, about 24, with a hairless triangular face, pouty lips and half closed eyes that say VERY DRUNK. He sways back and forth, more to his internal alcohol waves than to the music. Wobbling over to our group, he joins us. His heavy yellow sweater is stained on the chest and left elbow. The stains look fresh.

And he's all over me. He keeps putting his arm over my shoulder and whispering sweet Mongolian nothings into my ear. His breath smells like puke. He can barely keep his head up, let alone who-knows-what-else. I shake him off, looking at Oyuntseseg and then toward the ceiling. As the night wears on, however, the guy gets better and better looking.

Oyuntseseg sees what's happening and whispers in my ear.

"Tonight," she says, "I come to you tonight."

I put my arm over the drunk guy's shoulder. "I'm busy tonight," I tell him. "I'm going with her."

"You like girls?" he asks.

I nod.

"Sorry," I say. "But don't worry, I like EVERYBODY! What're you doing Monday?"

"TONIGHT! TONIGHT!" he yells, attracting the attention of the folks around us.

Oyuntseseg grabs me by the sleeve and pulls me off the dancefloor back to the table. She's ordered cokes for everyone there and put them on my bill.

"Tonight," she says, "Your apartment. Four people, okay?"

She points to herself, the petite co-worker and the guy with the black eye. I'm wary of him, but I'm not one to turn down an orgy.

"Ok," I say, "four people."

She points to one of her more secretary-looking co-workers. The woman stands next to a young man wearing very baggy jeans, a backwards baseball hat and a t-shirt that says LONDON GREAT UK.

"Six people," she says.

"No six people," I tell her, "too much."

Oyuntseseg bends to whisper in her friend's ear. I grab myself between my legs and point downstairs, toward the mens room. She nods.

Somewhat drunk, I stumble toward the stairs that lead first to a mezzanine, then the first floor bathrooms. I hear running behind me. It's Oyuntseseg.

She takes my arm and pulls me down to the mezzanine. We go to a small alcove under the stairs. She leans against the wall. I kiss her. She thrusts her tongue into my mouth, but pulls it out quickly.

Her hand fumbles at my zipper. Lightening quick, she's through the layers of underwear necessary to combat the Mongolian winter. Lightening strikes the lightening rod.

"Ok?" she asks. "Does it work?"

"Yeah," I tell her. "It works great."

I try to kiss her again, but she turns her head away. Instead, she takes her hand from my fly, carrying with it my little bald-headed friend.

Pressing herself back against the wall, she fixes her own fly so I have a clear passageway. Key into lock. Right there under the stairs for the viewing pleasure of any passing drunk. Standing up, her back against the wall, me doing deep kneebends pressed against her. Superfly, doublefly, interfly deep kneebends.

I try to kiss her again. She again turns her head, but presses her pelvis forward.

Not ready to become a Mongol dad, I finish before I finish — fixing my pants. There's still the rest of the night, right?

"I no come tonight," she says, making the mustache/throat slit sign again. "I come tomorrow. Three AM."

Well, there's still the drunk guy with the triangular face.

So I zipper up and head upstairs with Oyuntseseg. She meets her friends on the stairs. There's a long conversation. Then she turns to me.

"Tonight," she says, "six people, ok?"

"No six people," I tell her.

"Okay okay," she says, pulling me by the arm over to her table where she orders beer for everyone — on my tab. Figuring I'll be busy tonight and hopefully needing Sunday to recover, I write my name and address along with "Monday Night: 8PM" on a small piece of paper. I discretely drop this paper on the seat where the triangle face guy is sitting. He doesn't see me drop it, but he does see me.

He puts his arm around my shoulder and squeezes as if trying to get the juice out.

"You come now," He says.

I break away as gently as I can.

"Not tonight," I tell him. "Monday."

He doesn't understand.

By now it's closing in on 2AM. I'm tired of the disco, the uncertainty and "The Skatman," now on it's fifth rendition.

"Let's go," I say to Oyuntseseg. I motion to the waiter to bring me the check.

"No!" says Oyuntseseg, making that thumb-across-the-upper-lip/throat-cutting sign..."Let's dance."

She's back on the dancefloor with her friends. I'm disgusted, angry. Triangle face has left. It seems like Oyuntseseg will never. I still have to piss; I was on my way the first time, when she waylaid me under the stairs.

I pay the bill and leave. No one says good-bye.

Downstairs, in the men's room, I trip over triangle face. He's lying on the floor, blood gushing out of his nose, covering the side of his face against the tile. He moves slightly, making gurgling noises through his mouth. I relieve myself of the evening's beer and go over to help him off the floor. He's already being helped — by the Mongolian monster with the black eye.

'Helped' is not exactly the right word. He's being dragged to his feet — and pushed. With the support power of overcooked noodles, his knees buckle every time he reaches his full height. The big guy is right over him, holding him by the back of his sweater like you'd hold a puppy by the back of its neck. The drunk is a human marionette, more dangled than supported. Together, they march to the coatcheck room.

As if he's seen it all before, the checkboy casually takes the numbered tag and pushes the coat into Triangle's hands. Before he can put it on, the monster pushes him out the front door. I follow.

Triangle spots me. He wants to talk. Monster blocks his path. He pushes away the bloody mess, who can barely walk. The drunk slowly staggers off. I figure the big guy thinks he's keeping away a bloody drunken homo — doing me a favor.

I figure wrong. After Triangle walks away, the goon comes over to me. The light coming out of the Hollywood's front door reflects on his shiner. It's now a red donut around a sunken eyehole.

We're in a dark area in the empty parking lot. The Hollywood is ahead of me to my left. Behind me is a brick wall. In front of me is the Mongolian Monster.

"See noseblood?" he asks, pointing to the barely visible stumbling young man, "I do that...You buy me vodka."

"I don't understand," I lie.

He unzips his jacket and reaches in.

"Pistol," he says, "me pistol."

He's bullshitting. Handguns are unavailable in Mongolia. I think. Even the cops don't have 'em. I think. Still, that doesn't make him any smaller — or less drunk.

As we speak, he presses forward. I back up toward the brick wall. He takes a step forward. I step back. He steps forward. I step to the side. He steps to the side. I step to the side again. Mmmmm, disco!

Over his shoulder, I see three people leaving the club. There's a studenty-looking Mongolian guy, tall, youngish with wire-rim glasses, and two somewhat older girls.

I duck past the monster and shout, "Call the police!" tilting my head toward the black-eyed one.

"What's the problem?" says the guy, in excellent English.

My tormenter walks very quickly back into the club. He glances back at me, his good eye filled with 'I'll get you.'

I explain to the trio that I'm being threatened by a Mongolian gorilla. They laugh, but volunteer to walk me home, even though they live in the other direction. I thank them and accept the offer.

As we walk, I wonder if Oyuntseseg is in cahoots with the monster. I almost let him into my apartment for the 'orgy.' She still has my address. By now, they all do. She promised to show up tomorrow night. At 3AM. I wonder who else is coming?

NINE

No one shows up from The Hollywood. There is neither riot nor orgy. My life
returns to the usual madness. Lust still reigns heavy in my mind, as does the
thirst for new adventures. Only one of those two is solved by seeing...

A HUNDRED AND TWENTY-EIGHT—AT THE SAME TIME

It's 4:45. I wait in front of the National Sports Palace, a large brown building with massive Stalinesque pillars. A huge banner proclaims the start of the winter wrestling season. Tickets are expensive, more than a thousand *tugriks*, but I've got friends in the right places. One of them, a student's older brother, said he'd meet me at four o'clock, with a free ticket. I'm not worried. He's still punctual by Mongolian standards. The matches aren't scheduled to start until four. There's plenty of time.

Here he comes now. Tsegbataar, in a clean *deel*, holding a single ticket. We enter the old pillared building. Inside, we pass through a carpeted lobby. A statue of a famous Mongolian wrestler leans out from the wall. I've seen photos of the same guy — one on a calendar, next to the Dalai Lama.

Inside, my friend explains that the wrestlers need him backstage. I'll have to fend for myself. There are no vendors in the atrium. Not having eaten since breakfast, I hope they sell peanuts, or at least *buz*, in the stands.

Walking in, I find a seat on the bleacher-type benches along the sides. The half-filled arena holds about 2000 people. With me on the benches are lots of guys in *deels*, mostly older men. Only a few look as young as I expect the wrestlers to be. Among these are a dozen cops. Not guarding cops, but audience cops, in full uniform, sitting as spectators.

I'm the only whiteman. Great! I love feeling I've been let in on a cultural secret. Whoops, there's another, on the other side of the room. Missionary-looking with a trimmed blond beard, he wears a black *deel*. Nothing like a Christian who wants to out-Mongol the Mongols. Yeah right.

Down on the floor, a few old men sit on ringside benches and chairs. The ring itself is a blue carpeted area, maybe 50' x 50'. In the corner closest to me sit three ancient monks wearing priestly yellow robes. A younger man, head shaved like the rest, wears red. He sits at the table and chats with the monks. His loud laugh and wide gestures belong more to an athlete than a religious man.

Drooping from a pole set into a large stand next to the monks' table is a Mongolian flag. In the corner to my right is another smaller table. Like the monks' table, it's painted bright orange, trimmed in an intricate blue design. Behind this smaller table sits a hunchback, about 40 years old, around five feet tall and wearing a fancy *deel*. He leans on the table with both elbows and stares with studied intensity into the empty space in front of him, not moving.

Other people gather at ringside. Tall and wide, they're probably retired wrestlers. They wear traditional Mongol hats, with a high point in the center of a round brim. Two ribbons drape down the back of each hat.

There are three TV cameras on the floor. The one on the other side of the arena, points directly at me. Ads for Zhullchin Travel, *MIAT* Airlines, and Gobi Cashmere decorate the walls. No Marlboro in Outer Mongolia, yet.

The smell of incense wafts up from the monks' table. They pass a snuff bottle among themselves, snorting loudly when their turn comes.

At the far end of the room a group of men gather in conversation. They wear either maroon, royal blue or gold *deels* — all with pointed hats, a mark of their high status.

At the table in front, a couple of lamas join the monks. They dress like the monks, except for red trimmed yellow hats. A young one, round faced and fresh looking, about 14, brings a tray full of flat bread to the table. It's perfectly arranged in a tower. Little candies cover the top piece. The camera moves in for a close-up. It makes me even hungrier.

The boy leaves the arena and soon returns with an enormous bowl of croutons. He adds it to the food already on the monks' table.

By now, the seats are three quarters full. One section of padded chairs is still empty. I look around and suddenly realize there are no women here.

At 5:15 two women carrying large packages enter. A man in a brown business suit accompanies them. Dressed in formal *deels*, the women unpack a pair of traditional Mongolian instruments. The instruments are shaped like Bo Diddly guitars with very long necks, a square body and four strings.

They begin to play those instruments, using a bow to make a beautiful high warble. The man sings a slow deep song. His baritone voice bursts with the same pride as his hand over his heart. I don't know if it's the national anthem, but no one stands.

After the singing there's silence. It's now 5:30. At 5:45 someone in the audience starts to clap. Then scattered applause. Then more.

I've been in Mongolia long enough to realize that this does NOT mean something is happening. Instead, it means that the audience WANTS something to happen. People applaud to say "get your ass in gear!" not "job well done."

By now, a few women and men with medals on their *deels* fill the VIP seats. The wrestlers come out. They wear turned-up-toed Mongolian boots, skimpy red or blue trunks, and an upper garment closed at the back, but completely open at the chest — like a vest with sleeves. A string belt is tied at the waist.

There is a story that this costume was invented to detect and prevent women from wrestling. Supposedly, in ancient times, a woman beat a man wrestling and the men couldn't take the humiliation. They decided they had to find a way to keep women out. Bare chests saved their honor. A woman told me that story.

Half a dozen boys — no older than five or six — are with the wrestlers and dressed in the same costumes. Their appearance stirs the audience into loud applause. They smile and bow lightly. They don't, however, wrestle.

Those who do line up around the perimeter of the square, face in. An old man in a fur hat walks inside the line, kissing each of them on both cheeks. Then the wrestlers walk off the carpet. There's an announcement and 128 men walk back on, parading around, doing a little dance. They stand on one foot, then the other, moving their arms like the dying bird in Swan Lake.

The carpet is crowded with dancing wrestlers. In a moment, it's crowded with wrestling wrestlers. All of them. At the same time. Big against small. Fat against thin. One man, built like a sumo star, grabs a skinny adolescent. He puts his meaty hand behind the young man's neck, leaning into him with his full weight. Pow! The youngster is on his back.

The system works by pitting the strongest against the weakest. Then the winners fight each other. Those winners go against each other, until finally you've got the strongest fighting the strongest.

Right now, the wrestlers are all over the floor, throwing each other every which way, banging into the walls. There are 128 wrestlers to start. They wrestle simultaneously on the arena floor. The TV cameras maneuver through the jumble, focusing in on this pair or that.

I watch a squat man with shoulders as wide as his torso is long. He clutches a much younger man who's built like a Charles Atlas before model, a ham-sized hand holding a chicken-sized neck. In less than a minute, PLOW! the younger man slams onto the carpet, on his back.

As best as I can figure, you win when you throw your opponent. Some part of his body, other than hands or feet, has to touch the ground. If both wrestlers fall together, then the first to touch loses.

Around the wrestlers are referees — or managers, it's hard to tell. They wear red or blue *deels*, with Mongolian hats. There are at least a dozen of them. They shout at the wrestlers, use body English (body Mongolian?) to instruct them, push them back into the ring when they stray. For encouragement, they pat each wrestler's butt like a baseball manager sending up a pinch hitter.

Another stocky man throws another skinny guy. A referee, about fifty years old, thin as my forearm, walks up to the pair. He carries two hats. One is fur, the other a traditional Mongolian hat.

He unties the belt of the loser and lets the ends hang. The winner raises his arm in triumph and the loser walks under it, head bowed. The ref hands the loser the fur hat. He walks off in defeat. The winner gets the pointed hat. He puts it on. Then he walks to the Mongolian flag and does the bird dance around it. Next, he walks to the monks' table and grabs a handful of croutons. Some of these he eats. Some, he throws into the audience.

The audience calls "Nosh! Nosh!" (I shit you not.) They hope the wrestler will throw them food. By now I'm so starved that I'd eat a monk if thrown up here, but none of the flying croutons land anywhere near me. This same ritual goes on with every win. The flying food always misses me.

Two wrestlers, weight-lifter types, both about six feet tall, move around the floor holding each other, spinning like dancers. Smash! Right into a TV camera. One of the wrestlers loses his footing and falls. The other raises his hand in triumph. A referee comes over. The man on the floor shouts to him.

"No! Fraud!" is what I guess he shouts. "I tripped, I wasn't thrown!"

The referee strokes his chin in thought. Then he says something.

All three look at the hunchback at the table in the corner. The hunchback just stares straight ahead without blinking — like he's on drugs. That settles the matter. The fallen wrestler gets up to continue the match. That's the first of many times where they refer difficult decisions to the hunchback, the ultimate authority.

The winning 64 wrestlers pick new partners and the whole thing starts again. This time one of the wrestlers throws a much bigger man into the monks' table. POW! Down goes the bread tower. Milk balls and wrapped candy roll everywhere. They're crunched under boots, rolling into the audience. I'm so hungry, I'm tempted to run down and start stuffing my mouth. I'm barely able to resist temptation when a flying crouton hits me on the head. I pick it up off the floor and cram it into my mouth. It's bitter, with a hint of the flavor of old socks. I don't care...then I feel it.

During my even-more poverty stricken days, I'd scarf down instant potato flakes then drink a glass of water. It filled me up for hours, on almost no money. This crouton works the same way — without the water. It expands in my stomach. Full, for a half hour. Then, the pangs hit again.

Right at pang-time, there's a half-time ceremony. A dozen men in *deels* march out and stand at attention along one edge of the ring. A well-medalled man comes down from VIP seats. He makes a speech and gives some plaques to the dozen standing men. This would be unremarkable, except that the wrestling does not stop during the ceremony.

These guys are standing very dignified along the side. Banging around in front of them — occasionally smashing into them — are a bunch of near naked men trying to throw one another to the floor.

Three hours into the match, I'm famished again. I manage to scrape up one more crouton, but this time it only lasts fifteen minutes. Maybe you build up a tolerance.

They're down to 16 wrestlers now. Those left are almost all fat. One is nearly seven feet tall. I have a headache from hunger. I've got to get something to eat before I disappear. I hear that the wrestlers are so tired by the last match that they just hang on each other and fall asleep. It can last for hours. I can't! Ahh, someone's walking out. The other white guy. He's left before me. Three cops also get up, stepping over the crowd to the exit. I won't be the first to go.

I stand and walk, sliding sideways through the crowd to the door. Out through the atrium, into the fading sun. Lamb tonight? I don't think so. For some reason, I have the urge for beef.

TWISTER or A LESBIAN'S GUIDE
TO OUTER MONGOLIA

Maggie, my fellow English teacher, comes from Belfast. She's Catholic, but only by birth. Sponsored by the *VSO*, the British equivalent of the Peace Corps, she's 30 + years old, talks about sex continually and how her time in Mongolia has been her most sexually active. She vows celibacy after each fling. The longest lasting vow was three days. Despite my best efforts, I haven't been able to supply a mattress for her fall off the wagon.

She's got a pouty mouth and striking gray eyes with poor vision reflected in constricted pupils. She's not skinny, but nothing bulges that shouldn't. The tip of her right pinkie bends to the left. It doesn't say sex. Everything else about her does.

Eve is a friend of Maggie's, also *VSO*, in her late 20s. She's from Liverpool and works at the statistical office in *Ulaanbaatar*. Her mother and step-father are dead. Her real father is still alive, she says. She has no interest in seeing him.

With dark shoulder-length hair, her eyes are as gray as Maggie's. Her features are tougher though. Her body is bigger, taller, heftier, but not fat. Although she's more emotional than the other girl, they both drink like Mongols.

Not conventionally pretty, Eve is as sexy as leather pants. Her movements are sleek and her dress is enticingly sloppy. She'll be travelling with Maggie when they leave Mongolia later this month. The pair are going to Australia, where Maggie will meet an old fling. She talks marriage. Eve's going for the adventure — and the sex.

Eve is now having a New Years party. I take the already-wrapped bottle of "Champagne," a gift to me from the English Department at the University. Then I make my way to her apartment. At 10PM I knock on the door. The party is swinging with people throughout the livingroom, bedroom, kitchen, bathroom. I even see two Mongols in the crowd.

When I arrive, David, the Canadian-Israeli, is in the kitchen. With him is Morris, another Canadian Jew who has wrapped himself in blinking Christmas lights. There's a well-built blonde girl I don't know, talking to a less well-built blonde guy I don't know. Morris tells me the guy's name is Rick. The girl's name I hear and forget. She says to stick the "Champagne" out the window where it'll quickly chill. I recognize her accent.

"Komma Du fra Danmark?" I ask.

It's a nice opening line because so few foreigners speak Danish — especially in Mongolia. The girl turns her attention from the blond guy to me. She introduces herself and tells me she's from Aarhus. We talk about Danes. I tell her I know Kim Schumacher, Jan Sneum, Anders Rou Jensen, Paul Borum, and Sort Sol. I let the names drop like the winter snow. Oh is she impressed!

Then I turn to the blond guy. American. Despite his thinning hair, he looks young, well-scrubbed, weller-meaning — and heterosexually lustful. He wears a SAVE-THE-WHALES t-shirt. Three of those sea mammals frolic in an 'H' formation between the 'W' and the 'A.'

"You like whales," I say.

He nods.

"Me too. I think they're great. I had some in Japan — in a kind of soup."
He blanches slightly.

"I think they're better when they're alive," he says self-righteously.

"Did you ever try to eat a whale while it's alive?" I say, "Impossible!"

He gives in to the conversation.

"Did it taste like chicken?" he asks.

"Nope," I tell him, "it was more like beef in salt water."

He laughs nervously.

I drain my beer and go to the refrigerator for another. When I turn back to the Danish girl, she's disappeared into the livingroom. I follow, running into Eve on the way.

"Mykel!" she says, giving me a hug. "You come to my party and don't even say hello to me."

"Hello," I say. "I didn't see you."

She gives me a quick peck on the cheek and then moves to a guy about thirty, slightly taller with slightly more hair than I have. Thin, suavish, he seems a nice fellow.

"Mykel," says Eve, "I want you to meet Hamish. Hamish, Mykel."

"Hamish? THE Hamish????" I ask. "The guy that EVERYBODY IN BAGANUUR KNOWS who cost us big bucks on food and a place to sleep and frostbite in the cold? THAT Hamish?"

You bet your frozen socks it's that Hamish. All smiley faced and happy-new-yeared, as if nothing happened. He knows the story. Only the people we asked hadn't heard of him, he claims. Everyone else in the town knows him. I don't punch him. It's New Years.

By now it's a few minutes to twelve. Those of us who've brought something to drink gather in the livingroom with bottles in hand. The Peace Corps Volunteers have no bottles in their hands. They wait with empty glasses.

At 11:59 we don't watch the non-ball drop on the non-building in non-Times Square. At midnight, the corks pop, the "Champagne" flows and we get drunker.

I end up back in the kitchen. The "music" in the livingroom has become intolerable. The kitchen is the furthest I can go and still keep drinking.

Rick is the only player left from the first round. The Danish girl he was with is not there. Instead, there's Robert/Bob, an American. Robert/Bob is in his late 20s/early 30s. He's chubby, with one chin too many — especially when he smiles. Typically American, he's not ugly, but rather the type you meet, find likeable, and instantly forget you met. Very friendly. He wears blue levis and polyester shirts. During our conversation I learn he's lived in the same building as me — since I moved in. I never noticed him.

With Robert/Bob are two other male Americans, a tall one and a short one, both of whom say they were fat.

"Eighty five pounds," says the tall one, patting his stomach, "I lost 85 pounds since I've been here."

"I don't know how much I lost," says the short one, "but it was a bunch. I can only thank my counterpart."

[Cultural note: I don't know if it's the Mongol-American dialect or one of those linguistic changes that blitz through US-culture without me noticing. But since I got here, more and more Americans refer to their boy/girlfriends/husbands/wives as "my counterpart." It sounds like an alternate universe in a sci-fi novel. Doppelgangers. Spooky when folks casually use it to refer to real people.]

About then, Eve bursts into the room. Her face is drawn, her eyes glassy. I assume it's from the alcohol. It isn't. It's from tears.

She sees Robert/Bob and throws her arms around him. Her sobs echo against the hanging pots and pans. She speaks between sobs, her words muffled by big Robert/Bob's shoulder. He looks at us over her whimpering body, completely surprised.

"Americans...awful...don't know what to do...won't leave..." That's about all I can make out during the four or five minutes of crying. It seems like forever.

Those of us in the kitchen NOT being cried on look at our feet, clean our fingernails and gradually and quietly leave.

Did you ever notice, when travelling in a foreign country, that whenever you hear laughter, you assume it's about you? You check your fly, wipe your nose, make sure there's no lettuce stuck on your front teeth. It's doubly bad with tears.

"I'm an American." I think. "What did I do wrong? Vietnam has been over for twenty years. What's the problem?"

I leave with the image of poor Eve crying on the shoulder of poor Robert/Bob who looks completely mystified.

The next day is January first. I stay in bed.

The following day I'm able to again wake up with an erection. Right then, I decide to visit Eve. Perhaps the two are connected. I prefer to think I'm concerned about her psychological health and my possible past contribution to its breakdown.

At 6PM I knock on her door. I hear a scurrying inside, then the door opens.

"Mykel!" says Eve, "I was expecting Maggie. What are you doing here?"

"I came to see if you were all right," I tell her. "You were in pretty bad shape a couple days ago."

"Oh, I was just drunk," she says, "and those Peace Corps creeps really got to me. Two girls. They thought they were so smart. I sent Maggie in to chase 'em out."

"What happened?" I ask.

"Instead of chasing them out, she sat on their laps and told 'em her life story."

"That's too bad," I say.

"No!" corrects Eve, "that wasn't bad at all. Maggie inflicted a much worse punishment than I could've. They left quick after that. Lemme tell ya."

I chuckle at the thought of Maggie, perched on their laps, saying, "When I was born, things were tough. Being a Catholic in Protestant Northern Ireland isn't fun. Every day, even as a schoolgirl, I was stopped by the evil British Police..."

Eve offers me a cup of coffee and we talk about her plans for Australia. Maggie is supposed to be here at seven. At seven thirty, Eve and I leave.

"Lets go to dinner." I tell her, "I'll treat. I found a restaurant that takes credit cards."

"Let's stop in at Robert/Bob's house first." she said, "Maybe Maggie stopped there without me."

So we're at Robert/Bob's. Maggie isn't, but she's expected. I settle into a chair. Eve and Robert/Bob take the couch. Before long, I'm forgotten, while Eve and Robert/Bob discuss their lives. After awhile, the conversation steers to the New Years party.

"Pretty wild," says Eve, "all that sex stuff."

"Sex stuff?" I ask. "Did I miss it?"

"Yow," she says, "EVERYBODY ended up with SOMEBODY!"

"Who am I?" I don't ask, "NOBODY?"

"Yeah," she continues, "pretty amazing. Maggie going off with Rick?"

"Rick? You mean SAVE THE WALES Rick? Maggie let HIS harpoon into her tail fin?"

Eve nods.

"And what happened to that Danish girl?" I ask. "I thought he was with that Danish girl. Don't tell me. She went with one of those Peace Corps creeps you were crying about."

Eve shakes her head.

"Then who?" I demand.

"Hamish," she says with a smile.

"Hamish???" I say, suddenly standing. "Everybody-knows-me-cause-I'm-famous-in-Baganuur Hamish?"

Eve nods.

I sit down, feeling the color drain from my face as the energy drains from my body.

After a short time, Maggie shows up. That means booze. The vodka will flow like other people's semen on New Years Eve.

"Put on some music!" she says, breezing into the room.

[Cultural Note: Mongolians have AWFUL taste in music. They like Rock Ballads and Techno Disco. The only people with WORSE musical taste than Mongolians are foreigners in Mongolia.]

She goes to Robert/Bob's CD collection and picks out one by THE POLICE.

"ROX---ANN!" she sings before the song even starts.

Robert/Bob and Eve join her. I don't know the words. Maggie pulls out the vodka bottle she's brought and pours drinks all around. The drinks are drained and glasses refilled. I switch to beer. The others don't.

"EVERY STEP YOU TAKE....EVERY MOVE YOU MAKE..."

I take another swig of beer to keep from grinding my teeth at the sounds coming from the CD player. I should've enjoyed them while I could. After THE POLICE come THE EAGLES.

"ON A DARK DESERT HIGHWAY...COOL WIND IN MY HAIR...."

Eve, Maggie and Robert/Bob are up and dancing. I sit there. There are four of us. Two boys and two girls. A fine combination no matter what your persuasion. It must be new math. Four people and I'm the fifth wheel on the wagon.

"It's hot in here," says Maggie. "Does anyone mind?"

With that, she takes off her sweater, peals off her wool skirt and her outer tights. She's now in nothing but a tanktop and a pair of very thin black tights.

Oh yeah, her panties are blue — the color of a boy's baby blanket.

The drinks flow throughout THE EAGLES. I'm on beer number six. They're on vodka number can't-count-that-high. Then comes ROD STEWART.

They're dancing away.

"DO YOU THINK I'M SEXY..."

Ok, ok, when in Rome...er...*Ulaanbaatar.*

I get up and do my little disco dance. Shaking my shoulders. Making little kissy kissy motions with my mouth. Wiggling my knees. Singing along to words I don't even know.

"IF YOU THINK I'M SEXY AND YOU WANT TO KNOW ME..."

Only nobody wants to know me. The two girls are both looking at chubby Robert/Bob. Maggie grabs hold of his sweater and pulls it over his head. Then she reaches for his shirt and opens it button by button.

"I'm just trying to get you comfortable," she slurs.

"What about ME!" I don't say. "Don't you want to get ME comfortable?"

Robert/Bob's shirt is completely off now. Then Maggie goes for the belt.

"Whoa!" says the big guy, "not so fast."

She laughs and pours the vodka drinkers another shot each. Another can of Tiger Beer for me. I look around, counting the people in the room again. I come to the same conclusion. Four. A perfect number. How can anyone be left out if there are only four people?

The record ends and we talk. It's about 3AM. After a bit of random conversation Maggie says, "Why don't we play a game?"

"TWISTER!" I suggest. "Robert/Bob, you got vegetable oil?"

This reference will probably be lost on Europeans and Asians. Possibly also on Americans under the age of 30 or over the age of 65. Foreigners, ask an American. Young Americans, ask your mom and dad. Watch 'em blush. Older Americans, ask your kids, watch 'em blush harder!

Robert/Bob, being the only American, is the only one to get it. He laughs, but doesn't have the game. Instead we play 20 questions. We're all so soused by this time that none of us can count to 20. So the game, although boring, lasts three hours. By that time, Eve has fallen asleep. Robert/Bob goes off into his bedroom.

"Well," I say to Maggie with a hopefully-not-too-smirky-smile, "I guess that leaves just us two."

"Yep," says Maggie, "what should we do?"

I could feel my ears move up at the strength of the smile stimulated by that question.

"Oh, I know," she says, "let's talk."

My ears return to their normal position.

"When I was born things were tough," she tells me, "Being a Catholic in Protestant Northern Ireland isn't fun. Every day, even as a schoolgirl, I was stopped by the evil British Police..."

"Aaargh!" I don't scream. Instead, I let her talk. My attention comes back when the talk turns to sex.

"I've had jaw problems forever," she says, opening her mouth wide, then moving her jaw back and forth, "it comes from giving blowjobs. It really made me appreciate smaller endowments."

"Yoohoo!" I don't shout, "Over here! I'm friendly as a toothpick."

Not hearing my non-speech, she continues, "And for so long, I would only take it from behind. See, I was saving myself for marriage — like a good Catholic girl. But those big bruisers...I still have chronic diarrhea from being overstretched."

I don't stand up, nor do I do a little jig pointing the lights toward myself, singing (to the tune of "Do You Think I'm Sexy") "Don't you know I'm slender...It would only tickle...You would hardly know it's there..."

Instead, I just sit there and listen to her reveal her early sexual experiences. We're the only two awake people in the house.

"I don't really have a TYPE," says Maggie. "Sometimes I feel like I'd screw anything that moves."

I shift position in my chair.

The alarm goes off. It's 8AM and Robert/Bob has to get up for work. The noise awakens Eve too. She squirms a bit on the couch. A low moan escapes from her mouth into the pillow she's clutching. Robert/Bob covers his naked upper torso with polyester and tells us we can leave or hang around if we want. I suddenly realize that I have to teach in four hours and decide I should sleep for two of them. I take my jacket, hat and leave.

But, there's ONE MORE PARTY. This one Maggie is giving for the entire English Department. It's her good-bye present to the other teachers. She tells me that she also invited one teacher from the German Department, a guy she has, for some reason, nicknamed "Lipstick."

I had met the guy at the End-of-Term party in the fancy *Ulaanbataar* hotel. Tall, with jet-black hair cut into a 70s mod-style, he spoke no English. He asked me to translate his German. He wanted to say some things to Maggie. I agreed.

So he starts in on "Seine Augen sind so tief..." (Your eyes are so deep.) And other equally memorable phrases. And I, with a straight face, translate this stuff to her.

"I've had a crush on 'im since I started at the university." she says. "I just wanna snarf him before I leave."

I offer to come early and help her prepare for the party. So, on that day, there I am, three bottles of Beijing Beer in hand, sleeves rolled up, ready to peel those potatoes and plaster that Chinese patè.

Somehow, through the British Embassy, Maggie has been able to get commodities unseen by Mongols and unthought of by me since I got here. Oxo, Ritz Crackers, Heinz catsup, all kinds of herbs, spices and pots and pans to cook them in. I've never marvelled at a kitchen like I marvelled at hers.

Well, there's no time to marvel. It's time to work, and we're lucky the guests are late. The garlic bread is just being garlicked as the doorbell rings with the first of them.

They come in two bunches — either by one member's car or by "taxi."

I'm pleased to see that Lipstick is not among the first to arrive. I'm even more pleased to see that he's not in the second group either. He can't make it. He has to proctor a final exam.

"Aw, that's too bad," I say, straining against the sarcasm.

The party's a success. Typically Mongol, there's a lot of singing and dancing. I even join in the latter, terrorizing the guests in an impromptu tango with Namjil.

The food goes quickly. The speeches are properly sobbed at. The guests pack up, en masse, to leave.

"Can we take you anywhere?" asks Dr. Sumiya, the head of the Department.

"No, that's ok," I say, giving him a quick wink, "I think I'll stay and help clean up."

We bid the guests good-bye. I sit on one of Maggie's two couches. She collapses on the other, saying, "I couldn't've done it without you."

I smile an aw-shucks-it-was-nothing smile and don't say anything.

"I need a drink," she says. "Want a beer? There's still some in the refrigerator."

I walk to the kitchen, fetch one and return to the livingroom. She's poured herself a glass of vodka.

"Lipstick didn't make it," she says.

"So I noticed." I say.

"I don't know what I'm gonna do now," she continues. "I wanna snarf that guy before I leave."

"You told me," I tell her. "Maybe you can go to the German department and tell him how much he was missed and offer to make him a private dinner to compensate for it."

She sits up straight, spilling a bit of the vodka.

"That's a good idea!" she says. "Do you think it'll work?"

"He'd have to be a snarfin' moron not to get the message." I say, trying to put a little message into my own voice.

Then begins THE CONVERSATION.

"Did I ever tell you that being a Catholic in Protestant Northern Ireland isn't fun. Every day, even as a schoolgirl, I was stopped by the evil British Police..."

I remind her that I've heard her history. We began discussing our own omnisexual experiences. This evolves into a debate on the genetic component of homosexuality. Her: pro-homogene, me: pro-choice.

"It was like at this lesbian orgy I was at," she says, "all the girls were naked and fondling each other.."

I adjust my pants.

"And this one girl, Jane, wasn't into it at all. All those other naked girls, fondling her breasts, sunk between her legs. She told me just didn't like it."

"I can see how that would be annoying," I say, "Tell me more."

She does, telling me about her own pursuit by a tough looking girl at The Hollywood Disco.

"She wouldn't let any one else near me. She was all over me, right in the middle of the club."

"Are there bull dykes in *Ulaanbaatar*?" I ask in amazement. "Maybe you should write The Lesbian's Guide to Outer Mongolia."

She laughs.

"If anyone should write that book, it's you, Mykel," she says.

But still she continues, explaining how both men and women make her feel good. How men can show strength in adversity and women can provide emotional support.

"How 'bout you?" she asks. "How come you like both?"

"Well," I say, "Boys have nicer butts, but girls have smooth hairless bodies that you can trickle your fingers down."

Suddenly, she gets it. I can see the change in her eyes. It's subtle, but it's there. She no longer sees me as the kitchen help, but as an object. An object like a television set or a stove. An object that's gotta be turned off before you can safely go to sleep.

"Oh that's funny," she says, thinking quickly, "You wouldn't like me at all then. I've got a big butt and a hairy chest."

I look at her arms, her upper lip — not a speck, not a strand, not a dark area. Sure, she has a hairy chest. Yeah, right.

And here. Right here at this critical point, I fuck up. My move is so obvious. The retort so natural, that I bang my head against the wall when I think about it.

Why don't I simply say, "Show me"? But I don't.

Chivalrous, Maggie makes up her bed for me and then goes to sleep on the couch.

The next morning, she lets me take everything. Clean out the place, a coat, pots and pans, spices, Heinz catsup and Oxo cubes. She piles it all on. She offers me potatoes and tampons — both of which I turn down.

"If there's anything else you want, just ask," she says. "I don't care what it is, just ask."

I don't, although she often repeats the question.

Finally, weighed down under my load, I head for the door. I kiss her goodbye and thank her for the loot. It's a kiss aimed at the lips but landing on the cheek. She pulls one of those quick head-turns that girls can do. One of those "Euuuw cooties!" moves that shriek, "Whew! Saved by a millimeter."

"Bye," she yells after me. "Thanks for the help."

"Anytime," I tell her over my shoulder. "Anytime."

ELEVEN

Expat parties are bad enough, if there were only a way to get away from it. It meaning, the music. Between the Euro-pap taste of Mongol youth and the Adult-contemporary hell of foreigners, it's a constant assault. Strange there would be so much bad music in a culture where the music runs so deep.

Put two Mongols together and one starts singing. Music runs through their veins like lamb fat. Like lamb fat, it gets them through the tough cold times. And there are lots of tough cold time in Mongolia.

Most Mongolian music is slow. They sing about the countryside after too long in the concrete of the city, about sheep flocks roaming under starry skies, and about mother.

Yes, rock'n'roll came to Mongolia. But it came with a Mongolian flavor. Slow rock ballads about the countryside, roaming sheep flocks, the loneliness of the open plain, and mother. Mongolia's early rock bands were not quite The Velvet Underground, but even a daughter is better than nothing.

Their first full-fledged rock band called themselves (what else?) Chinggis Khan. Inspired by reports of the hippie revolution abroad, they scrounged instruments and a state subsidy. In 1970, they played their first show.

Immediately, crowds poured out to see them. Rock'n'roll in Mongolia. Made by Mongols! It was almost like being a part of the real world.

Since that time, Chinggis Khan has played in Russia and at Boudokan in Japan. Japanese TV viewers voted them one of the world's best bands.

They're big friendly guys with hair down to the middle of their backs. On the street, they stop to shake hands. In bars, they hang out with the locals.

Mongolia's Grateful Dead, they're the grandaddies of modern Mongolian rock'n'roll. You hear them on the radio. Other bands cover their songs. They even play live once or twice a year.

At their concerts, the crowd stands like in the Fillmore days of the 60s. People join hands and sway back and forth, singing together as one big happy family. Be happy. Love everybody. Love Mongolia. That was the message of Mongol rock.

Until 1990. That year is the low-point for Mongolian society. A crumbling Russia becomes a Soviet without a Union. It can't feed itself, let alone spare anything for the Mongols. Bang! Pack the bags and get out. Take what you can and scram.

After nearly fifty years of Russian support, Mongolia is in shambles. The economy is ruined. Unemployment is rampant. Store shelves are empty. People spend their last tugrik on vodka. They need to forget how bad their lives are. University students go on a hunger strike to end communist rule. The government caves in and has elections. The communists win. The future? What future?

In that year, a group of highschool kids meet in a stairwell after school. They bring their battered acoustic guitars. There's one snare drum gotten through "not very proper" means. They set up right there — on the landing... and practice.

"One, two, three...Yesterday, all my troubles seemed so far awaaaay....!"

They play The Beatles songs they've heard on the radio. They copy the Chinggis Khan tunes they've heard in concert. Anything that's not communist.

In 1991, Ganbayar, the oldest and the group's leader/drummer, gets hold of a cassette by the German band, HELLOWEEN. Fascinated by the power of the loud hard music, he decides THAT'S what he wants to play. He calls the others together.

Wow! They've never heard anything like this before. They too want to play *this music. This fast music. Quickly, they rehearse and perfect the style. SPEED is what they play. SPEED is what they like. SPEED is what they name themselves. The Mongolian word for SPEED is:*

HURD
(THE ONLY ROCK BAND IN MONGOLIA)

Pronounced "Hort," that's what they play, or at least the best of it.

A huge poster hangs on the wall across from the Central Post Office: skeletons play electric guitars against a black background. The name HURD drips in blood-like Cyrillic above the drawing. Five dates, all at the National Concert hall. Only HURD, no opener, two hours each night.

Skulls and guitars — in Mongolia! Yes!

I run to the theater to make sure I get tickets before it sells out. Lucky I do. Despite the 700 *tugrik* admission charge, the box office is besieged. I fight my way to the front and shove my *tugriks* under the little slot. Behind me, a young woman holding a bag of school books, presses against me. She's got stacks of one *tugrik* bills, each as thick as my fist, ready to slide in for the tickets.

The performances sell out quickly — every night, all 1500 seats of The National Concert Hall.

The night of the show, I get there early. I want to hang out. Meet the local rockers. It's cold, but I'm anxious to get into a scene I didn't know existed. I arrive at the hall an hour early. It's a bright white building with coffin-shaped pillars in front. It could be in Washington or New York. If it were, it would house the local philharmonic.

It's not the philharmonic that's playing tonight. It's HURD! An even larger cloth version of the skeleton poster hangs in front of the pillars. Outside, a crowd gathers.

Three longhaired Mongols, wearing motorcycle jackets, share a cigarette next to the far pillar. A thin teenage girl wears a tight leather dress that she must've bought in some other country. So much for the punks.

Two steps down from the longhairs, an old women in a worn red *deel* speaks with a policeman. Huddling near the entrance, a young mother carries her toddler tightly wrapped in a blanket. In a small group to one side, half a dozen men stand, their tan cashmere coats over black suits and ties.

On the steps, a ten year old, wearing baggy pants and a backwards baseball hat, shares a walkman earphone with an identically dressed friend. Every age, gender, and type of Mongol is here to see the band.

When the door opens, a city cop in a leather jacket and fur hat, stands next to the female ticket-taker. She ushers those with 700 *tugrik* tickets to the lower level. The 500 *tugrik* crowd is sent to the balcony.

Each ticket has a row and seat number. Inside are rows with plush velvet-covered seats almost matching the ticket numbers. A runway extends from the stage into the audience. A ruffled white curtain hangs in front of the stage. If it rose to reveal tap dancers with canes, it wouldn't look out of place. From the towering speakers, comes a weird musical mix. Some *Deep Purple, Anthrax, Skatman* and *Chinngis Khan*. The rest I've never heard before, slow rock ballads and la-la-la pop music.

At seven o'clock, the "starting time," the crowd begins applauding, whistling, stamping their feet. The canned music on the speakers gets louder. Occasionally, a ping! or a loud off-key chord comes from behind the curtain. To my right, a young couple kiss loudly in their seats.

Slowly the chords become on-key. The house lights dim. The faint sounds of high speed drum-bashing break through the applause. The bashing gets louder as the room gets darker. The curtains open on a black stage.

On that stage are large red and white boxes, some fifteen feet high, others smaller. They're oddly shaped and at odd angles to one another. In the back, on the biggest box, the drummer bangs away with a flurry of power.

Then come the guitar players, one at a time, two tall skinny guys, wearing black jeans and t-shirts with full-color pictures of bands I've never heard of. Over the t-shirts, black leather jackets.

Now the vocalist enters, carrying a cordless mic. He's dressed like the

others, except, instead of black levis, he wears Calvin Klein underpants. White, skin tight, stretching from waist to mid-thigh, they could be jockey shorts, or bicycle pants. It's hard to tell. What isn't hard to tell is that either the guy is all potatoes and no meat — or he stuffs.

Blam! They're off. Three speedy metal songs. Fast, powerful, with DLAM! DLAM! DA DA DLAM! hooks. Good enough to scare the pants off any visiting missionary. Beautiful: Mongolians who understand the music and make it — hard and with SPEED!

The singer runs to the drums, then out to the audience. He climbs on top of the huge speaker column, up over the rail to the side balcony, growling lyrics all the way.

The guitar players use cordless guitars. They race back and forth across the stage. Their long hair flies behind them like a horse's mane in the wind.

"Chonno (wolf)," howls the singer.

Though I don't understand the rest of the lyrics, I'm so impressed I'm on my feet. Standing, I raise my fist into the air and cheer them on.

The crowd is silent around me. The old woman, now two rows ahead of me, looks with her jaw hung open. The men in suits sit with smiles frozen onto their faces. The teens and moms with their kids squirm uncomfortably in their seats.

The smooching couple leans forward, brows furrowed.

After the third song the guitarist slows down. The singer moves to the front of the stage. He puts one leg up on the monitor. In a voice that could come from an American LITE radio station, he croons a ballad. It's slow, with plaintive guitar breaks. The singer pouts, cries, stretches his hands toward the audience. It's a love song.

The first slow chords set the crowd applauding. The first words send them smiling, swaying back and forth. The kissy couple leans back and holds hands. When they get to the chorus, the entire hall sings with them. Their unified voices drown out the sound of my teeth gritting.

The next song, too, is a ballad, agonizingly slow. It's the hit.

By the fourth slow song the Mongols are on their feet. They stand in their seats, swaying back and forth, arms over their heads. Neighbors' hands touch. They grab hold. A human love chain. Far in the back of the orchestra seats, someone holds a cigarette lighter, flame aloft.

The slow songs last another half hour. The crowd sucks it up. Then the ballads stop. There's a power chord. Two. A buzzsaw guitar. The click of the fuzz box. The drums: gaja gaja gaja gaja. SPEED returns.

With new energy, the band runs back and forth along the stage. A smoke machine pumps gray gas over the stage floor. Colored lights flash. The singer climbs to the far end of the runway, then zooms back. The guitarists and bass player lean forward, swinging their hair in unison. Faster and faster they go, along with the music. The drum beats madly. BLA DUM! BLA DUM! BLA DUMBLAD-UMBLA. BLADUM-BLADUM-BLADUM-BLADUM-BLADUMBLADUM-BLADUM. The band is a blur of action, running, playing, singing. SPEED SPEED SPEED.

The audience sits down. It's quiet again. They listen politely.

For the last song, the band plays a mid-tempo number with lots of time changes and hooks. When they're finished it's over. No applause. No "thank yous." No encore. Just curtain down, lights on and leave. The end.

◎ ◎ ◎

There is a factory in the Northern part of *Ulaanbaatar*. They make cement, industrial wire, and the big iron poles that form the centers of highway pillars.

A constant clang and whir comes out of the building. Inside, you're assaulted by the never-ending clatter of REAL heavy metal.

This factory complex, left over from commie days, was made with THE WORKERS in mind. Pictures of Lenin and *Sukhbaatar* still hang in the hallway. In back, the commies constructed a "workers' hall," a kind of auditorium.

Workers can use this area for whatever they want. With a large stage and hard wooden benches, this is HURD's rehearsal room.

I enter the hall, saying *"Sain bain yy"* to the man mixing cement inside the doorway. I walk past him to the main room where the floor is filled with bloody fur. A group of men work salting the meat and stretching the fur to prepare it for market.

I'm with Uyanga, a friend and translator who works at the new private radio station. Not only does she speak excellent English, but she knows the band and arranged this meeting.

We walk past the fur to a long table in front of the stage. At the table sit members of HURD, along with a few young men I don't know. All dressed in black leather jackets and t-shirts. You wouldn't associate them with the *deel*-wearing herdsmen at work on the fur. But this is Mongolia.

As we walk in, the band members smile and wave to us. A man I recognize as the drummer gets up and shakes my hand. He says something rather long to Uyanga. She laughs but doesn't translate it.

I apologize for being a few minutes late. He tells me not to worry because the singer isn't there yet.

While we wait, I show the band some tapes I brought with me: SubPop grunge, Dischord emo and Earache death metal. These cassettes help me get through Mongolia's aural Gobi. Maybe they'll help the band.

When I set the tapes on the table, half a dozen hands fly out for them. The band, their friends, groupies, whoever they are, grab them, open them, and drool over them like Russian Jews over smuggled matzo.

There's a flurry of questions. Uyanga tells me they've never heard of any of the bands: L7, MUDHONEY, NAPALM DEATH. What are they? Where are they from? Do they play them on the radio? Are they famous?

The drummer takes out the insert card to the TAD cassette. He studies it, sounding the words out as best he can. He asks Uyanga a question. She translates.

"He wants to know what GOD'S BALLS means," she says.

Before I can figure out how to answer it, the singer shows up. An hour late, he sits at the end of the table his legs crossed, his arms folded. He's tall and skinny, with a brooding look. He acts more like an undergrad art student, than the wildman I saw in concert.

Uyanga introduces the group: Ganbayar is the drummer. Otgonbayar plays lead guitar. Tomortsog is the brooding singer. And two guys, both named Naranbaatar, play bass and rhythm guitar.

"Should we start the interview?" I ask.

Ganbayar smiles and nods. The others pull up their chairs as if being closer would help me understand their Mongolian.

"What bands do you know in America?" asks Ganbayar. "What do people listen to? What do you call this kind of music?" He points to the MUDHONEY cassette.

"What kind of music does WASP play?" asks one of the Naranbaatars.

It's an hour before I can ask any of my own questions. I tell them I liked the concert, but my tastes were different from that of the audience. The fast stuff was great, I say. But the slow ballads...my mother might like them.

"Do mothers in America like metal?" asked Ganbayar.

"Humor doesn't translate," I explain to him. "Anyway, it seems with a name that means SPEED and all those good fast songs, you're only playing slow because of the audience."

"That's right," he says, "This is all new to Mongolia. We have to teach the audience. It's difficult. For now, we have to live."

"Do you live off your music?" I ask.

His forehead wrinkles in non-comprehension.

"Do you or the other guys in the band have other jobs?"

"Oh no," he says. "HURD is our lives."

"So you live from your royalties?" I ask.

My translator is having a tough time with that one. I explain.

"You know, the money you make from record sales and having your songs played on the radio."

Laughter explodes simultaneously from all the band members.

"Such things don't exist in Mongolia," says Ganbayar. "We have no records.

They play our cassette on the radio and we thank them. There is no pay."

"Our money comes from concerts," says Otgonbayar. "We play the big concert hall when we can, and small clubs other times. We can sometimes play three times a week."

"Do you play bar mitzvahs?" I ask.

"We play in some bars," says Ganbayar, "What kind of bar is that?"

"It's not important," I say. "I just wanted to know how you earned your money."

"We play one or two songs in some festivals. Sometimes we can do concerts like the one you saw. Sometimes people hire us to play at special shows for special groups."

"Does that pay the bills?" I ask.

"Not really," he answers, "but we also have the only big PA in town. Rent it to bands and concerts...THAT pays the bills."

"At least you're not salting skins," I say.

He laughs. Then he tells me the band's history: the high school meeting, the instrument scrounging...

"Sometimes someone comes from Singapore with a guitar. We buy them. Sometimes someone goes to Korea. They buy strings and sticks. We do what we can."

"Where do you get tapes to listen to?" I ask.

"It's better now. We get some cassettes from Russia or China, or travelers leave them." I see him gazing at the pile on the table. I nod. They grab 'em up, with plenty of *"Bayerlalaa's."*

"It sounds like a tough way to live," I continue. "How many others are doing it? In fact, how many rock bands are there in Mongolia?"

They laugh, again.

"There are less then twenty pop bands in Mongolia..." says the other Naranbaatar.

"But there is only one ROCK band," finishes Ganbayar, "HURD."

He asks me the difference between 'pop' and 'rock.'

"Rock is louder, faster, and more aggressive," I tell him. "Pop is smiley-faced."

He nods. "Then we are the only ROCK band in Mongolia."

"We're trying to educate the audience. We play the slow songs to catch them.

Then, once we get them around the neck, we shake them with the hard fast songs. This is all new to Mongolian audiences. They're not ready for it."

"But you're unique," I say. "Aren't you happy there's no one else like you?"

"Happy?" says the drummer. "Why be happy? We're alone! We want twenty bands to play like us. A hundred bands! But there aren't a hundred of bands in all Mongolia."

Otgonbayar jumps in; "Kids come up to us on the street. They say they want to start a band. They say they want to be just like us. We take them here. Show them our guitars. Teach them tricks. But we know they'll never make it. They can't buy instruments. They can't find places to play. There is nowhere to go. How can we like that?"

So they do what they can, living the rock'n'roll life in a very un-rock'n' roll country.

"We think we can play in Russia," he continues. "A man in Siberia called us. He likes our music even though he never heard us. He says it's only the idea."

I guess the novelty of Mongolian metal isn't lost on the rest of the world. The band may even make it to Moscow, someday. Like Jimi Hendrix going to England, maybe the trip abroad will bring them fame and respect back home.

But back home, fame and respect back home doesn't get you very far. Even when you're the only ROCK band in Mongolia.

Footnote: By 2004, the band developed a reputation for promoting Mongolian nationalism. The Chinese government suddenly cancelled a planned concert in Inner (Chinese occupied) Mongolia. They were afraid of appeals to independence. The story made the NY Times, though not exactly the front page.

Thrilled to discover Mongolmetal, a few weeks later I'm drawn to a ratty flyer half-blown off the door to the University: a black skull with the words ROCK DRAM in Roman letters. Underneath it is the Cyrillic address of the National theater, a stately building across from the post office. Yowee! More ROCK! I head for the theater. The place looks closed, shut tight. Around from the back comes a chubby young woman. She walks quickly, pulling her long coat tightly against her.

"Uchlarai," I say. "Tickets, khaana?"

She stops and turns toward me.

"Tickets for what?" she says in near perfect English.

"Rock Dram," I tell her.

"That's not for days," she says. "You come back on right day. The office there." She points to a little hut detached from the main building.

I thank her and leave, to return on the "right day." The box office is open when I get there...I think. The door to the hut is open, but inside is only a boarded-up ticket window with a small crack at the bottom.

A shadow moves beneath the crack. I bend down for a closer look. Blue deel cloth flashes by. I tap on the wood.

"Uchlarai," I say, "ticket jamar enteve?"

The cloth behind the crack morphs into flesh as whoever is on the other side brings her face close.

"No ticket. No ticket. No dance today. No no."

"I don't want a dance," I say, abandoning all attempts at Mongolian, "I want the ROCK DRAM."

"Ta, Rock Dram? No. No. Bish Bish Bish"

"Yes, me, Bid, Rock Dram."

"Tavn zuu" she says.

I pay my 500 tugriks. She slips a xeroxed piece of newsprint through the crack. Taking my "ticket," I go out to the main building. At the top of the wide staircase is a row of six doors. All are closed. None have knobs or handles on the outside.

It's 5:50. The show is scheduled to start at 6 o'clock. I'm the only one waiting. At 6, a young man climbs the stairs behind me. Ignoring me, he goes up to the second door from the left and pounds on it. Nothing happens. He pounds again. There's a shuffling inside. The door opens and the man enters. I'm right behind.

It's dark inside. The woman who opened the door wrinkles her brow in surprise. I hand her my ticket. She looks at it and passes it to the guy who went in before me. They discuss it.

The young man speaks to me.

"I'm Chinzorig," he says. "How did you know this performance?"

"I saw a poster," I say.

"Welcome," he says, "we really didn't expect anybody...not like you."

I smile, hoping it's the appropriate response. Chinzorig speaks to the woman and she smiles. He asks me where I'm from. I tell him.

"I have a friend from America," he says, "His name is Larry. He lives in California. Do you know him?"

I smile.

He smiles.

Chinzorig tells me he's one of the actors in the play tonight. "It starts soon," he says.

"Then I'd better get seated," I say, heading for the orchestra seats. There are six other people already there.

By showtime there's almost a dozen. The crowd peaks at about thirty. In the center of my row is a group of black-suited businessmen, each with a briefcase. Other audience members are older. A few are children, not older than eight or nine years old.

At 6:40 the play starts. At least the loud slow ROCK ballads start. A minute or two later, the curtain opens.

The set is pure German Expressionism, but on a low budget. The set designer has stretched three giant pieces of cloth across the stage, one red, one silver and one blue. They're pulled tight at oblique angles. Large holes in the cloth give the illusion of planets. A blue circle hangs on invisible wires at the right. We're obviously on another planet, a thought I've often had during my time in Mongolia.

Four people are on stage. A bearded middle-aged man looks like Captain Zarkov from Flash Gordon. Two indeterminates wear gas masks. They've pulled their jackets up over their heads, as if they tried to take them off without unzipping them. There's also a svelte girl in a leather harness that just covers the good parts. Pasted-on glitter glitters from the leather straps.

The girl wears silver boots with four-inch soles and eight-inch heels. She kneels in front of Captain Zarkov, who is pointing to something in the distance. They speak in Mongolian, so I have to construct the story in my head. Here's what I think happens:

The planet's dying. Captain Zarkov is the ruler. Harness Girl is his daughter. She has to go to another planet and find something-or-other. This something-or-other is the only thing that can save their home.

Suddenly the music starts again. Though not my cup of airag, it's well played. Local pop idols from the band Harrang recorded it especially for this performance.

Dad and the girl start singing to one another. Dad's plaintive pleas play off the girl's brave attempts to reassure him. Finally, the girl leaves and dad falls on the ground screaming.

Suddenly a bunch of guys in skull masks appear. With them are girls dressed like Mrs. Dracula. They dance around the crying man, stretching their arms out toward him and shaking them. The rest of the play follows the original girl from planet to planet, looking for the mysterious planet-saver thingamajig.

At her first stop, she discovers a guy who dresses like an Indian — feather, not turban. He wears a blue bandanna instead of a headdress,. He offers the girl some food. She refuses it, preferring to eat worms.

Spacegirl: You...you speak Mongolian?

Alien: Of course, everybody in space speaks Mongolian.

Among other things I think I understand are: "yaki-soba" "ein billig" and "Ho Chi Minh."

Anyway, when the guy gets ready to leave, he ties the girl to a post. She struggles and then falls asleep. She's discovered by a trio of vamps in short, low-cut dresses. Lead by a top-heavy middle-aged woman, they look over her body with more than a hint of lesbitude. When the heroine awakens, one woman demands that she answer a question before they release her. She answers it and they release her. Then they take her to THE WOMEN'S LAIR.

In THE WOMEN'S LAIR our heroine sits by herself, eating worms. The other women form a circle on the opposite side of the stage. They sit there talking amongst themselves, as if they're afraid of the newcomer.

She calls to them, saying something that immediately warms them up. Out comes the food and drink, more than just worms. Just before they serve it, the older woman secretly pulls a vial from between her breasts. She dumps the contents into the drink.

Zarkov's daughter falls asleep again. While she sleeps, the women rifle her pocketbook. Awakening before they find what they want, she pulls her pocketbook free of them and runs away.

She wanders for awhile, somehow ending up on yet another planet. There she runs into THE SPACE BUM, played by Chinzorig. THE SPACE BUM is alone, sitting and drinking his space vodka. Our heroine spies him and asks for help. THE SPACE BUM assumes she doesn't really want his help, but his vodka. He turns his back to her, refusing to talk.

Eventually, they warm enough to each other to sing a rock duet. That is interrupted by one of the guys in a skull mask, lowered from the ceiling on a cable.

About this time I notice a Portuguese friend of mine, Joaquin, in the audience. I'm slightly disappointed because I'm no longer the only foreigner. Still, he's a good guy, a journalist and a musician. Not a bad combination. It's nice to see him.

I don't know how long my attention diverts from the stage. By the time it returns, the SPACE BUM scene is over. Leather girl is now on another planet. Here, she meets SPACE STUD. This is a tall thin young man who wears a beret and black leather jacket on his upper half. On his lower half are extremely tight pants with wide black and white stripes.

It doesn't take many duets before we get to THE SEX SCENE, choreographed between our heroine and SPACE STUD. After much twisting, turning and middle bumping, both of them are on the ground. He lays face up. She lays on top of him — also face up, her back to his front.

Their bliss doesn't last long. SKULLMAN drops from the sky again. This time he carries a dagger. Throwing our heroine off SPACE STUD, he plunges it into the other man's heart. SPACE STUD dies, singing his own dirge, while SKULLMAN drags him into a special effects pit of smoke and flames.

Then comes the finale. Everybody comes from the wings. They dance to dark metallic music. A vocal chorus rises from the speakers: AAAAAHHHHHHHHHH! AHHHHHHHHHHHHHHHHHHHHHHH! OOOOOOOOOOOOOOO! OOOOOOOOOOOO-OOOOO!

Our heroine rises from the floor, hoisted skywards behind the gossamer silver cloth. Everyone else falls, laying face down on the stage. The music gets louder. The curtain falls. There's applause. And it's over.

After the play, Chinzorig, still dressed as the SPACE BUM, comes to talk to me. He asks if I want to go upstairs and meet the others to celebrate the opening (and closing — it's a one nighter) of the play. I tell him sure. Then he sees Joaquin.

"Is he a friend of yours?" he asks.

"Yes," I tell him.

"Well, then bring him along."

Together we go upstairs to the dressing room. Actors, propmen, director, the whole gang is there. Zarkov is peeling off his beard. The others sit around a table, some on a couch, the rest in chairs or on the floor. Two men I haven't seen before get off the couch to make room for us. They don't know much English, but they try.

"You American? You like play? You like Mongolia? How long you been here? You like rock music?"

The crew members introduce themselves. Stagehands, set designers, the director, all there and happy to meet us. I compliment the set designer for the most innovative minimalism since Dr. Caligari. He doesn't understand me, but knows I'm saying something nice.

The director has a guitar. A few strums, a few words and everybody joins in. Then comes the vodka. While we sing, the bottles keep coming, one after the other, like eggs from a magician's hat.

There is, however, only one glass. So while most folks sing, one-by-one we use the glass and pass it on. As usual, the Mongols drink it straight. No mixer. Why ruin a good drink? Whenever my turn comes, I chug it down. A full glass. Bang! It's gone.

"You sure you're an American?" asks Chinzorig. "You drink like a Mongol."

"Thanks," I tell him. "Wait till you hear me sing!"

And sing I do. I join in every song — especially after five or six glasses of vodka. Even though they're in Mongolian, and I never heard them before, I can belt out those tunes. Often I accompany myself pounding out the beat on the table.

The black-suited businessmen suddenly appear at the door. Chinzorig introduces them as co-workers from "my really job." Gradually, the rest of the audience appears: wives, husbands, children, of the cast members.

They don't stay. They've only come to collect their kin and leave. It is, after all, a worknight. I'm sad to see people go away when I'm feeling so good.

Eventually, Chinzorig says that the theater is closing. I thank him for the great time and stand up. Then, suddenly, the floor moves. POW! It slides right out from under me. Down I go, caught by Joaquin and Chinzorig just before my head hits the ground.

I try to stand again, but it's like walking in a spinning tunnel at the amusement park. Things get a little vague at this point. I remember Joaquin and Chinzorig each taking me under an arm. I remember going to someone's house, a nice woman with two little kids. I remember the kids giggling and the woman's face frozen into a smile.

That's it, until the next morning when I awake on a strange couch. Joaquin is asleep on the floor. There's an evil-smelling plastic bucket next to me, I'm not feeling so good.

My hostess serves me lamb soup and milk tea for breakfast. I don't have very much of it. It takes me a whole day to recover.

From the specific to the general. That's what my teachers used to say. Let them see it, then tell them how it works.

You've had your specific, though there'll be more. A lot more, in fact. You'll see why this chapter is called:

120 DAYS OF VODKA

(Actually, it's closer to 300 days, but I like association with DeSade. More fitting, however, would be Sacher-Masoch.)

Remember the Budweiser 'party animal' promotion? The one with the black-eyed pit bull at wild frat parties? The company pulled it because of complaints. It glamorized alcohol, caused vandalism and teen pregnancy, they said. Mongolians have never seen it. They live it.

Leave a Mongol alone in a room and she'll sit and watch the mountains through the window. Add another and they'll have a conversation. Wait ten minutes and one will burst into song. The other joins in for the chorus. Add a bottle of vodka and you've got a party.

Mongols can smell a party from miles away. Like vultures on a sheep carcass, they descend on the nearest gathering and pluck the guts out of it. No one minds. There's no concept of "invited" or not. It's a party, after all.

Mongolian parties are more unified than parties in normal countries. They're organized like summer camp activities. No little groups. No wall flowers. No breaking away to sneak into the bushes. Maybe it's a relic from Commie times, but Mongols do it collectively.

I explain American parties to Sainamdrar.

"In the US and most western countries," I say, "a party is actually an ever-changing group of small groups of people."

"How do the people from one group contact the ones in another group?" she asks.

"It's a ritual known as mingling," I answer. "People drift from group to group, carrying the same drink. Depending on the party, the minglers talk about music, art, politics, or sex. More often, they complain about how much they hate parties, and how boring they are."

"I don't wonder," she says, "if all they do is talk."

Pick a room, any room. (Not my apartment, please!) At one end is a table with a lot of bottles on it. A few wine, a few more vodka, maybe some beer. Food? Only if it's a dinner, or there are some whitefolks — and they brought it. Let's go to a teachers' party, typical of more than I can remember:

Besides me there's Al, Maggie's replacement. He's a big British raver, in his mid-twenties, fluent in Spanish and Thomas Pynchon. He's got a shaved head, thick-rimmed glasses and a modest demeanor. He's also incredibly sexually active, something the Brits must consider a requirement for the job.

It's party time. The door is locked, just in case a student should try to bother us with something academic.

Toila has pushed the desks and chairs into a large circle away from the center of the room. That leaves plenty of floorspace for dancing. Right now no one dances; we just sit on the sides talking about politics and religion. There is some beer on the table and a couple bottles of vodka. Al and I are the only ones drinking the beer.

Dr. Sumiya reaches under a desk for another bottle of vodka. He taps a spoon against it to get our attention. He fills the glasses around the room. After a toast, he dips his ring finger into the glass and sprinkles some vodka into the air "for God and nature." Then — down the hatch.

Each of us bottom up our glasses. They say it's 'unmasculine' to leave anything in the glass. The female teachers are easily more masculine than I am.

After two or three drinks the vocal chords loosen. Sumiya pours another glass of vodka and hands it to Namjil. Namjil stands and sings, holding the vodka glass high. After three words, the rest of the crowd (except Al and me) joins in. Soon, it's a rousing chorale of memories of lost relatives on the steppe.

After the song, Namjil takes a sip of vodka and passes the glass to Sainamdrar, my term-long crush, recently lost to the seed-spreading Al. Her repertoire is as familiar to the crew as Namjil's. A few lyrics and BANG — everyone joins in. Sainamdrar takes a sip from the vodka glass and passes it to me. Sumiya intervenes, filling it to the brim again.

"I don't know any songs," I protest. "And it's not fair. You have help. I have to sing alone."

"If you don't sing," says Namjil, "then you have to drink a whole glass of vodka. It's our tradition. Besides, you could always sing YESTERDAY. That's what the foreigners usually do."

I slug down the vodka, refusing to sing. Sumiya refills it. I pass it to Siirtbat, the next teacher in line.

Siirtbat not only sings, but downs the entire glass to boot. Sumiya is there with a refill for Al.

Al doesn't flinch. "YESTERDAY, All my troubles...!" he sings.

The crew joins in "Ahl my trahboos seem so fah awee!" Applause. He bows, takes a sip of vodka and passes on the glass.

While the others sing, each of us sips on the vodka glass in front of us. These are different from the passing/singing glass. These are our PERSONAL drinks. Sumiya, with an eagle eye and deft hand, springs to refill our glasses as soon as they sink to the half-way level.

"Mykel," says Doytseg, "it's your turn again."

She hands me the vocal glass.

"I still don't know any songs," I say, raising the clear liquid to my lips and sucking it down.

By the third time around, I've decided it's do or die. Wobbly, I rise to my feet, vodka glass in hand: "OH WHEN THE SAINTS, COME MARCHIN' IN..." I wail away in my best Louis Armstrong voice, expecting the crew to join in. The words aren't that difficult.

Instead, it's stone still silence. Twenty jaws drop as I stand there, clapping my hands, stomping my feet: "I WANNA BE AMONG THEIR NUMBER..." When I'm finished, there's nothing — not even the sound of breathing. I stand, swaying slightly in the vodka breeze. Quietly, Sumiya takes the glass from my hand and passes it to Siirtbat. It never reaches me again.

After the singing, comes the dancing. Bad Eurodisco, and "SKATMAN!" Everyone on the dancefloor. No slouchers. Me too. I'm afraid if I don't get up, I'll have to drink a glass of vodka for each song.

One thing about Mongolian parties, you never remember the end of them. They fade into the horizon, like the end of a long road. Concentrating on "what happened next" only brings a headache.

Expats in Mongolia also have parties. Most of the time, even though Mongols are invited, they're Western-style parties. The music is low enough to converse over and people break into small groups and talk.

"That's no kind of party," Sainamdrar told me. "Standing around and talking. That's a conference, not a party."

You've already read about Maggie's parties. Now that she's gone, it doesn't mean the parties have stopped. Julie, a VSOer who lives in my neighborhood, is having one tonight.

She's invited her fellow Brits and some Mongolian students. The party is supposed to start at 9PM. I'm there at 9:30. There are three Brits, proper-looking ladies in their mid-forties, and no one else.

Around 10, the Mongols show up — in force. Some of them were even invited. One is Tsetsesteg, the student who appeared at my apartment in a miniskirt at 11AM. Things are going to get interesting.

By midnight, a line winds into the kitchen from the bathroom door. From behind that door come gagging sounds and frequent flushing. Those who can't wait stand bent over the sink, running water to force the regurgitated vodka and mutton down the drain.

Bodies of passed-out students line the hallway. A girl, about 20, staggers over them. Chunk! Her foot catches the kidney of a prone Mongol. She's down, her legs folded over the body beneath her. She doesn't get up again.

Besides the Mongolian students, the party has an odd mix of Austrians, an Australian and a Canadian tourist, and a few Ukrainians. I'm the only American.

The tourists have been brought by the notorious 'BB from *UB*.' BB (real name BatBold) is probably the best English speaker in Mongolia. He's friends with the band HURD and interpreted when I met them a second time. He's got long hair and a longer sense of cynical humor. He was the first Mongol I spoke to, at the train station when he was waiting for the Monkey Business customers.

He works for Monkey Business. They take care of tourists in town for just a few days, usually on the trans-Mongolian railroad from Beijing to Moscow. He shows them around, taking them to places they would not normally visit, like expat parties. Tonight, he's brought two of his charges, the Australian and the Canadian.

The Canadian, a pleasant woman in her mid-twenties, is in Julie's bedroom sitting on the bed staring vacantly out the window. The Australian, a tall thick-bodied young man, sits on the couch in the dance room. Next to him, wrapped in his arms, her lips against his neck, is Tsetsesteg. Me? I'm dancing to "THE SKATMAN."

The front door opens. It hits hard against one of the bodies lying in the hall. A chubby European shoulder continues pressing from the outside. Inch by inch, the door pushes aside the stupored Mongolian on the floor. When it fully opens, in walks the European. Nobody notices much. All eyes are on his partner. Silence chokes the party guests like lamb caught in the throat. Into that party walks THE ONLY NEGRESS IN MONGOLIA.

The Mongols gawk in awe. Some of them have seen black men before, American soldiers in town on a good-will trip, some African students. But not one of them has ever seen a black woman. Thirty dancers stop dancing. Thirty Oriental faces turn toward the door. Thirty mouths hang open. Tsetsesteg and her labial partner part.

Slowly, the woman walks into the room. She might as well be Moses, as the sea of people parts in front of her. A short, slim woman, maybe thirty, she has a good natured smiling face. Like a queen nodding at her subjects, she turns to the right and left, smiling at the strangers.

Taking off her sleeping bag coat, she makes her way to the bedroom where the rest of the coats lie in a pile on the floor. Once she's in the other room, away from the dancers, the party returns to full swing. I go speak with her.

Her English has a French accent. She tells me her name is Claire and she's from Cameroon.

"I am married weez a man in zee foreign serveez," she says.

"A Mongol?" I ask.

She shakes her head.

"No, 'ee eez African. At zee embassy."

She tells me that while her husband plays government, she's become the head chef of a restaurant called THE WHITE HOUSE. She's turned it into a French-African Restaurant.

"I might bring my entire English class," I kid. "They'd come just for the thrill of meeting a real live black woman."

"Zat wood be great. You weell love it." says the woman.

The next class, I propose it to the students. "It'll be expensive," I tell them, "make sure you have enough money. I can't pay for you."

"How much is enough money?" asks Bishbataar, putting me on the spot.

"I don't know," I say, "but it could be as much as five dollars."

There's a collective gasp.

"So if you can't afford it," I tell them, "don't come."

Ten students show up.

Since I've called in advance, they provide a special, private room. Choucroute, bouillabaisse, pot-au-feu, coq-au-vin. There are also a few African dishes, both Senegalese. One is a kind of soup, the other a kind of chicken.

What is this stuff? My students want to know. There are English explanations next to each, but nothing has mutton in it. The students don't know what to do.

"Chicken is a bird," says Bishbataar. "People don't eat birds. Cats and dogs eat birds, not people."

"Try it," I tell him. "It tastes like lamb."

Eventually, everybody chooses something. Most enjoy their dishes, although the Senegalese food is too spicy for Mongol tastes. For me, it's the best food I've had here. It better be, the bill comes to $105.

No one has enough money. Fortunately, they take credit cards. Citibank covers the difference.

After the meal, Claire comes out to thrill the students with her presence.

"Do you get the spices here?" asks Tsetsesseg. (She doesn't, they're imported from China.)

"Does the food taste different in Africa?" (It does.)

"Do you like Mongolian food?" (She says she does.)

They ask her all kinds of questions, somehow managing not to embarrass me with "Do people wear clothes in Africa?" or "What does human flesh taste like?"

The restaurant adventure turns out to be a pleasant-though-expensive diversion from the main focus of *Ulaanbataar* life: MORE VODKA. That begins the next weekend. I visit a couple of my *VSO* pals who live near the State Department Store. It doesn't take long for the usually sensible and always proper Brits to pick up the native habits. At James and Hannah's, the second bottle of vodka is already open when I get there.

Here we are: me, Al, Hannah, a blond English teacher with a nosering and a light gypsy air, and James, a horticulturist who likes old punk rock and has nose hair so long it braids. Also there's Sebastian, another big English guy who likes 'football,' and has a smiling cynically joking personality. Loud and hilarious when he's drunk, he's the kind of guy whose simple proximity makes you want to giggle.

Despite the vodka, this is a Western party, so none of us sing or dance. A Dead Kennedys tape is on low volume and we talk.

"Thank God it's only freezing out," says Hannah.

"God is a ten foot woman in a leather bikini," I say, "with a whip."

"There is no God," says Sebastian.

After tanking up at Hannah and James's, Al, Sebastian and I go out to MOTOR ROCK. It's a new disco in the St. Petersburg Club, formerly known as The Lenin Club. There's a new disco every day in this city.

We start with a few beers, then comes vodka. I weave my way home at 3:30AM. Al and Sebastian are still dancing, working on a couple of girls who've previously agreed to 'slow dance' with them. Me? Though I've made the reluctant move from punk rocker to disco bunny, I have yet to find the courage or patience to ask someone to 'slow dance.' If you get tired of your partner while discoing, you just face the other way and dance with someone else. That's more difficult if your partner has a couple of arms wrapped around you. Besides, I have to get up at 11 to go to the graduation lunch the next day.

Ah, the next day. I'm hung over. Stomach ache, head ache, nausea. I feel like someone should take a sharp knife and slit me open, pull out all the bad stuff, empty my kidneys, then start again.

The graduation lunch is at the *Ulaanbataar* hotel. It starts at 2PM, I wobble in at a quarter to three. I sit at one of the professors' tables. In front of me are five glasses, along with the plates. Unlike the plates, the glasses are filled (from left to right): white wine, vodka, beer, red wine, champagne.

First comes a vegetable salad and soup. A meat salad and bread follow. Then comes the entree: 1/4 chicken with gravy, potatoes, and rice. Then comes the OTHER entree: steak in gravy, potatoes, rice and more bread. The second I empty a glass, a waitress refills it with the proper liquid. I eat slowly and drink as little as I can get away with, sticking to the beer. I figure, if I only get mildly drunk, my body can recover from the past week...er...month...er...

Mildly drunk, however, is not to be. You see, there's THE PROCESSION. The graduating students stand up and move to one corner of the room. I recognize Tuyatseg, the girl who tripped over the body at Julie's party.

They all form a line against the wall. Led by Tuyatseg, it weaves from table to table. One-by-one, students move from professor to professor. Each time, they drink a toast. Every professor drinks with each of the students. There are 127 students.

Lunch ends at 5:00. At 5:30, I have a date with some of my own students. We're going to dinner at a new restaurant. It's only fair. I went to The White House with one class. Now I've got to go out with the other. I've warned them, though. I told them they'll have to bring at least $5 each. It's an expensive place. I wonder what we'll have to drink.

THIRTEEN

The Russian-made film URGAA was a minor hit in The States. It was about — and filmed in — Inner Mongolia. The customs and people there are nearly the same as those in Outer, where I am.

One of the scenes critics described as `disturbing' was the slaughter-on-the-farm scene. Mongolians have animal-killing methods as carefully prescribed as kosher butchery.

In the movie, a herder holds a sheep on its back, between his knees. Using a very sharp six inch knife, he slits the animal's belly, just under the breast bone. Then he slices downward, from the breast bone to the pubic bone. Separating the sides, he reaches into the slit, like you might reach into a tissue box for the last kleenex.

He feels around the animals innards until he gets to the heart. Wrapping his hand around the large vessels leading to the heart, he squeezes. This prevents the flow of blood to the animal's brain — or anywhere else for that matter. The animal dies quickly during the surprisingly bloodless operation.

After it dies, the herder widens the slit and pulls the inner organs out of the animal. This is NOT bloodless.

The movie doesn't show the preparation. It just cuts from the slaughter to the dinner. I've heard though, at least with goats, that farm families cook them by stuffing the hollowed body with hot rocks. Then they close it up and cover it with other, heavier, rocks. The animal cooks from the inside. The skin, still on, keeps in the heat. After a half hour or so everyone digs in.

◎　◎　◎

In 1990, the Russians left Mongolia. Along with their troops, they withdrew their financial and technical support.

The Mongolian economy collapsed. Instant poverty hit like the winter cold. Families starved. No longer able to care for their children, they abandoned them to The State. They forgot, however, that The State, could no longer even take care of itself.

Parents left hundreds of children at the doors of the few orphanages. Most of the time, there was no room to take them in. Some parents raised children until they could walk and speak, then brought them to the big city and let them go. These became the street kids of Ulaanbaatar.

Except for the few taken in by orphanages, most abandoned kids live in the huge underground system that houses the pipes that deliver heat to city residents. The pipes keep them warm underground. In Mongolia, warmth is as important as food.

◎　◎　◎

It's 6:00AM. I'm walking past the bus station, wobbling home from an all-night vodka party. It's bitter-cold. My eyelids stick to the freezing tears.

Ahead of me, in the middle of the sidewalk, a manhole cover rattles. It shakes like the top on a boiling pot. THUNK! It flops open in the dawn light.

A tiny head with a filthy face pops up, looks around, and disappears for a moment. Then it pops up again.

Soon a crew of street urchins, like a rat pack, crawls out of the manhole onto the street. They begin a day's begging and stealing.

The newspapers report about three thousand street kids in Ulaanbaatar. My guess is the number is much larger. Aged between three and sixteen, they've developed their own culture, games and gangs.

Shift the scene a couple of weeks ahead to a spot in a more isolated part of town. A group of street kids has gathered in the courtyard of an old Russian apartment building. The leader of the group stands separate from the rest. He's about 15 years old, taller than the others, with narrow eyes and a face as dirty as the ground beneath his feet.

The leader points to another in the group, a small boy, about six or seven. This younger one wears blue shorts and a t-shirt. A jagged tear runs down the right shoulder of the shirt. Head bowed, the little boy walks toward one of the stone walls in the courtyard. Hunching his shoulders and tucking his chin tight to his chest, the boy stands still next to the wall.

The leader drops to his knees. He runs his hand in the dirt until he finds a fist size stone. Holding it up as a sample, the other boys in the group rummage in the dirt for rocks the same size.

The leader holds the stone in both hands, like a pitcher in the windup. He reaches back and throws it at the little boy. PACK! He hits him on the arm, just above the elbow. The boy's face tightens with the pain, but he says nothing. Then the others throw their rocks, one to the knee, one to the thigh, one to the neck just below the ear. The boy turns, facing the wall. Another rock slams into his back, hard. The little boy goes down. On his knees.

"Zogcox!" he screams.

He's given in and limps back to the others. The leader points to another boy, this one a bit older and tougher. Bravely, the new IT takes his place by the wall.

Maybe it's the kind of toughening you need for life on the street. Maybe, they're preparing for a career in law. It makes me cringe and I walk away.

Children play a big part in Mongolian culture. The average age there is the youngest in Asia. With that in mind, here are:

THREE STORIES ABOUT KIDS

STORY ONE: THE CURE

My $65 a month salary is not quite getting me through. It would pay for a Mongolian diet — without the vodka — but that's not enough. There's email. And discos. And fruits and vegetables every once in a while.

To support my addiction to minimal nutrition, I take on a few private students. Two of them are twelve year old boys. One is Korean. His family lives here for business reasons. His parents are raking in the post-Communist *tugriks* in "an enterprise." They can afford the extravagant $4 an hour I charge.

The other is Mongolian — a very bright kid who'd rather play computer games and talk than study from a book. Skinny, posterboy cute, Enkhtor, comes in with his schoolbag, Mongolian-English dictionary, and freshly sharpened pencils. Most of the time, I let him talk.

Today I have a cold: sneezes, runny nose, a convenient topic of conversation.

"There a special Mongolia medicine," he tells me, grabbing his dictionary and flipping through the pages. "Mongolians say that a man with an alive mother will never die," he says while looking through the entries.

Although I'm not worried that my sniffles are fatal, I appreciate the kind sentiment.

"Is that because he will always have a mother to care for him?" I ask.

"No," he says, "it because he can drink his mother's this."

He points to the word in the dictionary: *shess* (rhymes with `yes') in Mongolian. It means urine (rhymes with `yuck!') in English.

"If you are sick," says Enkhtor, "this is the best. You can also drink from your own body. It almost as good."

I nod, hoping he won't expect me to try it at the moment.

"I don't like the taste, though," he says, "and it has a bad smell."

"Is that strange?" I ask. "Why do you think most people in the world would rather drink Coca Cola?"

"All medicine tastes bad," he answers.

I concede his point.

"But if my mother boils it in a pot and I do this..." he pulls his sweater half over his head and makes sniffing noises like he's inhaling from a vaporizer, "it not so bad. One day, I sick. The next day I not sick. You try it."

"My mother is in New York," I tell him, "I don't think she'd pee in a jar and send it to me."

"Maybe my mother will help you," he says.

"That's all right," I answer quickly. "I think I'll try some traditional American medicine. It's often suggested by old doctors in the American countryside. It's been used for ages by our people."

I explain the traditional American treatment for the same disease. How we go to the old apothecary and say: "GimmesomeContac." He's never heard about this before.

"Then, we cut a cardboard box and pull out some small plastic beads sealed into a large flat sheet." I mime the action. "Inside the plastic beads are even tinier beads of all different colors."

I can tell by his squint and protruding lower lip that he's not sure if I'm telling the truth.

I continue: "We push a clear bead out of the bigger plastic sheet. Then we put it in our mouth and drink water at the same time. We're not allowed to chew the bead, because that would let out the healing spirits before they can get inside us. We have to swallow it whole."

I draw some pictures for him and he puts them in his notebook. He's fascinated, but can't fathom what it would be like to swallow plastic.

"In America then," he says, "you don't need your mother when you get sick."

"That's right," I tell him, "we don't need anything as long as we have plastic."

STORY TWO: A CHILD'S LAUGHTER

A great man (me) once said, Whenever you hear the sound of children's laughter, you know that somewhere close, a cat has been nailed to a tree.

It's good to know that no matter how strange Mongolia seems, there are certain things you can always count on. A child's cruelty is one of them.

Maggie told me about an adventure in her building. From inside her apartment, she heard scampering, up and down the stairway in the hall. At first there was also a yapping noise. Then it stopped, but the scampering, now accompanied by giggles, continued.

She put her ear against the apartment door. Outside: KRRRRRRR... KACHUNK...KRRRRRRRRRRRR...KACHUNK. The elevator door tried to close, but ran into an obstacle. Something hard, a piece of wood or a boot. The door slid partially closed, then hit the object and opened again.

Finally, the door closes completely. Then, TANGA TANGA TANGA: young footsteps on the staircase. After that, a second or two of silence. Then, eeeeuwww, eeeeeuuuuuuuwwwwww, eeeeeuwww: a muffled whining.

Venturing out of her apartment, Maggie walked down the dark corridor (no lightbulb — natch) and felt her way to the elevator. She pushed the button. The doors opened.

A little puppy swung by the neck from a rope tied to the elevator light fixture. Its eyes bulged. Its tongue hung out, dripping saliva. But it was alive, legs softly pumping the air.

Our heroine ran back to her apartment and got a large knife from the kitchen. She cut it down, loosening the knot around its neck.

She carried the dog into her apartment where she set it on the couch. After filling a bowl of water, she set that too on the couch. The animal sniffed at the water. Its tiny tongue came halfway out of its mouth and retracted. Again. It was trying to drink, but couldn't manage to slurp the liquid into its strained throat. Weakly it stuck a paw in the water, and brought it to its mouth.

For the next week, Maggie nursed the animal. She got it on its feet. As time passed, Maggie feared she was getting too attached to it. She had to leave in a couple of months and didn't want any more to worry about.

One day, she carried it out the door of her building and let it loose. It looked at the wide Mongolian world, tentatively walked ahead, then ran. Maggie closed the door behind it.

From that day on, once or twice a week, Maggie heard a loud canine howling from a nearby apartment. Coming from a much older dog than the puppy, it started at around eleven o'clock, lasted an hour, built to a crescendo, then whimpered out. After that: silence. The origins of the whimpering are still unknown. She has never seen a dog in any apartment in the building. She has also never again seen her puppy.

STORY THREE: IT DOESN'T PAY TO BE BISEXUAL

Americans don't talk about excrement. Mongolians don't talk about money. Germans don't talk about THE WAR. Every culture has its social taboos. One theme, however, runs cross culturally. Evaded and euphemized, nobody wants to talk about death.

But there are times when it comes under such unusual circumstances that talk spreads. Sure, it's in whispers, especially in a pre-tabloid society like this one. But it's there.

This story comes from my students. Bishbataar referred to it. Other students laughed nervously. Slowly, student by student, each filling in more details, the entire thing emerged. Here's how I've...er...pieced it together.

Tumor was a 60s teen idol, a pretty boy like David Cassidy or Lief Garret. Girls screamed and swooned when he sang teenage love songs. His picture was on every girl's mirror and in her wallet.

With The Beatles, then disco, Tumor faded into retirement and semi-obscurity. It was only this year — a few months ago — that his name reappeared in the papers.

Until then, he had been living quietly with a young boyfriend, just a kid actually. The love affair was well-known, but not news. In Mongolia, homosexuality is slightly odd, but not particularly startling. It would have stayed that way, except that our popstar had a wandering eye. This year that eye landed on a beautiful young woman.

One day, while his live-in lover is away in the countryside, Tumor brings the young woman home. It could be a scene from one of the South American soap operas the Mongols love. The young man returns, finds them in bed, and all hell breaks loose. What follows, however, could not be in a soap opera.

Walking in on the pair, the shocked youth runs for the kitchen. Curling his fingers around the handle of a large knife, he brings it to the bedroom.

According to the police reconstruction, the guy gets them both in bed. He stabs Tumor in the neck, severing something important. As the popstar bleeds to death, the young man attacks his female lover THWUMP! Right to the belly. THWUMP! Again. And Again. Blood galore.

When they're both dead — or at least helpless. The real fun begins.

First the young man removes Tumor's head. Cuts it completely off sawing through the cartilage and bone. Once separated from the body, he carries it to the kitchen and puts it on a wire rack in the oven. The dish, however, isn't ready to be served.

Now it's the woman's turn. Using his trusty Mongolian knife, he slits her right up the front, breast bone to pubic bone. He pries apart the opening, like you might pry apart a tissue box to get the last kleenex.

He scoops out the intestines, scattering them near the body. The heart too. That isn't what he's after. This is a man out to prove a point.

"You want this girl? I'll let you have her. You'll look good together."

He plunges his arms into the woman's body. Feeling toward the back, he finds her kidneys. He pulls them forward, cutting them loose. The police noted a strong smell of *shess* at the scene.

Then our young protagonist returns to the head on the oven rack. Using his still sharp knives, he slices the ears from the head and throws them on the floor. He takes the woman's kidneys and stands them beside the earless head, as if to replace the lost organs. Satisfied, he pushes the rack into the oven.

He does not turn it on, however, because that's how the police find it. Raw, and ready to go. Maybe the kid had to leave in a hurry.

FOURTEEN

If Anthony Perkins needs to play Tumor's jealous lover, Michael Douglas will have to star, as me, in this chapter.

There are new moral dilemmas and visual special effects. Bringing together two aspects of Mongolian academic life, this chapter is about

MINI SKIRTS AND FINAL EXAMS

I start my university job as a *Spoken English* teacher; the only "native speaker of American English," I'm supposed to give instruction in the American dialect. Free to design my own course, I need to insure that students speak and understand conversational American English.

"Instruction by Mongolian teachers is based on British English," says Dr. Sumiya. "Maggie, the other native speaker, is Irish. We need you to put some balance in the department."

"No prob!" I tell him, "I'll learn dose guys howta tawk good in no time."

"Okay, Mykel," he says. "Mongolian teachers will be instructing them in Grammar and Basic English. That is based on British English. The rest is up to you."

Gutalmaa teaches the other courses to class 2C. Sonya, a Russian-born/Mongol-married woman, teaches them to 2D, the wild and lazy class.

By three quarters of the way through the term, some of the students have become my friends. Though I'm wary of the hustlers, I like them all.

November First: At the end of class, the 2D students don't rush for the door as usual. Instead they gather quietly at my desk. Even Yontuya, a nut case who drifts in and out of class at random, stands silently by. Altanzagas, a pretty girl whose name means "goldfish," approaches my desk. Her head is bowed. She speaks more to the floor than to me.

"Mykel-*baksh*," she says. "We need you teach us Grammar and Basic. Sonya refuse."

"What happened?" I ask.

"She don't like us. She mean and angry. She Russian."

"Yo!" I say, "Dat ain't my job."

Her high cheeks wrinkle. Her almond eyes grow wet. Her lower lip slowly protrudes. "Please Mykel-*baksh*," she says. "We cannot finish term. We will have to leave university."

"Please Mykel-*baksh*," comes another female voice from the back of the room.

Soon there's a chorus of "Please! Please! We need you!" whines. Enough to melt an igloo.

"Okay, okay," I say. "Let me talk to Dr. Sumiya and Sonya and find out the story. If everyone agrees, I'll take over the classes."

Then come the "thank yous," the "oh thank yous," the "you are greats." Bishbataar shakes my hand. Tsetsesseg gives me a peck on the cheek. Tarbileg jumps up and down clapping her hands like a seal. I eat it up.

Sonya is a middle-aged woman with a gray crewcut and laugh-lined eyes. She has come to my aid in the past, helping me get a post office box and negotiate the daily absurdities of Mongolian life. She's as far from "mean and angry" as I am from "mature and settled."

"What happened with 2D?" I ask her.

"I'm on my own private strike," she tells me. "They're lazy and disrespectful. They don't do their homework. I won't teach them."

I've never seen her this angry.

"Will the university really kick them out if no one teaches those courses?"

She nods. "And they deserve it!"

"Is it okay if I take over the classes?" I ask her.

"Do as you like," she says, "but you will be..." she reaches for a Russian-English dictionary. After fumbling a bit, she finds what she's looking for.

"SUCKER!" she reads.

◎ ◎ ◎

"Okay guys," I tell the class, "I'm your new teacher for Grammar and Basic."

"Waaaaaaaaaaaaaaaayyyyyyyyyyyyyyyyy!" comes the cheer.

"I don't know your work in those classes," I continue, "so all I'll have is The Final. If you study and do well, you'll get a good grade. If you don't, you'll fail. Okay?"

"We agree, of course," says Bishbataar. "You great man. We be great students."

I teach the remaining classes. It's a more difficult task than I expect. Sonya has been teaching them the Russian version of British English. She calls "conditional type II" what I call "subjunctive." She teaches "shall" and "might I," as if the students were going to tea with the Queen. I teach "yo!" and "punk rock!" as if the students were going to get soused at CBGBs.

"Look," I tell them, "you're gonna hafta unlearn dat stuff. Dat's British. I'm from New Yawk and I wanna teach you howta really tawk."

◎ ◎ ◎

December 30, 8:40AM: it's freezing outside. Inside, it's not much better. I've been wearing my Thinsolite™ boots. Guaranteed to twenty below.

"Those boots look warm." says Namjil.

"They sure do," I answer, "but they're not. They're not only cold, but painful. The super-duper Thinsolite(TM) acts like a vegomatic between your toes. The only relief is to remove the innersole. Then, you're even colder."

"Why do you wear them?" she asks.

"They're the only boots I have," I tell her. "I'll get new ones in Korea, where it's cheap."

I've already got my ticket. I'll be gone as soon as the final exams are over.

Today's the start of the last day of class: Bishbataar, the fast-talking car owner, gives me a bottle of vodka. It's from all the students, he says, to celebrate the coming vacation.

"Thank you," I tell him, "that was very nice."

"We need toast," he says.

Suddenly every student has a glass. I open the bottle and fill them.

"For Mykel-*baksh*!" says Bishbataar.

"Waaaaaaaaaaaaaaaaay!!" cheer the students. Then bottoms up.

"Another toast!" shouts Tsetsesseg. "To winter!"

By the end of the class, the bottle is empty.

Besides the vodka, the class gives me a snuff bottle with a picture of *Chinggis Khan* on it. I also get a *hatakh* — one of the long blue silk pieces symbolic of Mongolia. Bishbataar makes the presentation. His prepared speech is somewhat slurred by the vodka.

"Thish ish for our great teacher, Mykel-*baksh*," he says. "She teach ush sho good and make ush sho shmart. We give all thish."

Right then, Yontuya, the nut, stands and puts on a wide-brimmed straw hat.

"It suits me, don't you think?" she says.

"It's very nice," I say.

"Me too," she says. Then, she walks out of the class.

After she leaves, Tsetsesseg, the sexy student/model taps her own head to explain Yontuya's departure. "She hit it in car crash. She not so good here anymore."

During the class, we set the times and places for the finals. I have to give three, one in Spoken, one in Grammar, and one in Basic.

I've never written a final exam before. I know what I want to ask for my own class, Spoken American. But how should I test the rest? The other teachers suggest I xerox questions from the textbook.

For Grammar, I pick the areas of agreement between American and British English. There are enough of them that my teaching won't conflict with Sonya's. Basic English is another story. The teacher's book has its own tests. I give them the one on the units covered in class. Based completely on British English, there are questions I can't answer.

> **Find the error in the following:**
>
> **Notice outside a school library:**
>
> **All books have to be returned before the end of term.**

What's the error? Is the missing before term? In England, you're "in hospital" not "in THE hospital." So that's not it. How about "must" rather than "have to"? Maybe it's a question of formality, this being an official sign. Who knows? I sure don't.

I give the exam anyway. If I don't know the answer, I'll mark it right. That's fair.

◎ ◎ ◎

December 15: I walk into the class wearing my best scowl.

"Okay class," I say. "Communism is dead. We don't cooperate anymore. This is an exam. Your answers are your own."

Bishbataar looks up, puzzled.

"Now everybody stand up," I tell them, motioning with my hands. "Move to that side of the room."

I now speak to the poorest student, a woman on a visiting scholarship from Inner Mongolia. "You, Altandor. You sit there." I point to a seat on the bench closest to me. "Now, Bishbataar, you sit next to her."

I put another weak student on his other side, thereby making it impossible to cheat. Muted groans come from the students as I seat them in a way calculated to produce honest results.

Tarbileg, the best student, I put in the rear of the room, in a seat against the wall. Next to her, I put Batchaluun, the best male student in the class, and a country boy who is completely honest.

After seating everyone, I collect all the dictionaries and flip through them looking for cheat sheets. Oh, am I bad!

At exactly 4PM, I hand out the exam. In less important tests, I let students work an extra fifteen minutes. Not today. The English Department party starts at six. We have to be there a quarter hour before or we can't get in. They lock it up, us inside, them outside.

At 5:30 all the students are still frantically writing.

"Stop now!" I say. "Your time is up."

They continue writing.

"Okay," I tell them, "I'll wait one minute. After that, it's minus 5. Two minutes is minus 10."

"You can't. It's impossible," Bishbataar says.

"Mykel-*baksh*," says Altanzagas. "We are your friends, no?"

A wall of whining arises from the students. They scribble furiously while I count down the seconds.

"Five. Four. Three. Two. One...Okay," I say, "that's minus five. Next, minus ten...Sixty. Fifty nine. Fifty eight."

A flurry of paper comes at me. Carried, thrown, run to my desk.

"No minus five! Please! I came late!" complains Tsetsesseg.

"No minus five. This too hard," cries Altanzagas. "We need time."

Tarbilig brings her exam to my desk. She smiles and leaves. Altanzagas comes, pen in hand, scribbling out answers and writing new ones as she walks. Tsetsesseg stays at her desk, writing away.

"Ask other people first," says Bishbataar, glancing at the test on his right.

"Now!" I say.

And the papers come. They come with crossouts and arrows, but they come. When I have them all, I tell the class, "I was only kidding about that minus 5 stuff. I just had to get your papers. Happy New Year."

"Why you do that?" asks Bishbataar. "I could write more."

"Happy New Year!" I answer and leave for the teacher's party.

Five hours later, I stagger home and quickly fall asleep. I awaken a couple hours later, with a stomachache, headache and a thirst like a salt mine refugee.

A couple aspirin, a bottle of water and a blissful trip to the bathroom take care of those problems. I go back to bed.

My front door is breaking. Something's coming through. Pow! Pow! Pow! An insect-like claw pushes through the wood. Its pincers click as it blindly gropes for me. I try to run, but am frozen to the spot.

There's more banging. The huge insect tries to force its entire body through the door. Pow! Pow! Pow! The wood on the door begins to give under the force. Pow! Pow! Pow! I awaken from the nightmare and realize that the banging is real. Then it turns to ringing: the doorbell. I roll out of bed and slip into my pants — wrong leg first — as the doorbell persists.

When I get the fly in the front, I zip up and answer. It's Tsetsesseg.

As soon as she enters, she takes off her scarf and long coat. She wears a tight silk blouse with a green mini-skirt. The skirt is so short you can see...well, it's very short. I motion to a chair. She sits down, crossing her legs.

"I guess you know why I here," she says.

I shake my head, more to clear the alcoholic remains than to answer "no" to her question.

"I not have enough time for examination yesterday," she says. "Can you give me more?"

I glance at the clock on the diningroom table. It's 9AM.

I give her the first cliché that pops into my still befuddled head. "It wouldn't be fair to the other students."

"How not fair?" she asks. "Did they ask? Maybe you do same."

I shake my head again.

"Please," she says, looking at me through weepy eyes. "I need chance. It will not hurt anyone."

She stands up and smiles at me, patting down her short skirt, turning this way and that.

"You like my dress?" she asks.

I shuffle back to my room and rummage through the exams. I take her exam out to the living room and hand it to her.

"You have fifteen minutes." I tell her.

She sits at the livingroom table and works on the test. I go into the kitchen to make coffee — for myself. I need to wake up and figure out what to do about this.

After twenty minutes, I go back into the livingroom. She hands me the exam. Then she opens her purse and takes out a bottle of vodka. She gives it to me saying thanks. I grab my English-Mongolian dictionary to show her the word 'bribe.'

"It's not bribe," she says. "Bribe is make someone do something. You already do it. This no bribe. This present."

She puts on her coat and scarf and leaves, leaving the vodka on the table. After the door closes behind her, I open the bottle and suck down a mouthful. Ah, I needed that.

Later that day, I grade the exams.

Tarbileg, the best student in the class, wrote "act of controlling workers" as a definition of "management." Her handwriting, however, made it look like auction controlling workers. I laugh at the idea.

I don't laugh, however, at the definition of "management" given by Altandor and half a dozen other poor students: auction controlling workers. Those bastards, they cheated despite the seating.

"That's it," my hangovered brain says. "I'm going to fail them. I may be a sucker, but I'm not an idiot."

Minus 20 for every cheat. On the border? Bang! You're out of here. Zero tolerance. Take no prisoners.

A quarter of the class fails. I put the names and grades into my computer and printout a list to bring to the English department on marking day.

December 20, Marking Day: I sit in the English department waiting to see how to turn in the grades. I have my list of passes and failures.

"So many fails?" says Sonya, "I didn't think you were so severe."

"I'm severe," I tell her. "Soft on the outside, a rock inside...Now, who do I give the grades to?"

"Why, to the students, of course," she says.

"Huh?"

"The students will bring in their grade books. You write the grade in the book and then initial it."

"You mean I have to enter the grades in front of the students?" I ask.

"Of course," she says. "That's who gets them, isn't it?"

Tarbileg is first. I give her the `95' she deserves. Altandor is next.

50, I write in her book.

Her breath cuts quickly.

"Mykel-*baksh*," she cries, "if I no pass I go back. I must go back Inner Mongolia. They communist there. You American. You want me communist?"

I change her grade.

Altanzagas is next. She's going to have a baby, she tells me. Would I want her on the street?

I pass them all. Give them what they want. Make them happy.

And Tsetsesseg? She passes too, barely. I wonder what she would have offered if I'd refused her the extra time.

FIFTEEN

Most students and teachers visit their families in the countryside during the winter break,. Everyone has family in the countryside. Some foreign teachers return home to see friends and relatives. Not me. I want to go someplace new, see something different. If I'm in Asia, why not enjoy it?

HOW I SPENT MY WINTER VACATION

I wanted Thailand, but planefare alone is over $800. I decide to go somewhere surface rate — like a cheap slow letter: Hong Kong or Korea.

The barman at the embassy said Hong Kong was the most expensive city in the world. So, I'm going to Korea, where it's cheap.

Mongolia wouldn't be Mongolia if you could just walk into a travel agency and book passage to Korea. They can get me as far as Beijing, they say. Then I'm on my own. My China visa lasts 7 days. I lose a day on the train, so I've got to move fast!

Early Thursday I get up to catch that train. I don't take much, but it's way too much, a boulder's worth, stuffed into my sister's 30-year-old girlscout knapsack. The laptop hangs around my neck — millstone style. My wallet has thirty twenty dollar bills. I'm ready to go.

I'm leaving Mongolia for the first time since I got here in August. Good-bye to the cold apartment, the 87 steps from the ground floor, the cows wandering in the streets. I wonder if I could ever call it home.

It's -30° and not yet light. I wait for a Number 20 bus or Number 4 trolley. A bus pulls in, the number plate is frosted over, opaque. By the time I get close enough to ask, it leaves.

When more than one arrive together, it'd be logical for the first to pull up furthest and let the others spread out behind. Logical? This is Mongolia. A bus comes in, swerves, screeches to a stop at the nearest corner. The next one passes it, cutting in front, blocking the number of the first. I'm used to this. On a normal day, I sprint back and forth to make sure I'm catching the right bus. Today, I carry 50 lbs of baggage. My feet are starting out rubbed raw by the evils of Thinsolite™.

I'm at the back end of the stop, when the number 4 pulls in 10 yards ahead. When I get to it, the door closes in my face. I scream. Kick. People look at me and laugh. Boy, are they lucky I'm short and in pain!

It took 20 minutes for that trolley, I'm not gonna wait for another. The next bus is number 21. 20? 21? It's close enough, I think, not thinking too clearly. I get on. The bus has to turn left at the State Department Store in order to get to the station. It doesn't. I get out and wait, running back and forth at the next stop, trying to make out the numbers.

It's getting light now. Must be coming on 8:30. The train leaves at 9:30. In 20 minutes, I get on the same number 4 trolley I'd have gotten if I waited.

At the train station, a parked train says: BEIJING ←→ *ULAANBAATAR*.

There's no way into it. All the doors are closed. Locked. A load of people head down the platform, toward the last car. That must be the way. I've been in Mongolia long enough not to ask why they would only leave the furthest car open for passengers.

I follow this crew, hobbling to the last car. I watch as they go AROUND that last car and cross over the tracks to another train on a different track — not mine. I stumble back to the waiting room.

There I see it's only 8:30. My ordeal took less time than I thought. At 8:45, I check the Beijing train again. This time, lots of doors are open. I go in and find my compartment. Bed number 13, an omen I have yet to realize.

Twenty more minutes. Maybe I'll have the compartment to myself. That would be the best. Actually, the best would be to share it with people of unimaginable beauty, wealth and generosity who can't keep their hands off me. I consider this unlikely. Last choice: people of unspeakable hideousness and avarice who can't keep their hands off me. Next worst: a family with a bevy of little kids, all of whom count as one passenger so there'd be 6 people crammed into this tiny space.

Just before the train pulls out, the family with little kids comes barreling in, looking at the various numbers, one by one, down the train corridor. I pray they won't stop here. There is no God — or at least she isn't listening. Maybe she's gone deaf from playing in a punkrock band.

In comes mom, kids, suitcases, running around, babbling, climbing. Lesson of the trip: Kids lack the concept of "borrow," although the word might be in their (parent translated) vocabulary.

"Can I borrow a pen?" means "Do you have a pen you don't mind kissing goodbye?"

On the plus side, it's nice to see that Mongolian children are allowed to hit their parents. Nobody tells them they can't be angry. The little girl is mad at her mom, THWACK! right in the side of the neck. It's a great change. After all, I come from a culture where kid's anger is BAD and suppressed for 18 years, where it finally comes out with an AK47.

The trip, as a whole, isn't so bad. Two of the kids stay next door. They rarely barge in to tear up the place. In my four bedder, it's mom, one kid, two students and me. The students are going to an Asian student meeting in Hong Kong.

One studied in England and has decent command of the language. The other knows a few words. Mom speaks no English and her little girl is scared of me. In a half hour, the Mongols introduce themselves. A half hour after that, out comes the vodka bottle.

By 11:30AM the vodka is knocking me out. I'm glad I can say "no more," in Mongolian, one of many survival tricks I learned here. The others have long since graduated to the third bottle.

Our cubicle is cold. Coldest compartment on board, the students tell me. I never take my coat off. In the evening, the five of us combine our resources to make a pot luck dinner. We have two tangerines, some cold fat-sausages, cold *hoosher*, and a bowl of hot water. For some reason, I feel sick.

Beijing, 5:30 Friday: 32 hours on the train. I'm sick, cold and tired. Tonight, I'll spend the bucks on the $60 a night luxury hotel I stayed in on the way to Mongolia. For one night, on a credit card, I can afford it. Later, I'll be cheap.

I pull out my map, say my goodbyes and leave the station, my backpack mysteriously having gained 20 pounds during the trip.

Outside, a cab driver, rail thin with a pockmarked face, grabs me by the jacket sleeve.

"Tak-she, tak-she" he says, trying to pull me into his cab. I shrug him off and am instantly clutched by another driver. It's like that grabbing-hands-from-the-wall scene in every horror movie since *Repulsion*.

I escape. And walk. In circles. Every few feet, I hail a hapless pedestrian, show him my map and start yelling. I point to the map and then to the street I'm standing on.

"Where am I?" I ask. "Where am I now?"

They smile politely, shrug and walk away.

I ask another, getting more and more frantic. My shoulders ache. Thinsolite is dicing the toes on my right foot, puncturing the soles of my left. I'm shivering, more from the trainride than the merely freezing weather of Beijing.

"MYKEL-*baksh*!" says a Mongolian voice behind me. It's Altandor, the worst student in my lowest-level class. She's with a few friends.

We talk as best we can. Me, using the 100 or so Mongolian words I know. She, using the 100 or so English words she knows. They're staying in a "nearly hotel" for $15 a night. With no luck finding my luxury place, I say, "Let's go."

They take me through back alleys, into a nightmare parody of Chinatown. A mysterious old man, with a skull cap and Fu Manchu mustache just stares at us passing. A women peeps out a door and quickly closes it when we get close. We walk over tiny stone bridges, straddling a network of open sewers. I shuffle along like a Chinaman on my painful feet. I have to duck, stand on tiptoe or turn side-ways to negotiate my massive backpack through the tiny passageways. At the

end of the maze is a yellow and orange neon sign in Chinese: the hotel. In the hotel are Mongolians. Dozens of 'em. I can smell the lambfat as I walk past. The halls are teaming. They look like people I avoid at night. My small fortune weighs heavily in my pocket as my computer does in my backpack. Altandor and her friends, like football guards, clear a path for me.

She walks in to talk with the management. Altandor argues, pleads, begs. I hear my name, and "Mongolia." Eventually, she turns to me, pleased with herself.

"You can stay here." she says triumphantly.

"How much will it cost?" I ask.

"Seventeen dollars a night." she says.

"OK," I tell her. "Do I get a bathroom with hot water — and HEAT!"

She nods. "But two beds in a room." she says.

"That's ok." I tell her. "I'll only sleep on one."

She shakes her head. "You no understand. Two beds. Two people."

"You mean I have to share my room?" I ask, thinking about my computer, my camera, my moneybelt and my special needs of the night.

She nods.

I thank her and take off. Outside the hotel, I negotiate a $2 cab ride to the $60-a-night place. Only the $60 a night place is no longer $60. It's $75. Tired, in pain and nauseous, I take it. It's only a credit card. Also, there's a still open travel bureau in the hotel. I can book my trip to Korea right there.

No I can't. Only one place in Beijing handles the Korean boat. It's closed. This is Friday night. It won't be open until Monday. I have seven days to get out of the country. Monday I'll have four.

Although the hotel travel agent can't sell me boat tickets, they do tell me that the boat leaves "every five days."

"Which days are those?" I ask.

"We have no such information." Says the woman who speaks English as well as I speak Urdu, "We just know five days."

I harangue her a bit more. She tells me the boat leaves from the port of Tianjin city. That city is about three hours away from Beijing.

"Can I get a ticket there?" I ask.

"We have no such information." she says.

"Could you find out?" I beg — near tears, "Call someone."

"Who to call?" she asks.

"How should I know who to call?" I yell. "I don't work in a travel bureau!"

The woman smiles and shrugs her shoulders, obviously not knowing what to do with me.

"Would it be better for me to go there — to Tianjin?"

"Yes," she says, "You go. It better. You go. Good-bye."

The next morning, Saturday, I'm off to Tianjin. I check out of the Beijing hotel, pack on my back, computer around my neck and head for the bus station. I'd planned to transfer to the Qianyan hotel in Beijing, recommended by friends who know my taste in nighttime hotel company. Beside the obvious advantages, it also houses a Mongolian tourist bureau that could help me plan my trip back. I chuck those plans in favor of catching the boat before I end up in jail.

The hotel checkout lady wrote "Tianjin Xin Gong" (Tianjin port) in Chinese on a piece of paper for me. I show the paper to a cop at the bus station. He vaguely waves to someplace "over there."

I walk over there and show the paper to an old man carrying a shopping bag. He motions for me to go back where I started. This time, I ask a heavy set, tough-looking guy with a scar that runs from the edge of his right eye almost to the corner of his mouth. He nods, grabs me by the arm and pushes me toward a car parked across from the buses.

"Tianjin Xin Gong," he says, "300 Yuan" (There are 8 Yuan in a dollar.)

"No," I say, starting to talk like them. "I take bus."

"Bus no good," he says. "Bus Tianjin — no Xin Gong. 200 Yuan."

"150 Yuan," I say.

"Okay, okay," He says. "You inside."

He opens the trunk and I put in my luggage. Then I get in the front seat.

"Wait a minute," he says. "Wait a minute. We go soon."

He tries to hustle up other people for the ride. I wait five minutes, but he hasn't found anyone. I get out of the car.

"No, no," he says. "You wait. Three people. One people 300 yuan. Four people 150 yuan. Okay. Okay."

I check the clock. It's getting late. I've got to get to Tianjin, find a hotel, maybe even get the boat tonight. I don't have time to wait for this gangster to hustle more passengers.

"5 minutes," I tell him. "Then I take bus."

"I no understand," he says.

I point to my watch and hold up five fingers. Seven minutes later, I'm ready to leave. Take the bus. The guy is nowhere. Gone. Out of range. My luggage is in the trunk. I've got to get to the port. If I miss a boat I could end up in jail.

I get out of the car and walk around it, banging my fist on the trunk. A few other cab gangsters laugh at my predicament. They point me out to their friends who also laugh. I'm not laughing.

I try the back door of the cab. It's locked. I slip my hand between the bulletproof plastic and the back seat, scraping my knuckles. I manage to get the fingertips of my left hand through and under the lock. I pull it up.

Opening the back door, I climb in. Then I start to take the car apart. I try to pull out the back seat. No luck. I pull off the plastic sill under the back window. Using this space as a lever, I create an opening big enough to reach into the trunk. Bracing my knee against the seat, I wrestle my luggage through the hole I made. There is a ripping sound, but it's not from my bags. Once I get it all out, into the back seat, I load it on my back — much to the ever-increasing amusements of the cab drivers now crowded around me.

I get in the bus. Cost: 25 yuan. It doesn't leave, however, for another hour.

Why? Because it isn't filled. The bus won't leave until all the seats are filled — and at least a dozen people are standing.

When the bus eventually leaves, the guy sitting next to me starts speaking. His English is pretty good. He lives in Beijing. He's visiting his mother in Tianjin. He knows a cheap hotel there, he says.

It's about 6 o'clock, Saturday night when we get to Tianjin. It seems like a pretty big city for a port town. I might have to walk a bit to get to the boat.

"How many people live here?" I ask my new friend.

"Eight million," he says.

It's a three mile walk to the hotel. The port is another 20 miles away. On the way to the former we pass the International Ticket Agency. The only place in town where you can buy boat tickets to Korea. It's closed. It opens 9:30AM — on Monday.

At the hotel, the young clerk looks at me like he's never seen a whiteman before. My friend fills out all the forms, including writing my name — in Chinese. Then we go up to my room.

In China, you don't get a room key. Instead, you get a room card. You show the card to floor matron and she lets you in, using a key on a huge ring of keys. My room has a decent bed, running water, a desk, and a TV. It does not, however, have heat.

"They're fixing it right now." My new friend translates for me. Yeah right.

My friend leaves me. I unpack and then head off to find someplace to eat. A restaurant right around the corner advertises "Cantonese Style" food.

Inside, a young man holds an armful of menus. He bows slightly then waves me to a table for four. I sit down, the only one at the table. Smiling, he hands me a menu, all in Chinese. Then he waits while I decide what to order. I smile and look around at other people's plates.

"Gimme one of what he's having and some mu shu pork," I say.

They don't have a clue. The owner taps a tallish studenty looking Chinese guy on the shoulder. She speaks to him.

"Can I help you?" he says to me in pretty good English.

"Yeah," I tell him, "I want some of that and a vegetable."

I look around, and at a table next to me there are folks eating something green. I point to it and make the thumbs up sign with a questioning look on my face.

The diners nod "OK."

"That one," I tell my translator.

He says something in Chinese to the waitress. She says something back.

"They don't have any more," he says and disappears in the kitchen. When he returns, he's carrying a bunch of what looks like giant clover.

"How about this?" he asks.

"I don't think so," I tell him. And he's off again. This time he comes back with a cucumber.

"OK," I say, "I'll have that. With those pancakes and the meat on 'em."

He does some more Chinese talking. Before I know it, I get a plate of cut up cucumbers. In the meantime, my translator sits by himself at another table for four. People come into the restaurant — in large groups. They look at the tables and lack of empty ones, then leave.

"Why don't you come over to my table?" I say to the guy. "That way there would be more room for larger groups."

"Good idea," he says and sits down at my table.

We start talking. I tell him I teach English in *Ulaanbaatar*. He says he works for a trading company.

"Oh?" I ask, "What kinds of things do you deal in?"

"I deal death," he says.

"Pardon?" I answer.

"Death," he repeats. "I sell weapons, guns, rifles, automatic weapons."

"Er...who do you sell these weapons to?" I ask, checking to see if he has any packages with him.

"Some foreign countries..." he says, "and mercenaries."

What is it about me? Is there a WWW (World Wide Weirdos) network that signals my every move? Do they wait with walkie talkies, hiding around each corner — "Here he comes. Send in another weirdo." What attracts them to me? Out of nowhere?

The death-dealer and I talk about politics, religion, guns. Did you know the AK47 is NOT a submachine gun but an automatic rifle? There's a difference!

He tells me his name is Bill. I'm suspicious. He pays for my dinner. I'm more so, but care less.

Oh yeah, he also tells me that the hotel I'm staying in is owned by the PLA. "PLA?" I ask.

"People's Liberation Army," he says. "I bet there's never been an American staying there before. You're probably very safe — and very well watched."

Sunday passes without incident — or interest. It's cold, wet and unpleasant. But before long I'll be cruising to Korea. I hear it's ten hours and $90. Not bad to a cheap land of civilized Orientals.

The ticket office opens at 9AM Monday. My China visa expires at midnight Thursday, still plenty of time. The odds are way in my favor.

This takes some higher calendar math, but I figure: if a boat leaves every five days, even if a boat left yesterday (Sunday), there would be another one on Thursday. The only way that I could strike out, would be for the boat to leave that very day, Monday — too early for me to catch it. But what are the odds of that happening? They couldn't possibly be stupid enough to schedule a boat leaving when you can't buy tickets for it, could they?

Yes, they could.

I'm at the ticket office door when it opens. The boat leaves an hour later. Seven-to-one odds — in my favor — and I lose. There's no way I can get from the ticket office to the pier in less than two hours. Plus my bags are still in the People's Army Hotel. My only choice, says the travel agent, is to take a plane. Of course, there's only one travel agent in town that sells plane tickets — a different one — and it's "far away."

Eventually, I find it and buy a ticket for the plane that just hops across the bay. An hour flight. Tianjin to Seoul. $350. I COULD'VE GONE TO THAILAND! I buy the ticket and take off for Korea the next day.

Korea is awful: cold, unfriendly, snowing, as expensive as Japan. Buying almost nothing, I spend $100 a day. The YMCA cost $30 a night. But there is heat — sort of.

People speak less English here than in China. When I approach a store, the employees push one another toward the door, "You deal with him." "I don't want to...YOU deal with him." "No you."

Not only don't people speak English, they don't want to know. Ask them a question and they run, unless you get a street vendor.

I stomp down a small side street near the electronics mart. I tried to buy an ink replacement for my printer. Those few vendors who would talk to me tried to convince me that THEIR cartridge would fit my printer, even though it didn't say so on the box. I'm worn out and angry.

A squat heavyset man grabs my sleeve. He's about 40, with pock marked cheeks, as if he once had cat whiskers and someone pulled them out.

"I got porno videos," he says, pulling me toward his little table set up behind a pedestrian bridge.

I brush off his hand, saying "No."

He grabs me again. "American porno. You like. Look here." He pulls on my coat, tugging me toward the table.

I brush off his hand, harder this time. "No!" I say, trying to continue walking.

He grabs me a third time, digging his nails into my upper arm. "Little boys. I got little boys!"

I karate chop his hand, yelling NO! as loud as I can.

He shrugs and looks at me, "I know," he says. "We still friends, ok?"

Let's see, what else can I tell you about Seoul except that the expense, hostility, and climate made me shorten my trip from three weeks to one. Oh, I know...

Koreans are gobbers. It's not that they spit more than others, that distinction goes to the Chinese. It's just that the Koreans work harder at it.

Possibly, it's because nose-blowing is taboo and smoking is so common. But there's a stubborn collection of hockers, lugers, phlegmballs and general lung excrement deep down in their collective alveoli.

And they work on it. There's never a silent moment. Starting with a mild throat-clearing, the sound moves deeper, becomes more hollow, as they half gag, forcing the dribbly goop gradually up from the depths.

Their chest muscles contract like a toothpaste tube as inch by inch the offending mucus is brought closer to expectorability.

Like a parody of German, the Koreans achhhh and achhhh, retching and contorting until gradually they succeed in forcing the viscous fluid into their mouths. Then, they roll it around a bit, savoring the sweet taste of victory, before expelling it in the nearest waste basket, ashtray or sidewalk. Then it starts again.

Mongols, on the other hand, are snot-blowers. Men only. Anywhere on the street. Wham! Direct from sinus to sidewalk. Big yellow balls, nasal projectiles. No handkerchiefs for these guys. No unecological tissues. Get in touch with nature.

Put up a hand. Press a forefinger against one nostril, a short inhale, then pow. Splat. First a force against the ground, then a little squeeze off of the remaining. A shake of the hand to get rid of the finger residue, then the other nostril.

There are flocks of 'em. Squeezing, squirting, blowing, blasting, clear, white, blood-flecked, yellow pasted. You've gotta dodge the flying ones.

Teams of 'em. Walk down a *Ulaanbataar* street to honking flying globules. On a typical day, the sidewalk is polka dotted with these white glisteners. You have to dance around them to get anywhere. In the winter, they freeze into an ice grating that'll trip you up in a second.

Back to Korea:

I decide to leave, buy my boat ticket, get out as fast as I can. I still have the lure of the Qianyan Hotel and cheap prices in Beijing. I buy a $30 heater in Korea and have a $12 zipper put on my coat. My Timberland's are still iron-maidening my feet, but the boots here are way too expensive. Beijing, Beijing. That's the place.

I go to a Korean travel agent to book boat passage back to Tianjin. I try also to book passage from Tianjin to Beijing, then back to *Ulaanbaatar*. They can't do it. There's only one place in Seoul that can sell boat tickets. It's "far away."

So far away I go. The $90 boat ticket cost $120 "super-economy class." The next boat leaves in two days, letting me off in China on January 30. My birthday is the next day. The 10 hour boatride, by the way, takes 36 hours.

The travel agent can't sell me the train tickets, however. I have to take care of those arrangements when I get to China. I've got seven days.

On the boat, I discover that "super-economy" is the 90's word for what, in the 40's, was called "steerage." There's one large room with straw mats on the floor. Every 18 inches, along the perimeter of the mats, is a brick-sized pillow and a thin gray blanket. That's it. My accommodations. I choose a spot close to an electrical outlet so I can keep the computer charged.

It looks like I'm the only whiteman on board. People stare at me, but are afraid to talk. When I take out my computer they gather, look over my shoulder, watch as I type. They're watching me type these very words! I turn to speak to them and they jump back. Rise into the air as if I'd said "Boo!" Back off. When I return to typing, they slowly crowd around again.

I go for a walk outside the cattleroom. That's when people STOP ignoring me. They want to discuss — in Korean. They refuse to believe I don't speak it. When I convince them, they start to use sign language.

I explain my 88 hour train-bus-boat trip to one of the overly inquisitive Koreans. He's a big man, with a bulbous red nose.

"You are SUPERMAN," he says. At least, I think he says "super."

Another big guy, this one with a craggy gray face and cheeks that touch his eyebrows, asks if I'm married. I tell him no. He points to my crotch and then makes an x-sign, as if saying, "if you don't get married, you might as well cut it off."

I want to tell him that's how I feel about using your head. But I don't.

I get to be friendly with the few Mongols on the boat. (I almost wrote "other" Mongols.) There's a guy and two girls, all in their mid-twenties. They're Korean language students, returning from a trip to practice. They too are the objects of much Korean curiosity. One of them speaks a bit of English. Although it's barely there, I know more Mongolian than I know Korean. The makings of a friendship if I ever saw one.

The Mongols are also going to Beijing. They say I can stick with them. They'll show me how to get from Tianjin back to the Chinese capital. They tell me they know a hotel in Beijing, close to the train station.

In Tianjin, the immigration man is suspicious. He asks me lots of questions and examines my passport carefully. In Mongolia, the US Embassy sewed in new pages because I had run out of visa space. Maybe this guy wants to make sure they're legit.

He brings the passport to the other officers. They look at it, show it around, say a lot of stuff in Chinese. Finally, I'm through, meeting up with my Mongol friends on the other side. After collecting my backpack (last out of the truck — natch), we're off to the bus for the three hour ride to Beijing.

My fellow Mongolians and I squeeze into one corner of the bus. Next to me is a young Korean couple who study in Japan. The rest of the bus is also

Koreans, with the exception of the driver and conductor. It's about 7PM by now. The three hour ride should get us to Beijing at 11. (I know math, but you don't know China!)

About an hour into the ride, the Korean guy next to me stands up and starts shouting at the passengers — in Korean. Then he starts shouting at the conductor — in Chinese. The conductor shouts back. Other people stand up and shout.

Meanwhile, the bus is picking up speed. The speed, lack of shock absorbers and road condition cause those standing to fall into those sitting. When they stand again, they continue shouting from where they left off, until they fall again.

This Chinese-style discussion, I find out from my Mongolian friends, is about the fare. The guy next to me warned his fellow countrymen that they shouldn't pay more than 50 yuan for the ride. The conductor wants more.

Eventually, the shouting stops. The conductor stamps his feet a couple times, sits down hard, and folds his arms AND legs. Not a happy sign. I guess he lost. That guess is confirmed, when we each pay our 50 yuan.

Once in Beijing, I want to go right to the Qianyan hotel. Although that hotel is not on my map, there is one called the QianyUan. I figure the two must be the same because there's so much variation in transliteration between English and Chinese. What's a little 'u' anyway? Right?

The Mongolians, however, tell me they know a nice hotel near the train station. It's cheap and will be good for a first night anyway. I still have four more.

"Do you have to go through a bunch of back alleys and winding roads to get there?" I ask.

They look puzzled. "Oh no," says the chubby woman — the best English speaker of the group, "it's very close. Only big roads go there."

I'm a bit skeptical, but the Qianyan (or Qianyuan) is far from the center of town...and these guys have been so nice to me...OK, I'll go.

When we get out of the bus it's Mongolian cold out. Must be -20°. Right away, I can feel it through the double pair of gloves I'm wearing.

My backpack w/computer pulls on my shoulders. The cord from the heater I bought in Korea cuts into my hand — through the gloves. My fingers will become so brittle they'll break and fall off from the pull of that cord. At least

I won't lose them. They'll stay well-preserved in the gloves.

The young Mongolian man takes charge of the short walk to the hotel. We DO stay on the major roads. It is, however, NOT a short walk. We follow the highway, over a bridge, scampering across six lanes of traffic, me with my backpack and heater tied to my hands. At least the fingerpain is gone. I'm too numb to feel anything.

We walk miles, following highway, main roads — no back alleys this time. After what seems like a month, we come to their hotel. It's a tiny place with a huge yellow and orange sign in front of it. There's no English, but there is Mongolian. Yes, it's the same place as that last group of Mongols took me. The same double rooms, the same Mongolian speaking staff. The same smell of boiled lamb.

It's now well after midnight. I'm too exhausted to do anything else, so I stay. It's $15 a night, payable in cash — US dollars only. Not a bad deal. The matron of the place treats us to free *buz*. At least I know my roommate. He's the one who led me here.

In the hotel there's heat and nearly-warm water. People are friendly, joking, open. There's a vodka party in the room next door. We're all invited. What an idiot I was not staying here the first time. Mongols, Mongols, Mongols, I love them!

At 7 the next morning, the construction next door begins. Sleep? Who needs that? It's up for breakfast. My new Mongol friends leave by plane later that day. Right now, they want to take me out for my birthday. They're going to sing Happy Birthday to me. It's the only song they know in English anyway.

Where do we go? To a Mongolian restaurant, of course. They're out of *buz*, though. So I get the lamb salad, with milk tea and Mongolian-style steamed bread. No candles, but they do sing. My birthday in China and the only people who care are Mongols. Why would I ever want to leave that country?

After breakfast, we bid each other farewell, exchange addresses and split up. Although still tired, it was nice to do SOMETHING for my birthday. Anyway, I'll have a "more intimate" celebration later at the Qianyan (Qianyuan) hotel.

I take my belongings from the Mongoltel and carry them to the train station. It's Tuesday. I have six days to get out of the country and I want to take care of that right away. I'll buy my ticket for *Ulaanbaatar* before anything else!

At the train station I'm shown to an office. A sign above the door says:

Ticket Office For Passengers To Hong Kong, And Foreign Places And Other Foreign Passengers.

It's closed. Lunch time. It's 11:30. It'll open at 1:30. I wait, taking off my pack, pulling out a book and watching the crowd grow around the office door.

At 1:40 the doors open. The stampede begins. The pushing, elbowing, clawing to the ticket window. Finally, I make it.

"No tickets to *Ulaanbaatar*," says the infuriatingly unruffled woman sitting behind the protective glass.

"Where can I get one?" I ask in a not-too-nice a tone of voice.

"You go to International Hotel. Buy there."

"You mean I can't buy train tickets at the train station?" I ask.

She nods.

"You mean I waited two hours for the international office to open to find out I can't buy international tickets here? Why isn't there a sign?"

She shrugs. "You go," she says. "Can't buy here."

What can I do but go? I put my bags on my back, pick up my heater, stumble under the weight and leave the train station.

Fortunately, the International Hotel is only a fifteen minute walk away. Unfortunately, no one at the hotel knows anything about train tickets.

After an eternity of being shuffled from one shoulder shrug to another, I find a tiny office stuck in the outside wall of the hotel. A worn thimble-sized sign outside says:

TRA S-SI ERIAN TI KET O ICE

There is a counter inside with two windows and tiny sticker representations of a MasterCard and Visa. I ask for a ticket on the next train to *Ulaanbaatar*. It leaves Friday and costs 632 Yuan. It's a little more than I paid coming down, but not bad — especially since I can charge it. I order the ticket.

They go into a little back room to prepare it. When it comes out, I have my MasterCard out and ready.

"Sorry," says the cashier (like she really means it), "we only take cash."

"What are these signs?" I ask.

"I know," she says, "but the bank says no. Only cash: 750 yuan."

"750??!!!" I yell, question marks and exclamation points included, "he told me 632!" Of course, the 'he' in question is nowhere to be found.

The cashier shakes her head. "750 yuan. Cash only. You pay."

I storm out of the place. Slamming the door open, then slamming it behind me. I head for a travel bureau. It's almost the same as a plane, I figure. If a plane leaves tomorrow...any time before Friday...I'll take it. I just wanna go back!

There are no planes till Friday. They cost triple the trainfare. And, although they have little MasterCard/Visa stickers at the airline agency — they only take cash.

I don't have enough. Sheepishly, I go back to the TRA S-SI ERIAN office. They smirk as I slink in.

After getting my train ticket, I have a few days to shop and enjoy the Qianyan (Qianyuan) hotel.

I carry my bags from the ticket office and hail a taxi, putting my things next to me on the back seat. The driver is a thuggish looking man with a checked cap and an undoubtedly, more checkered past. He makes no motion to turn on the meter.

"Qianyan Hotel," I tell him.

"80 Yuan," he says.

I get out of the cab, dragging my luggage. There's not another cab in sight, so I put on my backpack again and trudge onward. There's a tugging at my sleeve. It's the thug.

"I give you discount." he says. "40 Yuan."

"I not go with you even free!" I tell him, trying to speak his own language.

"30 Yuan," is his reply. "It far."

Another cab passes, I hail it. Right in front of this guy.

"How much to the Quinyan?" I ask.

The driver points to the meter. My kind of cab. I get in, NOT making a provocative gesture to the other driver, still outside. It turns out that the hotel is some distance away. Despite that, the meter only reads 10 yuan. The driver lets me out on the wrong side of a large highway.

I can see the hotel on the other side. It's much fancier than I expected. I struggle with my bags, finding a pedestrian tunnel not too many kilometers from where the taxi left me. I cross under the highway and head toward the hotel. Pretty fancy for a student hotel, I think. There is a row of red flags leading up to the entrance. There's also a row of soldiers, all standing perfectly at attention, as if waiting for a visiting dignitary. Well, I guess they heard I was coming.

I walk down the path between the row of flags and soldiers, limping under the weight of my backpack, computer and Korean heater. From the looks on their faces, it doesn't seem like I was the one they were expecting.

As I get up to the front gate the last (first?) soldier in line steps in front of me blocking my path. He says something in Chinese.

"Thanks for the welcome," I tell him. Actually, I say "Sorry, I don't speak Chinese."

He says something else. Then he points to the hotel.

I nod.

He makes a motion with a two-hands-in-prayer position, then putting these hands under his tilted cheek, as if he's sleeping.

"Yes," I say, "I want to sleep here."

"No here," he says, expending his entire English vocabulary but one: "Closed."

I don't ask any more. What can he tell me? I turn around, walk to the highway and prepare to jump in front of the next large truck. I don't. Instead, I walk and walk until I get to a subway. Then, I go to the same sexless expensive hotel I stayed in during my first trip to Beijing. At least they take credit cards.

[Economic Note: This is possibly the ONLY place in Beijing that really takes credit cards — though you'll see the MC/VISA stickers all over. The Chinese use them for decoration, like smurfs.

When I try to buy at other places, they tell me, "sorry we only take German cards." (This despite their sticker for the JCB card — only issued in Japan.) Another time I'm told, "Why are you using the card now? You should buy something more expensive." At the $75 a night hotel, they even smile when you show them the plastic.]

So I shop and eat. Some noodles, some Kentucky Fried. (OK, I'll admit it. After six months of lamb and vodka, I did it!) I buy a $9 pair of boots — a dozen times more comfortable than my hellish Timberlands, a hotplate, a John Updike book, a canned ham. The rest of the time I stay in my hotel room savoring the heat and hot water.

I haven't looked forward to leaving anywhere with greater joyful anticipation since I left the Buffalo city jail in 1969. But that's another book. On the day of the train departure, I'm at the station three hours early. I just hope I don't get a mom with her gaggle of kids, all stuffed into one tiny compartment. I don't. It's much worse.

At first, it looks like I'm lucky. When I go to put my bag under the seat, I find that the last passenger left his beer there. A dozen bottles of China's finest. Under the other seat: another dozen. Wowee! What luck. Their loss is my gain. I open a bottle and toast to my birthday and my return to Mongolia.

The joy does not last. This, it turns out, is the smuggling train. Merchants of all kinds, bring anything they can get in China back to Mongolia to sell. Boxes of fruit, cases of liquor, silverware, radios, TVs, coats, cases and cases, boxes and boxes. Every passenger has his weight tripled in baggage. My three compartment mates — a married couple and one guy from Inner Mongolia — have the place so stuffed with boxes, bags, cases, and knapsacks, that it's impossible to straighten my legs. There is five square inches of floorspace, and that's it for movement. I'm not happy.

They try to be friendly. Introduce themselves. Make nice. I'm in no mood. All that crap. And my new beer! They put it out in the middle of the floor. They've used the space under all the seats. It's filled with their contraband. Now I'm gonna have to offer the beer to everyone!

The train takes off. I curl up in a corner and read a book. The ugly American. Gradually, my ugliness eases and I offer the crew a beer, explaining that I found them here when I came into the compartment. They decline the offer, and instead buy beer from someone selling it in the corridor. They offer me one of those.

"Why?" I ask. "Why don't you drink this stuff I found here?"

"It's not ours," comes the answer.

I don't get it.

By the time we get to Erlian, the last stop in China, I'm reluctantly friendly with the guys in my compartment. They try so hard to be nice, offer me food, talk as best they can. Such a wonderful change from the Koreans and Chinese. I give in.

In Erlian, there is that six hour stop while they change the wheels from Chinese width to Russian/Mongolian width. I've been through that before. This time my new Mongolian friends offer to take me to an outdoor market while we wait. We go by taxi. Not any old car, but a horse-drawn open cart with padding on the sides. It's still -20°. My hands, feet, nose, are so cold I can't stand in one place for fear of freezing there permanently.

The market is the cheapest I've ever seen. I buy ten candles for a dollar. Two dinner dishes, a dime each. A travel alarm clock, a dollar. A pair of gloves, 75 cents.

After shopping, the Mongols (my compartment mates and a couple of their friends) suggest we go out to eat. And where do we go? A Mongolian restaurant! Their treat, of course. How can you stay mad at people like that?

After eating, I go to the train waiting room. The married couple go out "to do some more shopping." I can't imagine fitting an extra toothpick in that compartment, let alone the things from the market. Somehow we manage. though the 5 inches of floorspace are now completely gone. We'll have to sleep in a little ball, on top of some of the softer packages, if we sleep at all. But where are the married couple?

They come back minutes before the train pulls out — with a lathe. Here they come, lugging this huge filthy machine: blades, gears, enough metal to build a tractor — and they want to store it in OUR compartment. Enough is enough! I'd put my foot down, if there were any place to put it. What can I do? They were so nice to me. All I can do is mope — and drink their beer and still wonder why they don't drink the stuff I found.

Back in the train, we go for twenty more minutes before we come to the other (Mongolian) side of the border. A customs guard boards the train. He goes from compartment to compartment, looking at the baggage and checking passports. He checks mine last. The others he takes, but mine he hands back to me. There's some discussion in the corridor.

A few minutes later an older officer comes over. He asks for my passport. He looks at it and takes it, calling over the other officers. They look at the Mongolian visa and the new pages stitched into the passport by the American Embassy in *Ulaanbaatar*.

The officer asks me something. The woman in the compartment translates, "Do you have any identification that you work for the University in *Ulaanbaatar*?"

I pull out my teachers card and show it around to the guards.

They talk some more, looking at the stitching in my passport and at the new pages.

"There is something wrong with your passport," translates the woman, "they think there is a false part."

"Those are new pages that the embassy put in," I tell her.

The guard speaks and the woman continues to translate. "They say that they will have to check with the embassy and the university. It is now Friday night. They cannot check until Monday. You cannot take this train. You must stay in the jail here until Monday, when they can check."

"The jail? In the middle of the Gobi desert?" I ask.

The woman nods.

I could feel the tears well in my eyes. I love adventure, but carted off by the cops to a bordertown jail? Was I destined to meet the end of my own sexual Gobi in a Mongolian prison?

I imagine the "Free Mykel" marches in cities around the world. Amnesty International ads and campaigns. I'd be a poster boy. Interviews on Larry King. The works.

"Please try to talk to them," I beg the woman. "Show them that the Koreans stamped the new pages. The Chinese too. Tell them the American Embassy in *Ulaanbaatar* added them because my passport was filled. Show them the stamps."

By this time all the customs guards are in another car with my passport. The leader had just tried to call somewhere on a mobile phone — without success. I tearfully walk into their compartment with the the lady.

She starts talking, pointing out my stamps, the emblem from the embassy in *Ulaanbaatar*, the official seals. On and on it goes. Finally the older guard looks at me, then at her. He nods. Then he hands me back my passport, and says (in

English), "Here, we are sorry," and they all leave the train.

I look at the woman who saved my ass and then kiss her. A big smackeroo, one right on each cheek. God, I love Mongolians. If this were Korea I'd be gone. Wham! In the clink! No one would've come to my aid.

Back in the compartment, I clear a tiny space and sit down. I'm shaking so hard I can't get the beer bottle opened. I finally manage and drink it in two gulps. Then, the train takes off.

Murphy's Law: When anything can go wrong. It WILL go wrong.

Board's Law: Even if nothing can go wrong, it STILL will go wrong.

An hour after we pass the border, the conductress comes around. She is not here to check our tickets. Rather, she is here to collect the beer she has stashed in various places around the train to avoid customs detection. The entire train crew are smugglers and they use the train to thin out their merchandise. After safely passing the border, they collect it. My compartment mates try to cover up for me with hear-no-evil-see-no-evil-I-don't-know-what-you're-talking-about shoulder shrugs. It doesn't wash.

The conductress turns her wrath on me. I'm afraid she's going to hit me. She rants, flinging her arms in the air, pointing to the empty beer bottles and then to herself. She's not going to leave. My compartment mates look at each other, then to me. Then they take their own beer — ones they bought for themselves, tie it to the remaining bottles of the conductress's beer, and then hand it to her. Satisfied, she goes to the next compartment. I offer to pay them for the beer, but they refuse. I LOVE MONGOLIANS!

In just another twenty hours, we pull up to the station in *Ulaanbaatar*. I give my friends a goodbye hug. They move my bags out of the compartment and on to the platform before the REAL unloading starts. I wave good-bye, put on my pack and make my way out to the front of the train station.

A man asks me if I want a cab. I tell him where I live and offer $2. He asks for three. I nod ok. I put my bags in the trunk and get in the cab. He gets in the front seat, puts the key in the ignition and turns it. Nothing happens. He tries again. The cab won't start. I open the cab door, get out and start pushing. A nearby street seller helps. When we get up to speed, the cab starts. I hop in and we're off. Before long, I'm back where I started...HOME!

SIXTEEN

Back from Korea and the winter term has just started. Maggie is gone. Her replacement is Al, a laid-back Brit with a fine sense of humor.

Tsagaansar, Mongolian New Years, comes early in term. It's still cold but that doesn't stop the frantic business of the town. Supermarket prices have doubled. Even eggs, lamb and flour are in short supply. These are the main ingredients for holiday fare. Along with vodka,

THESE BUZ ARE MADE FOR WALKING

They're about an hour late. No big deal. This is Mongolia.

It's Tsagaansar — white moon, white month…lunar New Year. There's some debate whether this is the first or second most important holiday in Mongolia. In any case, it's a biggie. Ulaanzul, my travel agent/student, has invited me to celebrate the holiday with her family. They're meeting me at "11AM" to pick me up.

The doorbell rings at just about noon. It's Ulaanzul to hurry me along. I put on my coat, grab my camera and wallet. She told me I'm supposed to give money to my hosts. No presents. In a flash, we're off.

They've hired a driver. There are four of us besides that driver: Ulaanzul, her mother, her husband and me. I figure we're going some distance — maybe to a lone *ger* in the countryside. I figure wrong. We stay right in *Ulaanbaatar*, but we head for the *ger* district. In the northwest part of the city, it's populated by city dwellers who prefer the comfort of a traditional Mongolian dwelling to the disadvantages of apartment living.

Here, the *gers* are packed so close they almost touch. Makeshift fences surround each subdivision. Residents cover some of those fences with green-painted plywood, decorated with traditional Mongol designs. Usually, the design is a kind of moebius chain, with the links intertwined and endless. Each link has right angles instead of curves.

There are no paved roads in this district. You just drive off the city street onto the side of the road. Then, you follow a dirt path to where you're going. Some of the entrances are just gated and numbered gaps in the fence.

We drive up to 27 and get out of the car. Ulaanzul tugs on the gate. It's locked. She bangs on it. No response. She bangs again. Still no response. She continues to bang until finally, a rustle comes from within. Then, a chain rattles on the other side.

The gate creeks open and an old woman looks out at us. She smiles and nods her head in greeting. It's like I'm one of the family, a long lost cousin from America. "Hi, how are you? Finally you're coming to visit your old Aunt Khartsetseg in *Ulaanbaatar*." She gives me a hug and leads me into the *ger* with the rest.

The *ger* sits in the middle of a small yard. In that yard is a large billygoat, alone in a low brown pen. Along the fence, on the inside, are nearly a dozen stalls with hay in them. Other goats wander from stall to stall.

We pass the billygoat, a little outhouse and then come to an atrium, made out of tin, that leads to the *ger's* entranceway. The five of us go inside. Two older people sit on a bed/couch in the round room. On one side of them is an ornate wooden dresser, painted Mongolian orange with yellow trim. The wood-burning stove in the center of the *ger* heats the place to toasty warmth. Steam pours from beneath a covered pot on the stove.

The place is incredibly clean. Not a dustspeck or dirtmark anywhere. The

occupants in their bright *deels* also look like they were just scrubbed clean. I know that if I rub anything, it'll squeak. Then I notice how immaculate the people I'm travelling with are. The only soil in sight is on my jacket and under my fingernails.

When the host sees us he immediately reaches for his fluffy fur hat. He dons the hat and takes a piece of blue silk. Then he bends both arms at right angles, the silk draped between them.

First the oldest member of our party walks up to the man. She puts her arms under his and says something in Mongolian. I recognize the words "good" and "body." They are not, however, said next to each other.

The man leans his face toward the woman. She kisses him on both cheeks, then takes a 500 *tugrik* bill out of her pocket and gives it to him. She then turns to the lady of the house, who has not donned a hat, nor holds a piece of blue silk. The same kissing and money passing ritual follows.

Each of the members of our entourage goes through the procedure. My host seems to blanch slightly when my lips touch his cheeks. I don't have a 500 *tugrik* bill, so I give three 100s. He smiles and thanks me just the same.

After the greeting, we sit on stools at the low table. Ah, the table. Usually, when we say food is piled high, we speak in metaphor. Not now. Pile is PILE. Two enormous columns of hard cakes tower well above my seated head. They're carefully arranged in overlapping folds, like bricks in a Roman column. On top of each stack is a fistful of hard candy, just like on the monk's table at the wrestling match.

In the middle of the table, in a big metal pot, is a cooked sheep, the whole thing, minus the legs and head. A fluff of wool still hangs from the end of the fatty tail. That appendage dangles over the edge of the pot.

Before the meal comes THE SNUFF RITUAL. The men of the house pull out their silk snuff bags and remove their ornamental snuff bottles. They exchange bottles in a complicated one-handed move that involves holding the bottle at the fingertips of their right hand. Then each places his bottle in the palm of the person to his right. That person, if it's a man, places HIS snuff bottle from his fingertips in the other man's palm. Women simply accept the bottle without an exchange.

Men, then take a bit of snuff and put it on their hand, or they use the built-in dip stick. They snort it back and trade off bottles again. Women open the cap and sniff at the bottle without actually inhaling the stuff. They then pass the bottle on.

No one minds my lack of a tradeable snuff bottle. I'm offered — and actually enjoyed — sniffing others. It's a fine rush.

"Dig in!" or the Mongolian equivalent comes from our host. So dig in I do. At first, I cut the fat from my meat pieces. When my host and friends comment, I remember where I am. Fat here is "the best part." It's a delicacy. People eat it on it's own. When you buy meat, lean cuts come cheaper than fatty ones. ("Who wants to eat that? It's all meat? There's not a bit of fat on it!")

I take a deep breath and gobble down the fat, with plenty of "mmmm amtatai" (delicious). Thirty seconds after the first bite of food comes the vodka. We each get a small glassful. As is the custom, you're expected to dip in your ring finger and splash some vodka into the air. It's an offering to God. The Mongolian God is one heavy drinker.

Knowing there is no such thing as one glass of vodka here, I make sure to offer God as hefty a shot as I can muster. To show that I'm a "real man," I down the vodka in one gulp. The host smiles and immediately fills up the glass again.

The next time, I sip. What do I have to prove, right?

There are no vegetables at the table, only the lamb and sweets. I fill myself up with the meat and am just about to dig into the sweets when the hostess gets up and goes to the stove. She opens the lid of the pot to reveal it's filled with *buz*, Mongolian lamb dumplings. There must be two hundred of them. All in neat little rows on a steamer.

Out come new plates, mirror clean. The hostess stacks them next to the pot and puts five or six *buz* on each plate. One by one we take the plates and start chowing down. To wash it down? Fill up that vodka glass!

It's an effort to down that last *buz*. I feel it resting right at the top of my stomach; anything else wouldn't make it.

Fortunately, this is when the next knock comes to the door. More guests. A new crew of super-scrubbed Mongolians come in. There are five of them this time, two children among them. One by one, they pass through the arm-touching, cheek-kissing money-passing ceremony.

New arrivals mean: More Vodka! This time I toss half the glass to God, who I'm sure is better able to hold his liquor than I am.

After the new-comers seat themselves, I ask my travel-agent friend how many guests the host can expect over the three-day holiday.

"At least a hundred," she says. "Sometimes twice that."

"It's better when they arrive in groups," she continues. "The host has to drink with each set of entrants. Usually three times. If too many people come alone, he will find it difficult with the last guest."

"Yeah," I say, "difficult."

Next comes the snuff ritual — a welcome relief from the eating and drinking. Having been in Mongolia long enough to always carry dental floss, I use this occasion to remove some inter-tooth gristle. It's a Sisyphusian task.

The newcomers are then offered lamb — and a delicious slice of pure fat. That signals it's time for us to leave.

My host and hostess stand up and I follow suit, although with great difficulty. We bid them good-bye and then head to the car outside. When we leave, the hostess presents me with a pack of cigarettes.

"I don't smoke," I tell her.

Ulaanzul kicks me and I take the cigarettes, thanking the old woman.

Outside, I'm informed that when guests leave a *Tsagansar* meal, they're always presented with a gift. It's rude to turn it down.

After we get in the car, I notice that the driver is not heading toward my apartment. I say nothing, figuring it would be rude to demand to be let off first, after they've been so kind to me. Still, uppermost in my mind is the urge to sit — or lie peacefully and just digest.

I turn to Ulaanzul, the woman who invited me to the meal.

"Where are we going?" I ask.

"It's *Tsagansar*," she says. "We visit families today. Now we're going to my in-laws house."

This time it's an apartment, not a *ger*. We slowly make our way up the unlit staircase. Step by step, I carefully kick the step in front before putting my weight on it.

My stomach rumbles from the churning meat gradually dissolving in gastro-intestinal vodka. I hope we're not offered "desert" or something in this next house. I couldn't handle more than a cup of coffee.

After ringing the doorbell, a young girl opens the door and invites us in. My presence doesn't seem at all strange to her. Inside, there are already a few people sitting around the table.

This host wears a conservative business suit, rather than a *deel*. When he sees us, he puts on his hat. It's big brown hat — maybe bearskin. He picks up a long blue piece of silk and drapes it over his outstretched arms.

One by one, we put our arms under his and kiss him on each cheek. When my lips touch his skin, he too blanches a bit, pulling away slightly. Maybe my breath has deteriorated from the fermenting meat in my stomach. Or maybe I'm just not a good cheek kisser.

After the twin smackeroos, I hand him a few hundred *tugriks*. I greet his wife, and slip her a few too. She hands 'em back. I don't get it.

"You act like you're ashamed of the money," says Ulaanzul. "You don't hide it. You present it with both hands, like this."

She puts the bill on top of both hands and pushes it forward as if giving a plate of peeled grapes to Cleopatra.

I try it and this time the money's gratefully accepted. None of this Japanese style "you shouldn't have." These folks spent *tugriks* on this festival and expect to be repaid for it.

We then walk into the livingroom where the table is set. There's a huge lamb, it's fatty rump sticking out over the pot. There is also the tower of cake and candy with a few little plates of salad.

The host brings out the snuff bottle, and the other males in the room bring out theirs. Snuff is traded and sniffed. I get to sample all kinds. After the snuff comes the vodka. Fill up those glasses. Drink to the New Year! Have another.

Out of the corner of my eye I catch the movement, a young woman carrying something, a stack of plates. While we drink, an older man, a friend of the hosts, begins to cut the lamb. Oh yes, meat for all ... more lamb. Sliced thickly. And for me — as the special guest from a foreign country — a huge chunk of pure fat.

I'm trying to think of a proper metaphor for how I felt putting that into my mouth. Stuffing too many leaves into a weak-seamed garbage bag is close. Trying to operate a trash compactor filled with concrete might also give you a better idea. But there I am, big smile on my face, a hunk of pure lamb fat in my mouth. And I chew.

Buddhists say you should chew each mouthful at least a hundred times. I would make a super Buddhist. The food just rests in my mouth. Will not be swallowed. I try washing it down with the vodka that still sits in the glass next to my plate. Now I have both fat AND vodka swirling helplessly in my mouth.

Eventually, somehow, it goes down. Lamb, fat, vodka, and even a table-spoonful of salad. Every time I empty the plate, it's filled again. Every time I empty the vodka glass, it too, is filled. If I'm too slow, my hosts motion to me to eat and drink up.

I surreptitiously unhook the top button on my pants and let out my belt a couple of notches. It's a struggle to catch my breath. Then comes the *buz*. Hundreds of them, all from a steaming pot. Another set of dishes. *buz* for everyone. "Only three? Whatsamatter you don't like 'em? We worked all day making 'em. They're different from others — fried, not boiled. Here, take some more."

I scoop two more *buz* out onto my plate. The hostess shakes her head and makes a slight "tsk tsk" sound, her tongue sucking against the roof of her mouth. She adds another four.

"Care for any more salad?" asks the man to my left in near-perfect English.

Relaxing my stomach muscles, I manage to expand to near pregnant size. The four *buz*, well dissolved in vodka, slowly make their way as far down as they can. There they sit, somewhere between my throat and my stomach, digesting in the wrong place like a tubal pregnancy. I need an abortion!

I no longer want to go home and lie down to let the food digest. I want to go home and stick my fingers down my throat. It is the dream that gets me through the meal. Seven, six, five, four more *buz*, a half hour or so and I'll be home, hugging the toilet, joyously letting out my over-intake.

A half hour passes, and we do indeed leave. I slowly pull myself to my feet and waddle over to where I put my coat. The host hands me a bottle of Chinese liquor as a present. I thank him. Our driver isn't outside. I don't mind. It's only about a mile for me to go home. I need to walk off enough for the vomiting to really make me comfortable. Together we walk, my friends and I...to the next meal.

Am I kidding?

No.

On the way Ulaanzul says, "Mykel, I need to tell you something. You're not supposed to kiss. When you touch your lips to people's necks...they think it's strange. It's only for families. Just put your nose next to them and do this..."

She sniffs in loudly, as if trying to hold back dripping snot.

"That's the way. No kissing, okay?"

I nod, the bloating in my stomach making speech impossible.

"And don't forget," she says, "this meal is important to these people. Refusing food is like doing this."

She spits hard on the ground.

We arrive at an apartment near the old Russian section of town. It's a large family. A picture of a stern official-looking Mongol hangs from the livingroom wall.

Cheek sniffing, money giving, snuff snorting, vodka drinking, fat slurping, yum yum. The soft white mass sits on my tongue. I chew, but it's useless. Like chewing mucous. Sipping vodka, I manage to make it slide to the back of my throat. I tense in a gag, fighting to keep from vomiting over the rest of the white jiggly slice.

Then comes the *buz*! The THIRD time! Served by a young woman, who I'd normally be flirting with. Now I sit like a slug, barely able to force a smile.

I can't! I just can't. I'm going to die. I'm going to be *buzzed* to death, lamb choked. I already have more lamb stuck between my teeth than I've eaten in the past ten years. When the *buz* plate comes around I look plaintively at Ulaanzul. I can't do it. Rude or not rude, there has to be a limit and I'm there.

I try shaking my head no. The rest of the dinner party thinks this is very funny. Hilarious. They pour some vodka as a toast. To my health. To the new year. To me. To the *buz*...now being piled up on my plate.

Ulaanzul whispers in my ear. "Remember, they will be very insulted if you don't eat it."

"But I'll die," I whisper back.

"It doesn't matter," she says.

So I eat them. Every one. Don't ask how, I don't know. There is something amazing in the capacity of the human body to endure things it was not meant to endure. Every second I spend at that table, I spend fighting the gag reflex. My shirt is now untucked and over my opened pants. The fly is completely open to allow ever more swelling.

When the doorbell rings, we know it's time to go. I press my hands against the table top to help me stand. I can't. I'm fixed to the seat, weighed down by the churning mass in my belly. I try to stand again, but it's no use. The new guests are already entering the livingroom, but I can't get up to let them take over.

Ulaanzul and the host, a jolly man with a stomach apparently used to large meals, each take me under an arm.

"Neg, hoyer, gurav!" they say simultaneously as they lift me to my feet.

I totter to the door. The host hands me another pair of socks. Ulaanzul opens the door. We're on our way...to another meal — two more.

By the time I'm finished, besides stomach difficulties and the Chinese wine, I have two packs of cigarettes, a datebook, two chocolate bars, and five pairs of socks.

Between the fourth and fifth meal, we get in another short walk. We need to stop to change dollars into *tugriks* to pay the hosts of the last families. I blank out, go on automatic pilot. I don't remember the last two meals, except that the last thing I'm offered before leaving is the traditional Mongolian drink, *Airag* — fermented mare's milk. I don't remember drinking it. I don't even remember the trip home.

I do remember how good that toilet looked. That brilliant white porcelain. That beautiful bowl waiting for me to give my all — and I do. And more.

The next day I don't feel so good. During the short time I'm on my feet, I meet Zolzaya, a Mongolian friend. She invites me to dinner to celebrate the New Year. I wonder what they're going to have to eat.

SEVENTEEN

Mongolian springs aren't flowers and young love. They're dust. The wind blows from the North. It races through the Siberian steppe, over the mountains and across the plains. In the winter the wind brings snow. In the spring it's dust, often in blinding storms. This year, it's fire. The wind-whipped fires have been spreading for a month, now. They cover an area the size of France, moving ever closer to the capital.

Every morning I pick the soot from my nose before getting up to practice tai chi. There's been occasional rain as the result of cloud-seeding, but not enough.

Today, I can actually smell the fire. For the last week the sky has been gray and smoke has hung like a fog throughout the city. Ulaanbaatar, like Rome, is surrounded by mountains. In the North is Chingeltai, a resort suburb, normally filled with summer houses, grasslands and herds of wild horses. Now it's filled with flames.

CNN shows a commercial for itself. A chubby senior news official, graying appropriately at the temples, says, "This company is structured in such a way, that no matter where the news is, no matter how far away, we can get there immediately with a bunch of bright, talented people."

Today, finally, comes the story about the Mongolian fire. They show a map. That's it. Just an outline between Russia and China labeled: MONGOLIA. The newscaster voiceovers about "a fire covering an area the size of Austria," and what do we see? A map. Not a filled-in map, with the fire areas in red. Nope. Just a lug of a map like they've taken a close-up of some multinational's boardroom wall. Maybe they ran out of bright, talented people.

Anyway, fire isn't the theme of this chapter. This chapter is about a changing civilization and the reality of dominant and recipient cultures. It's about respect and race and religion. It's about choosing west over east and what it means for those of us in the west. In other words, it's

ANOTHER WRESTLING STORY

As with the death salesman in China, my World Wide Weirdos network continues to grow in Mongolia. I guess Gibby Haynes, singer of the Texas band The Butthole Surfers, first noticed it. I told him about a meeting I had. It was right after The Challenger space shuttle exploded with those astronauts and schoolmarm in it. A girl approached me at a party.

"Hello," she said.

She was attractive, so I started a conversation. It didn't take too long before she was chatting full swing.

"I'm from Texas, and my dad's famous." she told me.

"How so?" I asked.

"He was the guy who started the *Teachers In Space* program."

"What is it with you?" Gibby asked. "Do weird people just stick their noses in the air and say, 'Hmmmm, that smells like Mykel Board. I'd better tell him how weird I am?'"

Gibby was right. Whatever it is, that quality hasn't left me in Mongolia.

BLACK ROSE, a Mongolian rap band with a large adolescent following, is playing at The Worker's Palace in western *UB*. I stand in the lobby, waiting for the doors to open. A man in his mid-thirties, dressed in a dark suit, walks purposefully over to me, swinging his arms like he's hiking.

"Hello," he says in English, extending his hand. "My name's Ganzorig. Do you speak English?"

I tell him I'm American. He says he's Mongolian. I tell him I figured that. He asks me what I do.

"Bi *Angli-baksh*," I say, stretching the limits of my Mongolian. "And what do you do?"

"I'm the fighting tactics instructor for the Mongolian Police Department," he says, without a trace of one-upmanship.

We talk about martial arts. I say I studied Tai Chi and Wing Chun Kung Fu. I don't mention I was the worst in both classes, and find it hard to keep my balance, let alone actually hit anything.

He tells me there is a special kind of Mongolian martial art and asks if I'd like to see it.

"Sure," I say, "I love that stuff."

"Fine," he answers, handing me a business card, "Here is my number. Call me and we will meet."

"Great," I say, putting the card in my pocket, ready to walk in to see the show.

"By the way," says Ganzorig, as I'm leaving, "I went to see Bruce Lee's grave in Seattle. He is my hero."

"Oh?" I ask. "Did you see any more of America than just Seattle or did you just fly in and out?"

"I didn't fly," he says.

"Wow that must've been some trip, then," I say. "You had to take a train to China somewhere and then a boat to Japan or Korea and another boat to the West Coast. How long did that take?"

"I didn't take a boat," he says, "I walked. Walking is my hobby."

The story is he took a train to Yakutsk in Siberia. Then walked, right through Siberia to the Bering Strait. Then across the ice to Alaska through Alaska to Canada's West Coast, then down the coast to Seattle to visit Bruce Lee's grave.

"Yow!" I say. "That's a pretty long stretch."

"Oh, I didn't stop there," he says, "I kept walking. I went south. To San Diego."

He continues, "This year I'm going to walk across Australia — or Greenland. I haven't made up my mind yet. Walking is my hobby."

The man speaks smoothly, matter-of-factly, as if he were talking about fishing or stamp collecting.

I check my watch. Time to go in to see the show. I promise to call him and set up a time to see Mongolian martial arts. Then, the concert.

The show is fun. BLACK ROSE is two guys with lots of back-up. Back up singers, back up dancers, two comedians who do an Abbott and Costello bit while the stars change clothes.

As a matter of fact, they change clothes at least half a dozen times during the show. There are the glitter boys, the homeboys, the JDs, the SS (with long brown leather coats and hats with skulls on 'em), the surfers, and a double Elvis.

The set is perfectly choreographed and synchronized. No live music, but this is rap. The background dancers of all sexes are clad skimpily enough to keep my interest, even when the ROSE gets a bit repetitive.

I don't see Ganzorig after the show and weeks pass before I finally contact him. We make a date. He meets me on a bridge close to my apartment. Together we go to the central sports palace to meet his charges. This is the same place I saw Mongolian wrestling a few months earlier.

A short but muscular guy, about 18, smiles at him and then at me as he approaches. I reach out to shake his hand, introducing myself.

"Hi," he says, "I Bruce Lee."

Gradually, one by one, the others arrive. There's Claude Van Damme, Chuck Norris, and a few with less memorable names. We can't leave yet, though, because Arnold Schwarzenegger has not shown up.

Schwarzenegger is half an hour late. He's a big guy with a flat nose and shoulders so wide he'd have to turn sideways to get into most rooms. Bowing, I say hello.

[Cultural note: Mongolians don't bow. They shake hands. On the other hand, martial artists do bow, so it's not so strange. Seeing as this guy is a foot taller and double my weight, with muscles from here to San Diego, I consider bowing to be the greater part of valor.]

There's some discussion, then we all hop on a trolley going West, toward where I live. We pass that and continue going to Suburban *Ulaanbaatar*. We come upon gray apartment blocks, one after the other, and an occasional monument with a faded red star on it.

It's by one of these monuments that we stop. We get out and start to walk. It's a strange part of town, even dustier than central *UB*, with no shops or even the kiosks that normally line the streets. We stop by a metal gate in a cyclone fence. Over the gate is an inverted crescent sign with yet another faded red star in the middle.

A wooden guard booth sits on the other side. Blotches of red paint cling to it. A dozen Mongols wearing thin blue slacks and long coats stand in front. They pace or just shift their legs as if waiting for someone.

Ganzorig leads us past the crowd and through the gate. He salutes the uniformed guard at the door. I trip over a pipe laying across the path. Looking up, I hear laughter. Suddenly, a lot of men in uniform are watching me. Just as suddenly, I realize I have just entered a MONGOLIAN ARMY CAMP.

Here I am among the Red Army, or whatever post-communist color it is now. Placards throughout the camp show pictures of stern-faced soldiers in fur hats. They gaze intently into the distance, some with bayonetted rifles, some in tanks, some with a wife, kid and dog. On each sign is a slogan. I don't understand any of 'em, but I can read the cyrillic "Lenin" as the author of at least two.

Jezus! If only I had known before I came, I could have made a bundle working for the CIA! How many Americans get to see the inside of a Mongolian army base? From the bug eyes and dropped jaws on the soldiers who see me, not many.

We go into the barracks following a maze-ish path until we get to the practice room. The crew I'm with go to change clothes. There are already some folks in the room. It's a dingy place, with dirty gym mats on the floor. Faint sunlight streaks in through the unwashed windows.

A short skinny guy wears long baggy shorts. Another guy, about twenty, wears an aikido uniform. A tall guy with a thick mustache wears a silk jacket with 'Jeet Kwan Do' on the back. Yet another is dressed like a ninja.

Lowering my gaze, I see — barefoot, in a gold robe, wearing boxing gloves ten sizes too large — a four year old boy. He's practicing his stance, kicks and punches.

Whack! Pow! He hits a foam tube one of the other fighters holds for him. Yaw! Hee! Swack! He kicks his right foot over his head, spinning on his left. By the time he's 10, he'll be a killer. Right now, he's got form, but I think I could beat him.

Padded punching boards hang on three sides of the room. A tall muscular guy, built like a basketball player, practices spinning high kicks against the board. Bang! to the right. Pow! to the left.

On the opposite wall, another tall guy, thinner and gawkier than the first, practices using his hips to power his arms into the punching board. He's got a big square head that seems to belong on someone else's body. If the Adam's Family's Lurch were a boxer, he'd look like this.

Things come to a stop as we walk in. All eyes are on me. The teacher introduces me to the class. He gives a short speech in Mongolian. A few of the guys there say something to him. He smiles and nods. Then he turns to me.

"I told them you were a Wing Chun expert," he says. "Now they want you to teach them."

I swallow hard, stealing a glance at the pectoral muscles of Arnold Schwarzenegger, who has just emerged, shirtless, from the changing room. Then I look around, frantically trying to find that four year old kid.

"Sure," I answer, swallowing hard, "but I don't want to interrupt your regular practice. Maybe next time..."

Bruce Lee is standing close and gets the gist of the conversation.

"Show me basics." he says.

"Ok," I tell him. "There are four gates. Top right, top left, bottom right, bottom left."

Bruce nods.

"Now," I continue, pointing to the area just below my stomach "say you punch me here..."

He does. Wham, right in the soft flesh. I'm down, cramped in pain in a curl on the floor. Slowly I get up. "We'll learn some other time," I say through clenched teeth.

Ganzorig smiles and nods. "Yes," he says, "this is an important practice. We're going to have Mongolia's first MAD DOG WRESTLING competition and my students are going to be in it."

MAD DOG WRESTLING, he explains, is the Mongolian equivalent of US Pro-wrestling. They bounce each other off the ropes, taunt the audience, jump on their opponent's neck, pull his hair, the whole kit and caboodle. I watch in awe as again and again they practice smashing into one another and simultaneously falling backwards to the mat.

Their costumes, every one different, lend a clownish air to the rehearsal. Claude Van Damme, just out of the dressing room, wears a spandex bathing suit with pictures of multicolored beachballs on it. I can only guess what the coach yells at his boys during their rehearsal.

"More elbow to the head!" "Grab him by his hair!" "Stomp on his face."

Near me, Chuck Norris practices a kick to Bruce Lee's head. Fake a punch, then wham! Spin, kick high. About eighteen inches before Chuck's foot is due to meet Bruce's face, Bruce is on the ground. The coach yells at him.

"You gotta let him touch you," says the coach. "Just a tap before you go down. Otherwise it looks bad."

They try again. The fake punch. The spin. The kick. Pow! Foot against jaw. Bruce's teeth click shut at the force of that kicking foot. Blam! He's down. On the mat. Staggering to his feet, shaking his head, he rubs his jaw.

In another corner of the mat it's Arnold Schwarzenegger against Lurch. I can't imagine which one's going to be the bad guy.

It's a ten ring circus. Hair-pulling here, neck-stomping there, knees to the groin, elbows to the neck, all at the same time. Blam! Chuck flies out of the ring — into me. I'm on the floor, ass first off the mat. He smiles, shrugs and gets back in the ring. I struggle to my feet.

Although they start on the weak side, within a few minutes, they've got it going.

"Grab him by the hair!" shouts the coach. "That's it. Now smash his face into the mat. Good! Again!"

Dutifully the guys follow instructions. It all would be convincing were it not for their clothes and the huge grins they wear — all of them, all the time.

Whack! Kick to the face. (Smile.) Blam! Punch in the stomach. Blam! Another punch. Blam! Blam! Blam! (Smile.) Only the four year old kid doesn't smile. But the look of angry brutality he tries to affect is so cute, I smile.

As for the others, no matter what they do, or how cruel they're supposed to be, they grin. All of them. Good guy and bad guy alike. Not a brutal, villainous grin, but a smiley-face smile like they're a buncha young Mongolians out for a good time.

When the rehearsal's over, the boys change back into civilian clothes. Then it's outside the barracks and into a city bus back to town. We agree to meet just before showtime on Mad Dog day. They'll get me into the match free. That's their part of the bargain. My part: teach them how to fight Wing Chun style.

"It's a deal," I say.

There's a week to go. It's going to be a rock/wrestling match, with a Mongolian rock band playing between the bouts. I never heard of the band, but it'll be weird to see the two in tandem. Rock and pro-wrestling, America comes to Mongolia.

That's when it hits me. I've been complaining about how Christianity has come to Mongolia to destroy it's culture. I've been complaining about how missionaries sucker in the mostly young and poor by telling them Christianity is modern and American. If they follow it, they'll have all the riches of America. I've heard Christians encourage youngsters to speak badly of their parents and their parents' religion, to denounce them as being lazy drunkards and idol worshippers. I've complained about all this, and here comes rock and pro-wrestling.

A friend e-mailed me this quote from the *San Francisco Bay Guardian:*
Globalization is wreaking havoc on cultural diversity by spreading Coca-Cola culture to every corner of the globe...

Aren't rock and wrestling 'Coca-Cola culture'? Aren't they as destructive to Mongolian society as Christianity? Mongolia, a country where wrestling is steeped in tradition and virtue...now turning it into American-style entertainment?

Mongolia, where traditional music, the horse-fiddle and the snake banjo have ruled the steppe, now gets invaded by rock'n'roll. Aren't I enjoying the same things I've condemned?

There are differences, of course. Neither rock nor wrestling is evangelized. There are no missionaries telling people wrestling is the culture of the rich and the modern. There are no people posing as English teachers and then preaching the rock gospel. Wrestling and rock culture is absorbed, not foisted, but is this difference enough? Is a McDonalds that people WANT any better than one built against their wishes?

Well, they're all here. Pro Wrestling, rock'n'roll, Christianity, and probably someday soon, McDonalds. Sadly, they're inevitable.

◎ ◎ ◎

It's the day of the match. I'm there early. I lay on the steps in front of the sports palace reading a copy of "SKIN FLUTE" zine that a friend sent me from the States.

A short professional-looking Mongol has a large TV camera on his shoulder. He occasionally points it at me. A few young men wait in front of the building. One has an eyebrow scar. Another, a chin scar. A third has one across his upper lip. Starting time approaches, but no wrestler does. How am I going to get in? I'd have bought a ticket if I'd have known, but now it's too late. I'll give it fifteen more minutes, then go home, a perfect end to an annoying week.

Flashback: On Monday, I'm waiting for a bus. My camera hangs around my neck. On it is the new flash I just bought in Beijing. The bus comes. As I'm about to board, a little girl tugs on my jacket.

Another beggar, I think. Get away kid, you bother me.

I brush her away. She tugs again. I free myself and get in the bus, annoyed. Then I look down at my camera. The flash was gone, obviously fallen while I was waiting. The little girl was only trying to tell me. Sometimes I feel like a real jerk.

So this morning I went with one of my students to buy a new flash. I knew it would be expensive. It'd have to come from China, smuggled under a seat on the train. We went to four electronic shops and one department store. They don't sell flashes in Mongolia. Wasted time. Wasted trip. No flash.

Now, in front of the next building, some people move a large wooden structure. It looks like a stage. I walk over to investigate. At that very moment a group of people leave the building. They're all young men. They pull at their ties and stiff white collars, looking very uncomfortable in their suits.

Ah, there's Bruce Lee, Claude Van Damme and Arnold Schwarzenegger.

"Mykel!" shouts Bruce, "What are you doing here?"

"I'm supposed to see you wrestle, remember?" I say.

"But it's cancelled. See the sign?" He points to a notice, written in Mongolian, near the wood structure in front of the building.

"Oh, of course," I say. "Why was it cancelled?"

"No electricity...The band can't play and there are no lights for us. They ran out of electricity. We can't do it until they get some more."

We talk for awhile. Arnold asks me to show him some Kung Fu moves. As I prepare to take a stance, Bruce jabs me quickly, just missing my nose.

"Is that how you do it?" he asks.

"Very good." I tell him, "Next week we'll have another lesson."

Claude Van Damme has taken something from his pocket. I ask him if I can look at it. It's a flash. A camera flash! A cheap one, probably costs a dollar in China, but this isn't China.

"Just what I need!" I tell him.

"Charge him $5," says Bruce.

"I'll give you $5," I say.

"Charge him $10," says Arnold.

"I'll give you $5," I say.

"Seven dollars," says Claude.

"Yours!" I say.

During this conversation, a large group of passing Mongolians has gathered around us. It's not every day they see an American pulling dollars out to buy something from a Mongol.

As soon as the transaction is completed, everyone in the crowd starts pulling things from their pocket.

"You want to buy a handkerchief? Used only once. One dollars."

"You want candy bar? One dollars?"

Bruce pulls out a cigarette lighter. "Here you are. Three dollars."

"Sure, I'll buy it," I tell him. "You can have this." I pull a hair from my nose.

He tries to make a mean face. I take a Kung Fu stance. He swings. Before his fist is half way to my nose, I fall back into the arms of a waiting by-stander.

I right myself and attack, slamming my arm against his chest, lightly, in fake-wrestling style, of course. Bruce comes back with a neck chop. The watching crowd cheers. My turn: a push to the chin. Him, a spinning kick...whoops, this is getting too close.

I raise my hands in surrender. The crowd cheers again. We shake hands all around and agree to meet again next Monday at 3:30. There'll be another rehearsal. By then, they'll know when the rescheduled date is.

At 3:30 next Monday, I wait in front of the sports palace. No one is there. Knowing this is Mongolia, and having learned one of life's great lessons: ALWAYS BRING A BOOK, I wait. At 4:30 I go home. Not angry, as I would have been eight months ago, but completely accepting, realizing how amazing it is that ANYTHING works at all here.

At the beginning of the following week, I start to see flyers for the rescheduled show. Hoping it won't be expensive, I decide to buy a ticket to insure that I'll get in. It cost 1500 *tugriks*.

I get there at the scheduled starting time, rightly hoping I'll be extremely early. Chuck Norris passes me in the hall, gives me a high five, and tells the guard to get me a box seat in the VIP section.

Inside, there is a huge stage to the left of the ring. Workers are putting down mats. The band is on stage tuning up and trying to weed the feedback out of the sound system.

A familiar thin, suited form approaches me. It's Ganzorig, the walker. He brings me to the other side of the room where the wrestlers are being made up. This is the second night. The boys gather to show me their wounds from the night before. A couple scrapes, one mat burn that looks like a giant hickey. I point to the make-up girl and ask if she did it. He doesn't get it.

I point the camera at Van Damme, as the make-up girl applies Gene Simmons KISS-like batwings to his eyes. He waves his hands, motioning for me to take someone else's picture. Mongols usually love to have their picture taken, but not now.

One by one, the boys sit while the pretty make-up lady draws pictures on their faces. Most of the stage names are in Mongolian. I can't understand them, so I'll call them by their make- up.

There's FLASH, with a lightning bolt starting at the right temple, and ending at the left jaw. LURCH becomes CRIMINAL MAN with vertical black bars from his hair line down to his neck. ACCUSED MAN has a single thick black bar across his eyes, the rest of his face painted clown white.

Bruce Lee and Chuck Norris get away with no make-up, as does the four year old boy. Schwarzenegger is treated to a different KISS-character — a Paul Stanley-like star around one eye.

Before the make-up is ready, Ganzorig escorts me to my seat. He tells me an important person who is both a high man in politics and an executive at a big corporation, will be sitting near me.

The place gradually fills up. It's not as packed as it was for traditional wrestling. Still, two hundred people applaud when the lights go down.

With the dimming lights, the amplifiers start squealing feedback. A troop of three or four people climb over me into the empty VIP seats. One of them is a t-shirted man, about 30, wearing a headband with a strange symbol on it. The other is an ordinary-looking Mongol wearing a brown suit with no tie. The third is a man in a tailored business suit. Tanned, he carries a new Sony video camera. He sits next to me.

His way of dressing, his video camera, his posture, all look more Japanese than Mongolian. Maybe he's the famous politician imitating a Japanese businessman. Maybe he's Japanese.

As soon as the lights dim completely, a form sneaks out of the cheap seats and makes its way to the empty seat on the OTHER side of me. He immediately puts his arm on my shoulder and starts talking. His breath stinks of vodka. He, I'm sure, is Mongolian.

The spotlight comes on. The band on the stage warms up the crowd with a hard rock instrumental. Then out comes the singer. He's dressed in a long black robe with a hood. He wears sandals and should be carrying a scythe. He takes the cordless mic from its stand and screams into it. The band gets louder, then moves from guitar diddling to a bass heavy BE DOP BE DOP BE DOP DEE DEE rhythm. The black robed man begins to rap.

As he raps out the words, he spins. His robe rises like the dress of a can can dancer. Underneath is a tiger-patterned jumpsuit. Faster and faster he spins. One sandal flies off his foot. Then the other. The band increases their musical pace. The singer increases the speed of his rap. The music speeds up. The words go faster. The singer spins faster. The music speeds up again. The singer whirls more wildly. Then he collapses to the stage. The music stops. There's polite applause and the spotlight shifts to the wrestling ring.

Canned rock music blasts from the speaker as the announcer tells the crowd what's coming. Two women march toward the stage. One wears a pair of loose black coveralls over a light-colored blouse. The other wears white. A white dress, frilly, cut high on the sides showing lots of leg, with white high-heeled shoes, and white gloves. They station themselves outside the ring, at opposite ends.

Then, come the first wrestlers. The canned music continues through the entire match. The first combatants are the two unpainted guys, Bruce Lee and Chuck Norris. They're dressed in thin robes with hoods. One red, the other blue. Chuck has an American flag cap on his head. Each takes a side and begins chatting with the nearest ring woman.

In the corners, the women help them slip out of their robes. Each young man is barefoot, shirtless, wearing gymshorts.

The referee is in a long-sleeve white shirt and black tie. He directs them to slap hands and start fighting. They do...well, sort of. Bruce raps Chuck on the chest, with his forearm. Chuck crumples to the ground. Bruce kicks him once. Chuck lays there, grinning. Then Bruce stomps around the ring, giving the thumbs up sign to the audience. Chuck lays there, grinning.

Bruce walks over to Chuck, grabs his hair, picks his head off the ground and smashes it into the mat. He does this again. Then he stands up and stomps around the ring, giving the thumbs up sign to the audience. Most of the crowd cheers. A few boo. Chuck lays there, grinning.

Bruce walks over to the prone Chuck. Chuck jerks to his feet, smashing Bruce in the chin with the back of his head. Bruce falls backwards. Chuck hits Bruce with his forearm. Bruce again falls back. Chuck picks Bruce up on his shoulders, holding him lengthwise, he spins him like a propeller and throws him to the mat. Bruce lays there, grinning.

Chuck stomps around the ring, giving the thumbs up sign to the audience. Most of the crowd cheers. A few boo. Bruce lays there, grinning.

Chuck returns to the prone Bruce. He puts one hand on his head and pulls it off the mat by the hair. Then he grabs a handful of Bruce's shorts and lifts him completely off the ground. Getting a running start, Chuck drives Bruce, like a battering ram, head-first into the padded turnbuckle.

Whack! Smash! Again! Then he drops him. Bruce lays there, grinning.

Chuck makes the rounds, arms outstretched, thumbs up. The referee strolls over to the prone Bruce. He looks at Bruce, slaps the mat ten times, raises Chuck's hand, and the rock band starts again.

The singer is even more energetic this time. He runs from the stage down to the floor and back up to the ring. He gets in the ring and screams into the microphone. The guitar player whammies away, bending each note as he stands open-legged, the guitar neck pointing ahead and upwards at a 45 degree angle.

Having forgotten my earplugs, I casually lean forward allowing my fingertips to fold the tragi into the earholes, plugging up as best I can.

The musical interlude is over none too soon and it's time for the next bout. This one is the heavyweights. ARNOLD SCHWARZENEGGER VS. LURCH. They introduce the gangly Lurch as: ABDUL JABAR.

The two giants emerge from behind the ring. Arms raised above their heads.

They're wearing the same robes that Bruce Lee and Chuck Norris wore earlier. On them, they only reach mid-thigh, looking more like prostitutes' evening wear than wrestling robes.

To add to the comedy, their faces are both painted, Schwarzenegger with that KISS star around one eye, Abdul/Lurch with the jailbars on his face. Oh yeah, the topper: Abdul is wearing those bathing trunks, the ones with the beachballs on them.

They de-robe in their respective corners, having a slight conference with their ring-side girl. Then, the match begins.

Schwarzenegger raps Abdul on the chest, with his forearm. Abdul crumples to the ground. Schwarzenegger kicks him once. Abdul lays there, grinning. Then Schwarzenegger stomps around the ring, giving the thumbs up sign to the audience. Abdul lays there, grinning.

Schwarzenegger walks over to Abdul, grabs his hair, picks his head off the ground and smashes it into the mat. He does this again. Then he stands up and stomps around the ring, giving the thumbs up sign to the audience. Most of the crowd cheers. A few boo. Abdul lays there, grinning.

Schwarzenegger walks over to the prone Abdul. Abdul quickly stands. He does not smash Schwarzenegger in the chin with the back of his head. Still, Schwarzenegger falls backwards. Abdul hits Schwarzenegger with his forearm. Schwarzenegger again falls back. Abdul picks Schwarzenegger up on his shoulders. Holding him lengthwise, he spins him like a propeller and throws him to the mat. Schwarzenegger lays there, grinning.

Abdul stomps around the ring, giving the thumbs up sign to the audience. Most of the crowd cheers. A few boo. Schwarzenegger lays there, grinning.

Abdul returns to the prone Schwarzenegger. He puts one hand on his head and pulls it off the mat by the hair. Then he grabs a handful of Schwarzenegger's shorts and lifts him off the ground. Getting a running start, Abdul drives Schwarzenegger like a battering ram, head first into the padded turnbuckle in the ring corner.

Smash! Again! Then he drops him. Schwarzenegger lays there, grinning.

While Abdul makes the rounds, arms outstretched, thumbs up, the referee strolls over to the prone Schwarzenegger. He looks at him, slaps the mat ten times, raises Abdul's hand, and the rock band starts again.

You can guess what happens through the next few bouts. The audience doesn't mind though. They cheer through the whole thing. Most haven't figured out the booing-the-bad-guy routine. Probably because it's so hard to tell which is the bad guy — except in the final bout.

This one again features Chuck Norris. Now, however, his opponent isn't Bruce Lee. It's the four year old kid. Chuck wears the ninja outfit: wide black pants with a black robe and matching belt. The four year old kid wears a gold robe over gold gym-shorts about three sizes to big for him.

The referee has them shake hands. Immediately, Chuck charges the four year old. The kid quickly takes a karate stance and POW! Front kick. Chuck flies across the ring and smashes into the ropes.

Shaking his head, Chuck prepares another attack. Head down, he runs like a bull toward the boy. Jump. Spin. High kick. The kid just reaches between Chuck's legs. Either Chuck suddenly learns to act or the kid really hits paydirt. Chuck crumbles to the mat, his hands pressed fetally into his crotch. He is not grinning.

Thrilled, the kid walks around the inside the ring, his tiny hands raised in triumph. The audience goes wild. The kid walks over to the now supine, and heavily breathing Chuck. He kicks him in the side and then grabs him by his hair.

Smash! He pulls Chuck's head up and slams it into the mat. Blam! Chuck struggles to his feet, a smile now on his post-pained face as he staggers upright. The four-year-old runs to the ropes and uses them to ricochet himself into the knees of the wobbling Chuck. BLAM! Chuck is down. Collapsed. The referee runs over. 1-2-3-4-5-6-7-8-9-10!

The referee not only holds up the arm of the four-year-old, but lifts up the entire kid. Putting him on his shoulders, he marches around the perimeter of the ring. The crowd goes wild, crowding the ring, banging on the sides of the mat.

Then the rock band comes on again. While they're playing, my pal Ganzorig brings the kid over to where I'm sitting. He introduces him to the man in the t-shirt with a headband. THAT is the important businessman? YES! I love Mongolia!

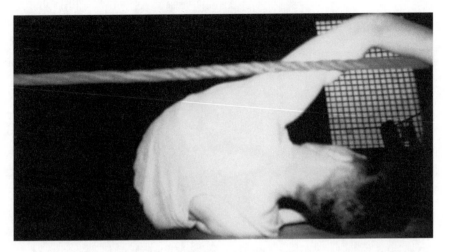

The band finishes and the t-shirt guy goes ringside to make a speech. There is a little ceremony. They present a trophy belt to the winner of the entire match. For some reason, it's Bruce Lee. Then the lights go on and we go home.

The day after this bout, I begin preparing for my dream trip: a journey to the Gobi. While I'm shopping for supplies, I see that one of the *Ulaanbaatar* newspapers has a picture of Hulk Hogan on its front page. It looks like he's a new hero here. It's the modern world, and Mongolia is becoming a modern country. I'd better see it quick.

EIGHTEEN

Mongolia has no town of Bayatov. I've changed the name to throw off the DEA and other perverts. Also, because our dealer was in the Peace Corps, we don't want to get him in trouble. They have ways of tracing these things, you know? The rest of this adventure is true, though not as obvious as its title:

OF COURSE IT'S HOT, WE'RE IN THE FUCKIN' DESERT!

School's out. Officially, it's the last week of finals, but I've given all mine. Now, I'm looking forward to my trip to the Gobi. Somehow that's the real Mongolia.

It's the day before we leave. We've managed to score some Bayatov Gold to spice up those quiet nights of sand and tent pegs. Marijuana isn't illegal here. It grows wild near the countryside village of Bayatov. Rumor is that Russian hippies planted it in the 80's. As a weed, it did what weeds do. The local cops don't even know what it is.

A Peace Corp volunteer teaches English in Bayatov. Every year, at harvest time, other volunteers join him to harvest the weed. Some come here to the capital to sell it to the expats. Last week a dealer was in town. Nice guy, young with reddish cheeks and just a hint of facial hair that was yet to develop.

"Here, check it out," he says.

We do and are convinced. In Sebastian's apartment, cozy, with his bad-taste posters on the wall (Sting, Genesis, Dire Straits), we talk.

"We're going to the Gobi soon," I tell him, "travelling free-lance through the desert. No tour, just adventure."

"That's not adventure," he says, "that's suicide."

I laugh.

We smoke. Eventually, we get to the crux.

"How much?" I ask.

The young volunteer scratches his head.

"Aww," he says, "you guys are taking a trip into hell. Why should I tax you for it? It's a gift."

"Into hell?" I ask.

He smiles like a sage. But we get the stuff for free.

Who is we? Well, there's me. There's also Sebastian, the big Brit I met at the *VSO* party. With a chronic cold sore on his lower lip, at twenty-four he's the youngest of us. We've become good friends in the past few months, though his glasses fog at some of the most awful music this side of the planet. He's just graduated from college and Mongolia is his first big trip outside England. He's quick-witted and funny, though a bit high strung.

Then there's Al, my fellow teacher, the one who took Maggie's place at the university. He's also big, with close-cropped red hair, flecked with gray. In England he was a raver. Here he's Mr. Mellow. Nothing riles him. At worst, when upset, he just turns off and sinks into a corner.

For some reason, girls find him irresistible. He's gone through two Brits, a Ukrainian and four Mongolians. One of the latter includes Sainamdrar, a teacher I've had an unrequited crush on during the entirety of my mateless stay. He's been here five months.

Despite my jealousy, I really like the guy. He has a subtlety and wry humor not common in today's elbow-poking "Get it? Dija get it? Really funny, huh?" world.

The fourth party in our adventure is the driver, Bishbataar, one of my students during the year. Although his grammar is awful and he missed half the classes, he's communicative, fun, and a hustler.

He has the only car in the class. Three times he'd promised to bring me to various places in the countryside. Three times he didn't come through. He often asks me to help correct his English in his love letters to a girl in Sweden. He promises her the world and his undying devotion. She only needs to send him an invitation that'll get him into that country. Once there, he told me, he plans to dump her and make his fortune in the free market.

Here in town, Bishbataar already has a leg up on the free market. He uses his car as a taxi. Cruising up and down the streets, he looks for fares — or girls. He's been through 'em all.

Now he's convinced us to let him drive us because he used to work for *Zhuulchin*, the state travel agency. He knows Mongolia like he knows his Swedish girlfriend's pubes, he says. Besides, wouldn't it be better to travel with a friend rather than some anonymous jeep driver?

He's a wiry guy, about 26, with a sparse mustache and a few chin hairs that embarrass him when they grow out. Tanned, he has good looks that instantly degenerate when he puts on his Mr. Suave get-the-girls act.

He's always looking for an angle, never satisfied with one hustle when there might be two. Chronically late, argumentative, headstrong, he would be unlikable if he didn't remind me so much of myself. He's promised us a Russian jeep for the journey. He can rent one from a policeman friend of his. His own car would never make it through the Gobi, he says.

Tonight, we're meeting Bishbataar at 7:30 to discuss the trip. Things have changed. After it was too late to find an alternative, he tells us he wants 'extra money' for gas and food. When you rent a jeep from a REAL place, you never have to pay for this. He also tells us — at the last minute — that he was unable to get a jeep, but has found an old Russian car.

"It's same strong," he says, "and we use less petrol. Better than jeep."

Sebastian, Al and I have a plan. I'm the bad cop. ("Bishbataar, you have to pay for everything. That's it.") Al's the good cop. ("Bishbataar, we understand. We'll give you whatever you need.") Sebastian's the compromiser. ("OK, we'll pay gas. You pay food. Fair enough?") We expect he'll agree to Sebastian's proposal.

We wait in Sebastian's apartment, puffing on a bit of the Bayatov Gold. Al and I make fun of the posters on the wall.

"You've got the same tastes as my mother," says Al.

"I'm glad your mum's got culture," says Sebastian.

"Of course," says I, "in England Phil Collins is culture. Boy, am I glad I wasn't born there. Pip pip, eh old chap?"

As we play, the gold burns down and the clock ticks on. At 8:30 we're annoyed. At 9:30 we're angry. We're also, for some reason, famished.

We decide to go to the Green Club, *UB's* only Indian restaurant, a 15 minute walk from Sebastian's. I write a note to Bishbataar:

YO JERKOFF!

We waited two hours for you! We're now at THE GREEN CLUB.
Meet us there. If you don't catch us, be at Mykel's place at 6AM
tomorrow. If you're not there by 6:30, FORGET IT!

Fuck you, S, A & M

For the next two hours, we slurp down curry, paratha, and beer. We also make plans on how we're going meet at the train station tomorrow if Bishbataar doesn't show up. We'll take a train as far into the Gobi as we can. Then we'll try to find a ride to the hardcore desert. Bishbataar can screw himself. At 11:30 I ask the waiter to bring the bill. At this instant, Bishbataar walks in.

"What happened to you?" I yell at him in my best irritated voice.

"You know..." he says, "this is Mongolia."

He has a point there.

So we pay the bill and go back to Sebastian's to discuss Bishbataar's pay. I do my bad cop bit, but the others are too stoned to go along with it. They make the final offer right away.

"Of course," says Bishbataar, "I'm just a poor man, from a poor country. You can do what you like with me. I can say nothing. You are so high and I am so low. I can say nothing."

Sebastian pretends to play the violin as Bishbataar spiels. He doesn't get it.

Anyway, we agree. He gets $75 a day. $50 of which he says he needs to pay for the car rental. The car is 'one of many' that this policeman friend has. Bishbataar doesn't explain any further except to say: "Mongolian police have lots of cars. They catch criminals, you see?"

Bishbataar will pitch in for the road food, to be deducted from his pay at the end of the journey. He'll meet me at my apartment at 6:30, now five hours away. Then, we'll pick the others up at Sebastian's.

"If you're not there by 7:30, I'm leaving without you," I tell Bishbataar.

"Yes, yes, of course," he says.

Tonight, too tired to finish packing, I set out what I'll need: an extra pair of jeans, my ancient Polaroid, a few packs of film that say "Best if used before January 1988," some New York City postcards as trinkets for the natives, a can of Cafe Pele spurious coffee, a box of prunes my mother sent me, a water bottle with a Daffy Duck stopper that Yoko brought me from New York, some handwarmers, a tent and foam sleeping pad borrowed from Ulaanzul, a roll of duct tape and very little else.

I sleep fitfully, awakening to the 5:30 alarm with vague recollections of a dream that involved Sebastian and a rabbit. I pack, then unpack the coffee to make myself some. After my early morning Tai Chi/Wing Chun practice, I sit in front of the clock and watch the hands turn. Bishbataar comes at 7:15.

"Mykel," he says, "I thought it better bring my own car. I not want to wake up policeman last night. We go get car now."

Quickly, I pack up my things and carry them down to Bishbataar's car.

"Everybody say not go today," says Bishbataar. "It Tuesday."

"I like leaving on Tuesday," I tell him, "It's near the beginning of the week, but you still have one day to take care of last minute buying."

"But in Mongolia, it's impossible," says Bishbataar. "It bad luck."

"We'll see," I say. "We'll see."

Then we're off to the parking lot where THE CAR waits for us.

At first, all I can see is that it's a big old Russian car, possibly used by *Chinggis Khan* himself to help conquer the Chinese. It's white, heavy, with a scratched side and a large crack across the windshield.

The cop and the garage keeper meet us at the lot. The cop is a big guy wearing civilian clothes. He's got a square face and a chest like a weight lifter. He and Bishbataar talk.

"Mykel," says, Bishbataar, "I go now. I put my car in garage. You wait here. I back soon."

He takes off. The two Mongols look at me and then look at the car. They smile.

The cop opens the trunk. He fumbles inside for something. As he fumbles, the trunk lid slams on his head. I quickly grab it and pull it up. He's unfazed.

I hold the lid open while he pulls out a hand pump. I let the trunk close gently. For the next half hour, he and the garage owner try to pump up the half-filled left rear tire. They put the pump on the valve, take it off, remove the valve, blow into it, use saliva to check for escaping air. They let half the air out of the tire trying to fill it. Eventually they succeed in filling it with exactly as much air as it had at the beginning. Grunting their satisfaction, they put the pump back in the trunk. Another half hour passes.

Then Bishbataar returns. He motions for me to come around to the front of the car. We have to push it out of its parking space. I help push it into the driving lane. Then Bishbataar gets in the driver's side. I sit next to him. The cop gets in the back seat.

The starter lock has been ripped out — a sure sign of theft. The car was obviously stolen and hot-wired. To start it, Bishbataar has to touch two dangling wires together and pump the gas pedal. After three or four tries, the engine turns over. We're on our way to the cop's apartment. He's going to bring us a spare battery, "Just in case, though you probably won't need it."

While we drive to his house, I survey the vehicle. If Webster needs a photo to illustrate JALOPY, I'll give him one.

There is a hole in the dashboard where the radio was. Imitation tiger skin seat covers are filthy and bunched up behind the driver and passenger's seat. The speedometer doesn't move. Neither do any of the other gauges: gas, oil, temperature. Everything is broken except the odometer.

A pair of black baby shoes hangs from the heat control knob. By now, the

owner of those shoes is probably stealing cars for himself.

After the cop brings us a replacement battery and bids us farewell, we're off to pick up Sebastian and Al. The two mile trip to Sebastian's apartment is uneventful. There, we pick up some more bags, some food (sugared donut holes, uncooked rice, a few cucumbers, half a dozen links of sausage, and an equal number of apples, already turning brown). Sebastian also has a borrowed 20 liter plastic jug filled with water in case the radiator needs a boost.

Bishbataar struggles with the trunk, finally opens it and we pack up. The wind catches the foam sleeping pad and nearly blows it away. Sebastian lets go of the trunklid to grab it. SLAM! The lid falls on his head. He's more fazed than the cop was.

"Now we get gas and oil," says Bishbataar. "I forgot to say you. Policeman told me we need oil a lot. We buy now. Also, very little petrol in car. I hope we get to station soon."

We're seated in the car. Bishbataar touches the starter wires together. Nothing happens. He does it again. There's a faint sputter, then a cough.

"We need change battery," he says.

Out of the car he gets, rummaging through the trunk to dig out the battery. He switches it for the one under the hood. Then he gets back in the car. Touching the wires, the car sputters and then kicks in. We're off.

First to the gas station. There, we wait for a short time before filling the car and a 20 liter metal can that came with it. Closing the can, the gas spills out through the poorly sealed spout. Bishbataar finds a bit of innertube in the station, removes the knife from his belt and cuts off a piece. By putting this between the spout and its cap, we're able to keep the gas in the can.

Now we have to find oil. That's not easy. The only garage that has AS-40, the oil this car needs, is on the other side of town. Of course, buying oil in Mongolia is not like buying oil other places. You don't ask for two liter cans, pay and put them in your trunk. You've got to give them a can to put the oil in. They pour it out for you, from a big steel drum. Then you pay them and put your can back in your car.

We have with us an empty metal can and an extra plastic jug. Both of these we fill with oil. I start the pay cycle, paying for both the first gas fill-up and the oil. It costs about 10,000 *tugriks* ($20).

Back in the car, Bishbataar tries to head us out of *Ulaanbaatar*. He can't. He's lost. He can't find the road that leads out of the city to the South. When we pass the same spot for the third time, I suggest going to a gas station to ask the best way out. We end up at the station where we first got the gas.

After getting directions, we get back in the car.

"We're off!" says Sebastian.

"Don't speak too soon," I tell him. "At least wait until we pass the city gates."

When we near the airport, we pass the first *ovoo* of the trip. This one is much bigger than the one Yoko and I saw near the monastery. It's about six feet tall. On it are empty vodka bottles with an entire horse head on it — not just the skinless skulls. In the middle is a stick with blue silk tied to the center. A single broken crutch lies on one side.

Mongolian tradition says that if you want good luck, you have to walk three times around an *ovoo*. Each time you walk, you have to take a stone from the bottom and throw it higher. I'm the first one to start the walk.

"No Mykel!" shouts Sebastian, "You're doing it wrong. You're supposed to walk CLOCKWISE, not counter-clockwise."

"Yeah," says Al, "who knows what kind of evil luck you've brought us now."

"And it's Tuesday," says Bishbataar.

The others do their best to reverse the curse. They walk the right way, flinging those stones. After the *ovoo*, we relieve ourselves of some bodily liquids, get back in the car and start the trip for real.

The 'highway' — a two lane road that must've been coated with concrete at one time — lasts for about 30 km. After that, it turns into gravel. Not exactly a gravel road, but parallel gravel-filled ruts.

The population is thinner here. Every quarter hour or so we spot a lone *ger*, or pair of *gers* in the distance. Usually, they're nestled into a niche on the side of a mountain. Even less frequently, we experience the joy of an actual passing vehicle.

I break out the box of prunes and offer them around.

"Mom sent 'em from New York," I explain. "They're filled with vitamins and great for a diet of lamb and noodles."

Everyone takes a few, swallowing them down, spitting the pits into our hands then tossing them out the front window into the desert. For some reason the back windows won't open.

For so few people, there sure are a lot of roads. Jeep tracks, truck ditches, bull-dozed streets and dried riverbeds branch off in all directions, winding into each other and then away. Our experienced driver takes advantage of every passing vehicle to make sure we're going the right way. Once an hour he pulls off the road to ask at a *ger*. He always returns with a smile and the news that we are indeed on the right trail. The way he squints through the dust and takes a random left then a random right is less reassuring.

Early on in any trip, you develop a special language with your co-travelers. Expressions communicate a lot with a few code-like phrases.

One of those phrases came after I related the story of my friend's father who spent several years in jail on a rape charge. While he was in college, his dad and a few of his friends invited a girl to their dormroom for 'a party.' When the girl arrived, she saw there was no one there except the boys.

"Where's the party?" she asked.

"You're the party!" they told her.

And the rest is court record.

"You're the party," became our first motto.

Another phrase develops from an expression I heard from a New York friend. Whenever I'd say anything vaguely double-entendrish, he'd say, "That's what the whore said to the bishop." Once, when Sebastian asks if we expect to take a long time (before reaching the first town), I use this line. He mishears it as "That's what the HORSE said to the bishop." It sticks.

The third key phrase comes when we leave the central *aimag* and enter Dorngobi (middle Gobi). The sun beats down on us. The ground radiates heat.

"It's really hot," says Sebastian.

"Of course it's hot," I shoot back. "We're in the fuckin' desert."

That one sticks too.

Let's go back to that first day. Morning passes quickly and painlessly. We see a herd of gazelle. At first a flash of white tail then the bounding graceful animals, running parallel to and eventually passing our car.

We pass a few more *ovoos*, including one that has a grotesquery of recently dead horse and camel heads on it.

Looking out the window, we see the desert here isn't pure desert. The sand is gravelly. Scrub patches pimple the landscape. Marmots and hamsters scatter at our approaching car.

Just before noon, we pass a group of camels lounging within walking distance of the road. I've never seen so many before. They look tired, bored. They chew their cud lazily, scarcely noticing what's around them.

I ask Bishbataar to stop. We get out and approach them. I stroll boldly in front of the other guys.

"Careful!" says Bishbataar, "they sometimes attack. Especially when they ready for female. They afraid you will steal one. They fight for their female."

Headlines: GOBI TREKKERS KILLED BY STAMPEDE OF ERECT CAMELS!

I take pictures as close as I dare. The camels don't seem to be particularly aroused. Up close I can see they're losing hair worse than I am. Bishbataar says that's only a summer phenomenon. It grows back in the winter so they can make cashmere.

One camel lays in a lump on the ground. Its long neck stretches limply in the scrub. Flies cluster around its eyes.

"It's dead," I say. "Lets cut its head off and throw it on an *ovoo*."

"I don't think so," says Sebastian, "Why don't you get close and see if it chases you?"

Slowly, I approach. It doesn't move.

"See?" I say. "It's dead."

I walk more bravely now...Suddenly the head rises and the back muscles ripple. It turns, raising its nose into the air as if trying to identify my scent. If it can smell permanent horniness, I'm in trouble. I turn and run back to the car.

"Enough camels," I say, "lets get in and get going."

"That's what the horse said to the bishop," says Al.

By early afternoon we're in the town of Erlinge. It's a creepy little place. When we drive through the city gates, the locals stop and glare at us. Dust blows over everything. It's like something out of the Old West, a dying town where only the badguys hang out, waiting for suckers from the East to wander in. For the first time, we roll up the windows and lock the doors when we get out of the car.

There are a handful of gray buildings, many with broken windows. Holes in the plaster expose the inner brick to the wind. The few old propaganda signs in the central square are worn illegible by the desert dust.

Just outside the main gate, we see a bunch of young men. Wearing dirty *deels*, they're sitting or crouching on the ground, passing around a bottle of vodka. A man with a filthy face and narrow piercing eyes spits as we pass.

We need a watercan, some bread, some gas and some water. We hope it won't take long to get them. Bishbataar asks one of the less threatening-looking people, a girl, about ten years old. She says something and points to a shack about twenty yards away.

"That's the store," Bishbataar tells us.

The store is two shelves behind a wooden counter. On one shelf are two kinds of cigarette packs, both Russian. On the other shelf are a couple of bags of rice and a large jar of something brown.

Al buys a pack of "Stewardess" cigarettes and we leave.

At the gas station another crew of young men, unshaven, dirty, sinister-looking, just hangs out. They sit in front of the station on a large piece of pipe.

We pull up to the pump. The crew laughs, showing as many black spaces as teeth. Bishbataar gets out of the car and opens the gas cap. He sticks in the nozzle. Nothing happens. More laughter.

A young man in a *deel* that was once blue points to a fenced area about ten yards from the gas pump. He uses his arm to make a motion like cranking a car.

Sebastian walks over there. It is a crank. He's got to turn it to get the gas flowing.

"Why me?" complains Sebastian.

"You're the party," I answer.

Sebastian cranks. The gas flows. The pump notches up five liters at a time. When it overflows onto the ground I yell.

"Stop crankin'!"

He stops.

The young tough in the blue *deel* asks us for money. He wants *tugrik* for five more liters than the pump shows. Bishbataar asks him about it.

"It was going to jump another five," says the tough, "just before you stopped."

Bishbataar argues and then borrows a canister to check. He asks Sebastian to crank very slowly while we watch the liquid go into the canister. Sure enough, in a few seconds it jumps. We pay what they ask. They keep the canister and don't look very happy.

Somehow Bishbataar finds the town well, not too far from the gas station. A round gray brick structure, there are mostly children around it, collecting water in huge cans. We go to fill our empty water bottles, including the one with the Daffy Duck stopper. Another one, for some reason, has about three finger-widths of vodka in it. Right now, water is more important.

"Anyone want to drink this?" I ask. "We need the bottle for water."

No one wants it.

"Should I dump it?" I ask.

"No!" shouts Bishbataar, as if I'd ask him to remove one of his testicles, "It's impossible. It's not water. It's vodka."

"Well then," I propose, "maybe we should give it to the kids."

"No!" repeats our driver. "Those are our future. We can't drunk our future."

"Do you want to drink it?" I ask.

"I driver," he says.

"Then I guess I'm going to have to dump it out," I say.

"You can't! It's impossible!" shouts Bishbataar. "It's vodka! You understand. Vodka!"

Exasperated, I throw the bottle to Bishbataar. "You take it! You decide!" I shout at him in the first of many hissy fits.

He catches it and offers it to a young woman who just arrived at the well. She declines the offer. Then looking over his shoulder, he opens the bottle and throws the contents into the air, covering Sebastian and I who are both standing close.

"Let the Gods enjoy it," he says.

Neither the wet, vodka-smelling Sebastian or I feel much like Gods at that point, but we have our empty bottle.

Back on the road it's smooth sailing for the next fifty kilometers or so. We stop for dinner at a 'Guansa.' Actually, it's a wooden wagon and a *ger*. Tied to the front of the wagon is a lone sheep pulling at the rope.

"I guess you're the party," I say to it as we walk in.

Inside there are a few more people, including a very fat old driver with a large birthmark right at the tip of his nose. Bishbataar talks with him.

"He will drive to South Gobi tonight," he tells us. "It better to drive in the dark. It cooler."

It never occurs to us that he won't be able to see where he's going in the dark. It's not like he can follow the streetlights. He's Mongolian and that's enough.

We're treated to a meal of milk tea, noodles, very fresh mutton and mutton fat. There's also some garlic, onions and a pleasantly sour green sauce.

"It comes from China," is all we can find out about it.

Tiny grains of sand mix with everything. We get used to it. After awhile we like it.

The dinner cost us a dollar a piece. Our host, a thin middle-aged man, is intrigued by us. Bishbataar explains. We can tell he's playing ole' hand Mongol to our naive tourism. We just smile, nod, and lust after the barefoot teenager fetching water from outside and stoking the fire.

Fortunately, it doesn't get dark until eleven. We're done with dinner by six, so we keep going. Bishbataar's map says there's a lake somewhere close. We plan to camp there for the night.

After a few hours of driving, asking directions, driving some more and asking more directions, we arrive at a compound. A wooden fence surrounds about a dozen *gers*. Besides the *gers*, a couple of wooden structures — a shed and an outhouse — are also inside. We pull up to the fence. An old man comes out to greet us. Bishbataar talks with him and reports back.

"The man says me the lake twelve kilometers away," Bishbataar says. "We can TRY drive part way. But there is sand."

"Of course there's sand," I say, "we're in the fuckin' desert!"

"I love this car," says Sebastian. "It's built like a tank."

"We'll make it," Al says, "just ask the guy directions. I have a good feeling about this."

Bishbataar speaks with him. The man points toward a flat area with a few trees around it. He shakes his head as he speaks. In a few minutes we're off. In a few more minutes, we're stuck in the sand.

The wheels spin. Sand flies. The car sinks lower in the same spot, as if digging its own grave. The engine smells like melting wire. The radiator percolates. The pistons cough. We look around for some wood or something to put under the tires. There's only sand.

We get out and push. From the front. From the back. We rock the car. Take out the trunk luggage. Put it back in. Nothing works. The sun heads downward toward the horizon. I don't want to die.

"Lets jack up the car," I suggest. "That way, when we push it, we can give it a jump."

"Lets put something under it after we jack it up," suggests Al.

"Your foam mattress!" says Sebastian. "And the tent material."

Bishbataar jacks up the car and we unpack the trunk again, looking for the right stuff. We slide it under the wheels and set the car down on it. Then we move to the front.

Bishbataar sets the gear to reverse. He touches the wires together to start the car. We push. BLAM! It skids backwards...into another sandpit.

We know what to do this time. We again jack it up and again free ourselves. This time we're on real dirt — clay. We're proud of our team effort and success. We also figure that's enough fear for this trip.

"OK," says Bishbataar. "Let's go to the lake."

"Fuck the lake!" says Sebastian. "I've had enough." Al and I agree.

We sheepishly limp back to the old man who laughs when he sees us.

"How was the lake?" he asks.

Wiseguy.

Anyway, he lets us set up our tents outside his little compound and feeds us that night. We take a Polaroid and give it to him to say thanks. He tells us there is a well nearby.

◎ ◎ ◎

The next morning, buoyed by news of the coming water, Sebastian and Al use most of what we have left to wash their hands and shampoo themselves. Me? I've never been a cleanliness fan. I'd rather drink it than wash in it. Still, I do my hands.

We thank the old man. The car sputters as Bishbataar tries to start it. It eventually turns over and we head for the well.

Strangely, there are no animals or people around this well. It's just a brick hole in the ground with a piece of scrap metal over it. We take off the metal and Bishbataar pulls up the bucket. Sebastian puts his hands in the water and brings it to his mouth. He spits.

"It's awful!" he says. "Smell this."

We don't have to. At the bottom of the bucket we can see a dead lizard. It's intestines spiral out, floating languidly away from its belly. Looking down the well, floating under the surface of the water, we can see several other decomposing critters.

So, we're headed out into the Gobi Desert with only five liters of drinking water, the car gradually getting worse, the day gradually getting hotter.

After a half hour of driving the radiator boils over. We get out, letting the car cool as much as is possible in the middle of the Gobi. Munching our sugar coated peanuts, we stroll over the sand looking at the scenery. There are a few mountains in the distance. That's it. Up close there is sand and scrub. Up closer it's teaming with life. Insect life. Spiders. Dung beetles (despite the lack of dung). Ants everywhere. Little brown ones, red ones, big black ones. Crawling from hole to hole. Lugging chunks of green and brown twice their sizes. All over. Not an inch uncovered.

Three of the four of us set a place amongst the ants. Sebastian, his cold-sore grown to immense proportions, goes off to attend to his personal needs. He's in somewhat of a bad mood due to my constant teasing.

"I don't 'ave 'erpes!" He whines. "It's a spot. Just a spot on my lip!"

"Maybe you don't 'ave 'erpes," I say, "but you HAve HERpes. That's what a cold sore is!"

"It's not 'erpes!" he shouts. "It's a cold sore. My mum gets 'em!"

Grabbing the roll of toilet paper from the car, Sebastian turns toward the nearest ridge. It's not very near.

"Be careful!" warns Bishbataar. "There is a desert thing that hides in bushes," he says. "It's like a this...." He points to a dung beetle, digging into the sand.

"You mean an insect?" says Al.

Bishbataar nods.

"It is very big though. And has spiky hands that grab. Even if you kill it, it never let go."

He digs his fingers into Sebastian's thigh.

"If it get you, they have to cut it out. Chop! Chop!" he says. "One time, this guy was taking a shit. This insect come and get him. Right here!"

He moves his hand between Sebastian's legs. I've never seen a big guy jump so quickly.

"They had to cut it off. Yep, chop chop!" says Bishbataar.

Sebastian decides to hold it in.

By this time the car has cooled enough to allow us to drive. We get back in. Sebastian takes the box of prunes and hides it under the seat.

Roads still branch in all directions. I figure we're going south, though. That's the most important thing. I can tell because it's morning. That means the sun's in the east. That puts it over Avenue A. I'm looking down Broadway. The Village is to my right, that's west. Behind me is Tower Records — north. We're headed to the Staten Island Ferry. Like I said, south.

It's about 11 o'clock and warming up considerably. Bishbataar asks me to hold the wheel and steer while he takes off his outer shirt. I hold it with my left hand while I scratch the back of my neck with my right. There is a bump there, like a small scab. As I scratch, it moves.

I lose control of the wheel, but there's nothing to hit and no road to go off of. Bishbataar grabs it back, letting me examine what's under my fingernail. A gray tick, legs wiggling in the air. I throw it out the car window, shaken a bit.

"I just found a tick in my hair," I report to the crew. "I don't think it got me, because it just came off into my hands. I didn't have to pry it loose...Still, it's scary."

"Usually they're not dangerous," says Al, reassuringly. "It's only a rare occasion, like this girl I know who got encephalitis."

"Yeah, thanks," I say. "That's a morale booster."

The next few minutes pass in silence. Then Al speaks again.

"Did the tick look like this?" he asks, showing me a gray bug exactly like the one I picked from my neck.

"Yep," I say.

"I got it out of my neck." he says.

"Well, it probably isn't dangerous," I tell him. "Ticks can bring Lyme disease — but those are only deer ticks. We don't have to worry about that."

Then we pass the deer.

"Just the disease I need," I say.

"That's what the horse said to the Bishop," says Sebastian. Actually, he doesn't say this completely, but instead stops after the word 'horse.' No need to go on. We all know it.

Fears of Lyme disease dig in the back of our minds like the ticks dug in the back of our necks. It's our main concern as the texture of the "road" changes from hard dusty gravel to rock. Bishbataar decides to speed up. Sebastian, Al and I are flung up and down over and under throughout the inside of the car.

"Slow down!" yells Sebastian.

"That's what the ho..." starts Al.

Before he can finish the syllable, a rock slams from the front wheel to the underside of the car. The poltergeist enters. The steering wheel wrenches in Bishbataar's hands. He pulls left. It pulls right. It spins completely around, nearly throwing the car over on its side.

Bishbataar stops.

We get out, our bowels loosened by the near spill, yet all of us more afraid of the giant grabbing beetle.

Bishbataar looks under the car. He makes a clucking noise with his tongue.

"Looks like we're the pear tree," he says.

"That's PARTY! Not pear tree," I tell him. "What's wrong?"

"Look!" says Bishbataar.

The three of us drop to the ground and look under the car. Not that we know what we're looking for, but we can see there's a piece with a bolt hanging loose under one wheel. About eight inches above is the piece that bolt should be stuck into.

Bishbataar slides under the car and tries to pry up the drooping piece. It won't budge. Sebastian gets under there with him. The dual strength gets them as far as the single strength. Nowhere.

The midday sun beats down on us. Sebastian wipes his brow.

"Of course it's hot..." I start.

A fierce glance from him shuts me up.

There is nothing for miles. Only flat rocky desert. No *gers*, no vehicles, no animals other than ants. Horizon-to-horizon. Nothing. I don't want to die.

"I don't want to die," I say.

"Stop that!" says Al. "Let's think."

"Why don't we jack up the car?" I say, offering my universal solution to any automotive problem.

"Wait a minute, that could work!" replies Al. "Get some rocks."

So Bishbataar jacks up the car while the rest of us get some stones. We lay them under the piece with the bolt on it and slowly lower the car. Jeezus fuckin' Christ...it works.

The little pile of stones forces the bolt up until it meets the boltee.

"We did it!" shouts Sebastian. "Now all we have to do is hammer it in."

"We haven't no hammer," says Bishbataar.

He tries smashing the piece with a rock, but it won't go in. While he works, the rest of us, off to the side, play 'hit the brown rock with the gray one.'

Just when we feel the buzzards circling above, we hear a motor. It's the RUMMMM-RUMMMMMMMMMMMM of a motorcycle. Dust rises in the distance. It approaches, carrying a man and his teenage son, both dressed in heavy *deels*.

We wave at them and they stop. Bishbataar talks to them. They listen carefully, both with their arms folded. The man speaks slowly, pointing vaguely to the southeast. Then, the two of them get on the bike and take off.

"They live forty kilometer away," Bishbataar tells us. "They bring hammer."

"They're going to travel forty kilometers, get a hammer, travel another forty and bring it to us, then another forty to take it home again?" I ask. "That's a hundred and twenty kilometers for somebody they don't know!"

"This is Mongolia," he says. "They are Mongolians."

After an hour and a half waiting, I'm ready to throw that 'this is Mongolia' line back in Bishbataar's face, along with the rock in my hand. But Sebastian spots some rising dust in the distance.

"It's them!" he shouts.

"It's the wind," I say.

I'm wrong.

They're back, bringing a hefty hammer and good cheer. Bishbataar climbs back under the car and bangs in that bolt. I take a Polaroid of the motorcycle pair and give it to them as thanks. Bishbataar and the man talk.

"We follow them," says Bishbataar.

We get in the car and do. They head off at right angles to where we are. They're making their own road, travelling at motorcycle speed. Bishbataar does his best to keep up, bouncing over the rock and scrub.

Tiny rock missiles smash against the underside of the ancient car. We can't slow down. We'd be lost in a second. We can only grit our teeth and hold on tight.

We've been led to a well. Deeper than the others, this one needs a pump to raise the water to drinkable level. The pump is a huge metal pipe, bent at a right angle — like an 'L' with the short end stuck in the ground. A boy, about 8 years old, leads a camel tied to the long end of the pipe. Around and around they go, drawing water to the surface.

The well acts as a kind of meeting place, a town square where there is no town. People from all over have come here to discuss life and politics, as well as fetch water. The latest complaint? No rain.

"Of course there's no rain," I say. "It's the fuckin' desert."

Bishbataar does not translate this for the locals.

Most of the people have come by camel or horse. Their steeds now water themselves at the trough. Stories of this ancient Russian car with three Westerners aboard will keep them entertained for months.

There's a rumble of giggles as we walk toward the well with our empty plastic bottles. I've kept the one with the duck on the top as my own private reserve. I don't want Sebastian drinking from it, spreading his 'erpes. Sebastian, by the way, is off behind a hill taking care of what the beetle monster previously scared back into him.

The giggles turn to laughter when he returns and we make him turn the crank where the camel was.

"Why me?" asks Sebastian.

"You're the..." I don't have to finish.

Through Bishbataar, I ask one of the herdsmen if I can ride his camel. Not ride it exactly, but just get on it. Enough for a picture. The herdsman nods and dismounts. In order to do so, he commands the camel to kneel — first on the foreknees then on the hind. He slips off. I slip on — between the humps. Conveniently, Mongolian camels are two humped rather than one.

Bong! Up go the rear legs. I hold on to the furry front hump to prevent myself from being pitched forward over it's head. Bang! Up go the front legs, tilting me back like an amusement park pirate ship ride. Howls of laughter rise like I do, into the desert sky.

The herdsman leads me around in a little circle. I tip to the right, then the left with each step. Al takes a picture.

"Enough," I say.

I've forgotten, that to get off this thing, I again have to go through the pitch forward and back routine. Before my feet hit the sand, I'm seasick.

After me, Al, Sebastian and even Bishbataar take turns on the beast. Each of us has the same reaction. By the time we're all done, tears of hilarity stream down the eyes of the local herdsmen — and their kids.

After the show, we take Polaroids for the herders, get back in the car and head back to the "road." It takes us much longer to find it than it took to get away from it. Eventually, however, we're on that dirt track, ready to continue our journey.

We bounce along for forty or fifty kilometers. Sebastian shouts, "Slow down Bishbataar."

Bishbataar tells us he can't slow down because the engine needs the fast-moving air to cool itself.

"That's why Mongolians drive fast," he explains. "It saves the engine."

We've just taken a Dukes of Hazard-type leap over an open pit. When we land, the rear of the car crashes against the gravel. There's a scrape of metal. Suddenly, the car sounds like the motorcycle.

Bishbataar stops and gets out. He looks under the car, clicks his tongue and walks back along the trail. He picks something up and returns with it. It's the muffler and end of the tailpipe. Non-chalantly, he opens the trunk and drops them on top of our luggage. This would be only the first of many car pieces to fall onto the "road" and be stored in the trunk.

That night we stop at a *ger* to ask if we can camp nearby. As we pull up, Bishbataar shouts something like "Lord Haw Haw a railroad," (call off your dog), a necessary phrase when approaching any country *ger*.

An old woman, frail, on a cane, comes out to speak with us. Nearly blind, she squints at Bishbataar as he hints about dinner. She doesn't look too happy.

"She says we can stay here," says Bishbataar, "but I think we should go."

We say good bye and drive for an hour. We stop at another lone *ger*. This one is extremely welcoming. We have some delicious yogurt before the noodles and mutton dinner. Everything is served by a beautifully flirty 14 year old. The whole family is there, but none of us notice anyone else. The girl has a small mole on the upper right eyelid, a narrow face, skin slightly lighter than the Gobi sand. She smiles continually at us and follows us around, completely silent. Since no one in the family speaks a word of English, we're free to say what we want, as long as we maintain the proper facial expressions.

"She wants me," says Sebastian, while we're drinking tea.

"Fat chance," I say, smiling pleasantly at the hostess. "We're gonna have to tie her to the back of the car and drag her along behind."

Al bursts into giggles, spraying the half-drunk tea out his nose. Sebastian and I look at him like he's gone insane.

I turn to the girl, shrug, and touch my finger to my temple. She smiles in an understanding way.

After dinner, we set up the tents. I have a slight nauseous feeling and a headache. Maybe it's the tick bite.

Inside the tent, Bishbataar says he's worried about the oil. We brought an extra five liters to take care of the car's dripping engine, but he says it wasn't enough. In the last town, we bought more.

"We shouldn't mix that oil with the city oil," Bishbataar tells us.

"We need AS20 oil," I say. "Didn't you buy AS20 oil?"

"Yes," says Bishbataar, "but city AS20 oil is different from countryside AS20 oil. No good to mix."

After nearly a year in Mongolia, statements like that make perfect sense. I don't ask further.

It's getting late and the car is acting up. We can rarely go more than 10 kilometers without having to stop and let the engine cool. Our dipstick says the city AS20 is down to less than half. The slightest incline is the Alps for the car.

It gets later and our goal of THREE NICE MOUNTAINS seems as far as it was when we started.

"Look!" says Bishbataar, pointing to the distance.

There is something mountainish ahead: the vague outline of a large shape.

At 10:30 the sun is down to the horizon. The tall silhouette looks exactly the same.

We pass a crippled jeep. The green vehicle is off the road, the hood opened, steam pouring out. A Mongolian wearing a dirty blue *deel* waves frantically to us.

"Let's stop and help him," I say. "People always help us."

"Not in this car," says Bishbataar. "We can't take more people. Only us. Other people too heavy."

I feel bad about abandoning this man in need, but Bishbataar might be right.

The car's bottom is awfully close to desert floor.

"No worry," says Bishbataar, quickly forgetting the sad scene, "we get to tourist camp. We stay there. Cheap. Usually $80 a night, for each. Now not the season. I get it cheap. No worry."

By this time, that's-what-the-horse-said-to-the-bishop has become a simple 'B-B-B-B-B' bilabial horse sound. Sebastian makes it.

It's coming on midnight. Our faint headlights barely illumine the barely-a-road ahead of us. As we approach the mountains we peer into the darkness, trying to imagine how a "Gobi tourist camp" might look. I search for the gate with the "Arbeit Macht Frei" sign.

"Look!" says Bishbataar, pointing somewhere ahead.

Al, Sebastian and I look in that direction. We see black.

Bishbataar turns the car off the trail and heads into the nothingness. A shiver of uncertainty passes through the rest of us.

There's the camp. Right there. A bunch of very clean *gers* behind a cyclone fence. It's closed. Locked tight.

"What now?" I ask, realizing that if I commit murder, there will be no one to get us back.

"Another camp," says Bishbataar.

"It'll be closed," says Sebastian.

"I'm going to sleep," says Al. "Wake me when we don't get there."

"It open." says Bishbataar.

"Look," says I, "if it's not open, we're not paying you a cent...a *tugrik*. Get it?"

"It open. It open." says Bishbataar.

We get back in the car. Bishbataar again drives. Into the darkness. No roads. No signs. No nothing. And we get to THE OTHER TOURIST CAMP. It's open.

A young man in a safari shirt and khaki pants meets us. Bishbataar and he discuss our accommodations. Eventually they shake hands.

"The manager wants $80 a night from each" Bishbataar tells us, "I make deal. Twenty dollars a night for two nights. It including meals. We must pay for drink."

It turns out that we must also pay for Bishbataar.

The manager leads us through the rows of bright white *gers*. Most are padlocked shut. He unlocks one with three beds in it. He then says something to Bishbataar, shakes hands with all of us and leaves.

"There warm showers in morning," Bishbataar tells us. "We still have dinner tonight."

A Japanese tour group and a few Germans are the only other people in the camp. We unpack in the *ger*. Al empties a few Stewardess cigarettes and refills them with Bayatov Gold, lighting up. Soon after, we're more than ready for dinner.

On the way to the restaurant, Bishbataar says, "Please don't ask anything to the Japanese. I turn red. The pretty girl. She often in Mongolia. Last year, I fucky fucky with her."

"So what's wrong with that?" I say. "Maybe you can fucky fucky again?"

"It difficult," he says. "The Mongolian tourguide. She from *Zhuulchin*. I used to work there. I fucky fucky with her. Now they together. It difficult."

"I wish I had your problems," I tell him. "You get around."

"Oh," he says, "I have all tourguides. If they work for *Zhuulchin*, they must go through me."

This is Mongolia. I don't question him further.

The meal is decent, if sparse. There are real vegetables: carrots, cucumbers, cabbage. All those colored things that grow in places far from the Gobi.

After the meal we relax with a couple of beers. We buy one for Bishbataar. When he finishes, he orders himself another.

"You're going to have to pay for that one," I tell him.

"I forget," he says, "You American. You European. Mongolians and Russians, we special people. We don't think about money. We have friends. 'Come come' we say. We don't care about money. Americans/Europeans always think about money. 'Just drink' we say. But we Mongolians and Russians."

"We bought you a drink," says Sebastian. "We're not rich."

"Of course you're rich." says Bishbataar. "You American. You European."

I know what's coming next. I'm right.

"I only a poor Mongolian," continues Bishbataar. "I so low. You American. You English. You so high."

If he bows to us, I'll punch him.

"Wake me when this is over," says Al.

"You special kind of tourist," continues Bishbataar. "You like to do things cheap. But you still tourist."

All three of us jump. He's touched a raw nerve. We rush to defend ourselves. We talk about how we're not tourists, but residents. We talk about how we travel, we don't tour.

"You're tourists who learn to do it cheap," he says. "You no like hotels and you no like pay a lot of money. You work here, but you leave. You can't be part. You see things like tourists. You look and then you leave."

The more we talk, the more we realize the truth in what Bishbataar says. It hurts. We think of ourselves as adventure-seekers. We take risks, go places others don't. But we're not part of this. We come to see, to experience, to take pictures, to leave. He's right. It's depressing.

Back at the *ger*, we empty the tobacco from more Stewardess cigarettes, filling them with more Bayatov Gold. Bishbataar says he's going out to 'see the girls.'

"Bring 'em back here," I suggest.

"Sure," he says, "let me take one of these to invite them with."

He picks up a Bayatov Gold Stewardess.

"Anything that'll help," says Sebastian.

"B-B-B-B-B-B," says Al.

An hour passes. Sebastian and Al sit at the doorway in front of the *ger*. They gaze into the star-filled sky, convinced they've seen a UFO, wondering what they should take if they're abducted.

Me, I want my Stewardess worth. I go looking for Bishbataar. He's outside the restaurant, talking to both the Japanese girl and the tourguide. I sit down next to him.

"These are my friends, Kyoko and Gantseseg," he says.

"Hajimemashite," I answer. (How do you do? — in Japanese.)

"Nihingo hanashimasuka?" asks Kyoto. (You speak Japanese?)

I nod. "Ninen Nihon-ni sunde imashita." (I lived in Japan for two years.)

"Sugoi!" (Great, terrible, awesome, awful.)

Bishbataar is getting nervous. He shifts in his seat. He tries out his Japanese. Then he says, "I speak lots of languages."

He starts in Mongolian. The girls laugh. (Evidently, the Japanese girl can speak some Mongolian.) Then he speaks some German. I answer him in German. He speaks some Russian. I manage to say in Russian, "I don't speak Russian." I pull out the Danish. He starts in French. I answer his French and raise him a Spanish. He sees my Spanish and raises me a Polish. I see his Polish and call him in Japanese.

"Nihongo joozu taberu," I say. ("I eat good Japanese.")

Their laughter almost loses it for me, but Bishbataar comes back with: "Kareno nihongo warui, ne? Demo watashi-wa kirei nihonjinno onanoko desuyo?" (His Japanese is bad, right? I'm a pretty Japanese girl, aren't I?) He means to say YOU'RE a pretty Japanese girl. His gaff gets a bigger laugh than my mistake. But that doesn't mean I score.

In fact, the girls quickly tire of our polyglottal one-upmanship and go off to bed. Bishbataar and I return to the *ger*. Al is still outside keeping track of the UFO, while Sebastian packs for the space trip.

"Do you think they'll like my R.E.M. t-shirt?" he asks.

Later that night, while floating to sleep on a Bayatov cloud, we talk about sex.

"How long is longest you ever go without woman?" asks Bishbataar.

Each of us gives a double digit number of months.

"Months?" says Bishbataar. "How you do that?"

I make a sign over my crotch, like I'm trying to get stubborn ketchup out of the bottle.

"You do that?" he says. "You mastrabute?"

"It's masturbate." corrects Sebastian. "You mean Mongolians don't masturbate?"

"No, never. It's impossible," says Bishbataar. "It's the communists. They teach us to be clean. We all clean. We don't mastrabute. We don't homosex. We only girls."

"What do you do when you feel the need?" I ask.

"I go through my book of numbers and call one up and ask to come over," he says.

"You got that book with you?" I ask. He doesn't.

After more stories about first times, and what it's really like to masturbate and homosex, we get to sleep.

◎ ◎ ◎

Just after sunrise, it's shower time. The other guys seem excited about this prospect. I'm dubious. Showers are not a major thrill in my life. I don't mind a little grit in my pores. I also don't believe there could possibly be hot water. This is Mongolia.

Reluctantly, I follow the crowd to the shower room. Again, I think of the ARBEIT MACHT FREI sign over another camp with showers. The stalls are open in the front with tile walls between. We strip, making glancing comparisons as boys in a shower are wont to do. I lose.

I also lose because THERE'S NO HOT WATER!

It's time for hissy fit #2!

"I told you there'd be no hot water," I say, stamping my foot in a shallow puddle. "I'm not gonna torture myself for a little sand. This is stupid."

I quickly dress and stomp out. Then I go to the *ger* and sulk. One by one the others return. Big smiles on their faces, sighs of pleasure, moans of delight, words about how wonderful it is to be clean.

"Fuck you," I answer with all my creativity.

After they carefully comb their wet hair and admire their newly hygienic complexions, we go to breakfast.

◎　◎　◎

After breakfast we're going to VULTURE'S MOUTH, a weird geological formation somewhere deep inside of one of the THREE NICE MOUNTAINS.

Bishbataar has found a "guide" for us, an old man with a single tooth in either jaw. His skin is as craggy and weather-beaten as the landscape. We're a bit worried about his extra weight in the car, but Bishbataar isn't concerned.

The car gets us to the base of the mountain. There's a museum there and a little souvenir shop. I buy some insect stamps for my nephew Kirk and some bird stamps for my pal David. I want a *Chinggis Khan* snowglobe. The man who runs the place doesn't quite get what I'm talking about.

VULTURE'S MOUTH is up in the mountain. Bishbataar assures us that our car wouldn't make it past the first bend. It's twenty kilometers through the desert, so we can't walk. He asks the souvenir man if he'll drive us.

"He wants 3000 *tugriks*," says Bishbataar.

"Will he wait for us?" Al asks. "We may want to spend some time there."

"He wait," says Bishbataar.

"If we had a jeep like you promised, we wouldn't have to pay this," says Sebastian.

"He'd just better wait until we're ready," I say.

Al doesn't want to get involved.

The half hour ride whizzes through a treacherous jeep track, past rare mountain goats, wild cows, marmots and little hamster-like animals none of us have seen before. Steep rocky mountains slope sharply to grassy hills. We're silent, just gawking through the windows as rocks, trees and running animals shoot across our sight. Suddenly, in the middle of nowhere, there's a small patch of dirt with a 'P' sign stuck in it. It's a parking lot.

"This a national park," says Bishbataar, "foreigners pay 1000 *tugriks*, but he talk for you."

The driver gets out of the car. He negotiates with a man on horseback. With him are two boys, about eight and ten years old. They agree to let us in for a Polaroid pic of the kids. We get out of the car and 'the guide' leads us into the valley.

As we walk, the scenery increases both in beauty and bizarreness. Like a Bride of Frankenstein hairdo, light rock formations zig zag down the side of dark mountains. Green hills fold into one another. A stream pops out of nowhere and disappears just as quickly.

I'm carrying a bag with three liters of water and the Polaroid. Bishbataar has a backpack with some food in it. We pass an open space and Bishbataar says, "Leave things here. It too much to carry." He leaves the pack. I leave the bag. It's not like a mountain goat is going to come around and steal them, is it?

The guide isn't guiding very much as we walk along the valley floor. There's no other place to go. Bishbataar, Al and he walk ahead. Sebastian and I take it slower, savoring the landscape. After a particularly twisty path, we come to the ice.

I still don't understand it. It must be something about the mountains providing continuous shade. But the river has a thick layer of ice over it. Here, in the desert, ice three feet thick. The ice thickens as the river deepens. Now we walk on a near glacier. Giant crevasses drop to the fast running river beneath. It's risky, walking here. Sebastian slips. I slip.

A huge ice crack, at least four feet wide, blocks our way. We've got to jump. From ice to ice. One slip, one false move, and this book doesn't get written. Sebastian jumps. His foot just catches the other side. He falls forward onto the ice. I get as close as possible to the crack. I look down the ten foot drop to the river beneath. I take a deep breath. I jump. Suspended for a second over the opening, I land upright on the other side.

We walk further, past a little grass ledge where cows graze lazily. Here, moving water has carved it's way into the ice. It's a river in the ice over a river. The water is ice cold. The cleanest water in the world. It tastes...it's impossible to describe. Nothing else will ever be 'water' for me.

Eventually Sebastian and I meet up with the others. They've stopped under a ledge as a cloud passes over. It doesn't pass. It stops. There's a downpour. Rain in enormous drops. Then hail, pea-sized iceballs pounding down on the ice in front of us. We push back against the rock, trying to protect ourselves.

"It never does this...what you call it?" says Bishbataar.

"Hail," I answer, "and it's doing it now."

"It's impossible," he says.

The impossible stops after about 15 minutes.

"We go back now," says Bishbataar. "We see ice. We go back."

"I wanna go on," I say. "The driver said he'd wait. Let him wait!"

"He already wait," says Bishbataar.

"Look," says Sebastian, "you go back. Tell him to wait an hour. If we're not back by then, he can go and we'll walk."

"Twenty kilometers through the desert?" I say.

"We'll be back," says Sebastian.

I look at Al.

"Whatever," he says.

Bishbataar and "the guide" discuss this. They agree to go back and ask the driver to wait. Al, Sebastian and I walk onwards. We soon come to the end of the ice. Here the valley narrows a bit. The rocky walls go straight up from the ground. They're dotted with ominous-looking caves.

"They have mountain lions here, don't they?" I ask.

"Sure," says Al, "they're a protected species."

"Are we?" I ask.

Almost in answer, we turn a bend and find a pile of bones in the valley. It was once some sort of animal. But it didn't look like this. A skull here, legbones scattered among ribs. Teeth marks fresh in the whiteness. Marrow sucked out. Everything picked clean. It was a big animal, maybe a cow. We'd only been walking fifteen minutes since we left the others, but I suggest we turn around and go back. Sebastian agrees. Al shrugs.

So back we go, nearly running to make sure we're there before the jeep leaves. We slip and fall. We jump over the ice pit. We're in too much of a hurry to consider our possible demise.

"Don't worry," says Sebastian, looking at his watch. "We've got plenty of time."

Slipping and sliding, letting the cold beauty pass us by with barely a notice, we trudge onwards. We pass the place where I'd left the water and camera. Both are gone, presumably retrieved by Bishbataar and "the guide."

Sebastian and Al, both much bigger than I, take larger steps. Before long, they've left me behind. I run up to them. Catch up, slacken to their pace, and am soon left far behind again. We join up just before the parking lot. When we get to it, the jeep is gone.

At least Bishbataar left us a few liters of water for our desert trek — like hell he did. Nothing. Not a drop.

We're stranded, facing a twenty kilometer walk through the desert, with no water, in the middle of the day. I don't want to die.

We head back to the valley to drink our fill of river water before starting the trek.

"Just wait till someone complains to me," I say. "'You think YOU have it rough,' I'll say, 'I walked thirty kilometers through the Gobi Desert with no water.' That'll shut 'em up."

"It's not thirty kilometers," says Sebastian. "It's twenty kilometers."

So we walk. And walk. The sun beats down on us.

"Hot, isn't it?" says Al.

"Of course it's hot..." I begin — and stop. I'm talking to no one.

Again, I can't keep pace with the British giants. Again, they ignore me plunging on ahead, leaving me straggler's bait for the local wolves and mountain lions. I am not happy.

About a half hour later, they realize there are no longer three of us. They wait for me to catch up. I'm furious. "Why don't you two just go on ahead and have my dinner waiting?" I yell at them. "Just tell 'em to make a feast, I'll be along any day...Unless I'm the dinner!"

They find humor in the situation. I don't.

"Look," I tell 'em, "you gotta back me up on this one. Don't wimp out. When we get back, we really give it to Bishbataar for leaving us."

"You bet," says Sebastian. "Whatever you say, we'll back you up. I can throw a pretty good fit myself."

"You in this?" I ask Al.

"Sure," he says, "you just set the stage, and I'll follow your cue. It was shitty of him to leave us like that."

Onwards we trudge. Across the forty kilometers of desert sand. Back to the museum, worn, dirty, thirsty.

We get to the car parked on a hill top. It's locked. Bishbataar is nowhere in sight. Sebastian goes to investigate. He asks at a *ger* at the bottom of the hill. Al and I wait on top. Before too long, Bishbataar appears from around the *ger*. He waves his arm in a "come on down" motion.

I wave my arms in a "Fuck you!" motion. "You come on up," I yell.

He disappears into the *ger*. In a few seconds, Sebastian comes out.

"Come on down," shouts Sebastian. "There's food here."

"I just want the fuckin' car keys!" I yell back. "I don't want to make nice to that asshole."

"That's telling him," says Al raising to his feet. He heads down the hill. I wait, stewing in my anger, but also incredibly thirsty and unable to get to the water inside the car. Thirst eventually wins out.

I stomp down to the *ger*. Looking in the door, I see Bishbataar, Al and Sebastian sitting with a local family, chowing down on mutton and noodles, sipping milk tea, friendly as neighbors. I'm not.

I stand outside the *ger* and shout at Bishbataar, "Give me the car keys!"

Bishbataar walks over to me. He wants to discuss it.

"I just want the car keys," I say — not shouting — but obviously angry.

"You act like woman," he says. "Why you act like woman?"

"You're offending these people," says Sebastian from inside, slurping down his noodles.

"Why you angry?" says Bishbataar. "You like woman."

I turn around and head up the hill — with no keys. Bishbataar chases me, giving me the keys, then walks back to the *ger* shaking his head.

"Just like woman," he mumbles.

I return to the car, drink a liter of water, eat the few crusts of bread left there, and brood.

"Thanks for backing me up," I say, when the others return patting their stomachs.

"You missed a really good meal," says Al.

I don't hit him.

We're back in our car, "the guide" in front with Bishbataar, the three of us squeezed in the back. We head away from the mountain over the flat, featureless terrain between there and the *ger* camp.

It's only five o'clock in the afternoon, but for some reason it looks very dark ahead. When we reach the darkness, we learn why. It's a blinding sandstorm and we're right in the middle of it.

It's as if a curtain swooped in and surrounded the car. We can't see anything. Sand blasts from all sides, coming through every crack. The wind howls as it pushes the car, rocking it like a ship in a typhoon.

The road is gone. We're on pure desert now. The "guide" peers through the window and points left. Bishbataar turns in that direction. A few seconds later, the "guide" points right. Bishbataar turns. Into the wind. Sand blowing into the car's grill. Into the car. Into our eyes, our throats. We cough. We gag.

The guide peers into the brown air. A vague outline is slightly visible through the pounding sand. It's the mountains, the one's we were driving AWAY from. They're approaching again. We've gone in a circle. Still no road, no idea how to get back.

Both Bishbataar and the guide hunch over the dashboard, squinting into the storm. The sand sounds like hundreds of BBs smashing against the side of the car. We feel it in our teeth as we grit them against the wind.

The guide points left. Bishbataar turns. He drives as straight as he can against the wind. The guide points right. Bishbataar turns. If I weren't so scared, I'd grab them by the throat — the both of them. Al, Sebastian and I cover our faces with handkerchiefs and press against the windows.

"There!" shouts Al, pointing to the left.

The guide points left. Bishbataar turns. We see the gate of the camp, an indistinct outline behind the sand-filled air. The car chugs along the desert, fighting the wind and sand until it reaches the camp gate. We seem to make it through the storm, because it's quiet here, although the air is still sinisterly brown.

At the camp we all get out.

"We must take care of the guide," says Bishbataar.

"I forgot my Smith and Wesson," I tell him.

He doesn't get it.

"He not want Polaroid," says Bishbataar. "Just give cigarettes."

This one isn't my problem. Al's the tobacco smoker. The cheap Stewardesses are gone — up in smoke with the Bayatov gold. He's only got his expensive Marlboros left. He gives them up. Somehow, I find that satisfying.

◎ ◎ ◎

We plan to leave the camp the next day. Bishbataar says he's found someone to take a look at the car and get it ready for the long trip back. He disappears with it. Sebastian, Al and I are left alone for awhile. The Japanese tourists, who were supposed to have flown to *Ulaanbaatar* today, are back.

"We can't leave," they tell us. "The weather in *Ulaanbaatar* is too bad. The cloud-seeding, a government project to help put out the fires, caused floods. *Ulaanbaatar* is under water. There was hail. Many people died."

There's more. "They also have gas rationing. You can't buy much. You can only get a few liters at a time."

We barely have enough gas to make it to the next town. And then there isn't a town for more than a hundred kilometers. A tourbus driver was supposed to pick up gas at the airport for us. They wouldn't sell it to him.

After a rather sparse dinner, I leave the others to take a walk. There are a few *gers* within walking distance of the camp. I go visit on my own. I figure I can make it without Bishbataar, on just my foreigner novelty value. As has been my ability throughout my life as a traveler, I manage to arrive at the *ger* just as supper is ready.

"Lord Haw Haw, a railroad!" I yell.

There is no dog. Instead a chubby Mongol, wearing a mustache and a burgundy *deel*, invites me to join him inside. He either has a very large family or he has visitors. About twenty people sit around the central oven. Mostly men, they range in age from an old man sucking on a traditional pipe to a baby sucking on mom's breast.

On the stove/heater/oven is a boiling pot of something. The smell of lamb fills the *ger*, as it does everything else in the country. I am suddenly the guest of honor. One of the younger men gets up from his low stool and gives it to me.

I take out my bottle of snuff (a gift from my students) and offer it to those present. They each take a snort — pleased that an American enjoys the custom.

The chubby man scoops some steaming victuals from the pot into a bowl. I'm the guest of honor, served first. Gingerly, they pass the hot plate to me.

Innards! Stomach, liver, brain, lungs, large and small intestine. All for me. A special treat. Each part looking exactly like what it is.

I smile as best I can when I'm handed this honoris offal. The others in the *ger* are aglow. See how much respect we've got for this foreigner? See how we treat him? Isn't it just heaven visiting a Mongolian?

I take a fork and poke at the various body parts in the bowl. Knowing what's in my own, I avoid the large intestines. The stomach has the texture of African hair and the toughness of a Goodyear tire. I skip that too. I can manage the liver. I only hate liver. It doesn't completely repulse me.

Using the fork to scoop up some of the brown gray organ, I put it as far back as possible on my tongue. Holding back a gag, I swallow and smile. The crowd beams in pride.

Piece by agonizing piece, I get through the liver and two five inch tubes of small intestine. The rest of the people help themselves to the lower status sections of the lamb, like the meat. Altruism glows in their eyes as they watch me eat the best parts.

When I've finished everything but the large intestines, I sit back and rub my stomach. "Full" I say. Hoping they'll understand the sign language.

"Eat! Eat!" says the big Mongol, words that are unfortunately the same in English and Mongolian.

Turning my gag into a cough, I saw into the large intestine. Cutting off about an inch, I press my fork into it and put it in my mouth. It's not as bad as I expect. It's worse. The closest I can metaphor is a garden hose filled with warm dirt.

After the meal I quickly excuse myself. The walk back to the *ger* camp is an internal debate on whether or not to stick my fingers down my throat. I don't.

I manage to crawl into bed, holding my stomach and moaning. Sebastian, Al and Bishbataar think it's hilarious.

"Sounds like you were the party," says Sebastian after I explain what happened.

"If you die," says Al, "We'll just serve you back to them. Tell 'em it's the food for honored guests."

◎ ◎ ◎

Early the next morning, after a divine time over the porcelain heaven, I feel better. We should be off before it gets too late. Who knows how long it'll take us? With the gas rationing, our first stop has to be the nearest city. Then we need to go to a *hiid* so we can pray we have enough gas to get us to the next city.

It's 9AM, Sebastian, Al and I are ready to leave. We're packed, washed, filled with the free breakfast (one egg and a slice of bread). The only problem is that Bishbataar is gone. So's the car.

We watch the clockhands turn. Once around. Again. Half again. At 11:30, the familiar sputtering cough of the car sounds in the distance. Slowly it putt putts to the gate. The three of us, bags in hand, go out to meet it.

Bishbataar is in the car. Along with him is a sinister looking post-adolescent Mongol. The young man has thick features and lips that hang open. His nose is typically Mongolian concave, except the end. That's been broken and now bends sharply downward.

"Can I have 3000 *tugriks*?" asks Bishbataar before we can ask him where he was.

"What for?" I ask

"I have to pay this mechanic," he says. "He just tune up the car for me. It work A-OK now."

"That's a mechanic?" asks Sebastian nodding toward the youth.

"No, not him," says Bishbataar. "Mechanic is an old man. He help. He fix engine. 3000 *tugriks* cheap."

"Waddaya mean cheap?" I say. "This car is your fault..."

Al reaches into his pocket and pulls out a wad of *tugriks*. He peels off six five hundred *tugrik* notes and hands 'em to Bishbataar.

"It'll save me a headache," he says. I'm sure the money will go right into Bishbataar's pocket. If there was any mechanic at all, he "fixed" the car for a packet of cigarettes or less. What can I say?

Bishbataar tells Sebastian to sit up front. The young intruder joins Al and I in the back.

"No too much weight in the back," says Bishbataar. "Sebastian is big guy."

"What the fuck?" I yell at him, wondering how much he's been paid to take this thug to the city. "I wanted to help those people before. You said we shouldn't pick anyone up. You said the car couldn't handle the weight."

"This person I want," says Bishbataar. "What wrong with you? You don't like him because he Mongolian. You're American — so high, while we're Mongolian, so low..."

"Okay, okay," I say, "he comes along."

We're off for the *Aimag* capital, about 50 kilometers away. As we creep across the desert, I keep an eye on our passenger.

A bag of candy sits on the ledge under the rear window. We keep it handy for the kids at the *gers* we stay in. Within three minutes the bag is in the thug's lap. He's eating the candy by the fistful. I look at him, narrowing my eyes like Bela Lugosi does when he wants to control someone's mind. It doesn't work.

On the way to the city, we pass a *ger* near a fenced-in cattle area.

"That's where is the mechanic," says Bishbataar. "I get out and pay."

He runs out of the car and around to the *ger*. In a few minutes he's back and we're off again. Sure he paid the guy — and it rains in the Gobi! Yeah right.

As we drive, I watch the Three Nice Mountains shrink from view. It's sad leaving them. They, and the river of ice inside, were the most spectacular sights in Mongolia.

We gradually approach the nearest town. It's a small village surrounded by a wooden fence. There's a large gate in front of the fence. As we approach that gate, the car begins to make new noises. In addition to the mufflerless machinegun sound and the carburetor putt putt, there is now a grinding — like metal scraping metal. Bishbataar stops.

He gets out to inspect the underside.

"I must take off pipe piece." He says, "It catches in rod."

It's a cancer! One by one the parts are removed yet the disease spreads.

Once Bishbataar is half under the car, the thug taps me on the shoulder. "I want money," he says, rubbing his right thumb against his right middle and forefinger. It's the first English he's spoken.

"Fuck you!" I say with a pleasant smile and shrug of my shoulders. He scowls.

I go for a walk to get away from the troublemaker. As I leave the car, I see the thug talking with Al.

I walk to the city gate. There is a family: a man, a woman, and two little boys, camped out in front. They have their luggage stuffed into a cardboard suitcase and two large bags, the kind that usually carry potatoes.

The man, in a dirty burgundy *deel*, looks at me. He nudges his wife. The two kids look up too. They laugh and wave. I wave back. The man sees my camera and suddenly stands up. The others follow, dusting off their clothes. Posing in front of the gate, the man pantomimes picture taking. I pick up my camera, not taking off the lens cap. Everyone looks serious. I press my finger next to the shutter. The smiles return.

"*Bayerlalaa!*" shouts the man. Then they return to sitting in the shade of the city gate.

I walk back to the car. The thug is gone.

"Did he ask you for money?" asks Sebastian.

I nod.

"Did he threaten you?"

I shake my head.

"He asked me for money," says Sebastian, "and I told him no. Then, he pointed at me with his thumb and finger like he was shooting a gun. I got scared."

"Did you give him any money?" I ask.

"Nope," said Sebastian, "Bishbataar said something to him, and he left."

Speaking of the devil, he is now out from under the car, wiping his hands on a rag. We get back in and gas up at the local station. Apparently, they haven't heard about the gas rationing.

Bishbataar gets instructions for our return trip. It's simply a matter of going North. Just follow the "road." You can't miss it. Yeah right.

The sky is beginning to cloud over. A darkness is forming in the north, gradually moving toward us. I get in the front now. I want a better view.

We sputter out of town, onwards past the city gate. The road turns into a grooved pit, bouncing us against the roof.

It's hot. We're in the desert, heading toward a city that might be under water. Al's window won't roll down. On top of that, since Bishbataar removed the extra exhaust piece, the engine now spews it's gaseous waste directly into the car. Sebastian and I keep our noses close to the open windows. Al soon slumps in his seat, passed out.

"Stop the car!" I shout. "You're killing us."

Bishbataar stops. Sebastian and I get out of the car. We open Al's door. He nearly falls out.

"Let's break that window," suggest Sebastian. "It's the only way we can breathe back here."

"You can't break the window!" yells Bishbataar. "It not my car!"

"Who cares!" I yell back. "The exhaust is killing us."

"You're like baby!" says Bishbataar. "I never see such a thing! You have to breathe? Babies have to breathe. You just switch seats. It's easy. Every five minutes. Don't act like baby."

"Just lemme go back to sleep!" says Al.

"No!" I say looking around for something to smash the window.

"Ok ok," says Bishbataar. "I fix it for you babies."

He takes a screw driver from the trunk and goes to work on the door. Peeling off the panel, he takes out a single screw. The window works normally.

"Mongolian drivers make their windows not open." He explains, "then people don't steal."

"That's all you had to do?" I ask. "Take out a screw?"

"For you babies — want to breathe like babies — I take out screw." says Bishbataar.

Sebastian and I pull Al out of the car and stuff him in the front seat. I sit where he was, next to the now-opened window. Soon, we're bouncing along again.

"Why don't you ride on the desert, on the baked clay?" suggests Sebastian, "it's smoother."

Bishbataar shrugs and moves the car out of the parallel ditches. The ride smooths out. We drive onwards.

Al, now fully awake, though with a headache, turns to us in the back.

"What happened to the road?" he asks.

"It's right..." then I look. It's gone. We're in the middle of the desert. Three hundred sixty degrees of unbroken horizon. No road, no nothing.

I look at my watch. It's 6 o'clock; that should put the sun over Christopher Street. We want to go up Broadway, so Christopher Street should be on our left.

"Where's the sun?" I ask.

"In the sky?" says Al. Wiseguy.

"We want it on our left."

The sky is completely clouded over. It's impossible to tell where the sun is. There are no shadows. No *gers* with their South-facing doorways. No nothing.

"I know, I know," says Bishbataar, driving onwards.

"Look at that!" says Sebastian pointing to a faint outline in the distance, directly in front of us. "It's THREE NICE MOUNTAINS."

And so it is — where we'd left so many hours earlier. Now we're heading toward it.

"I know. I know," says Bishbataar, turning the car around and heading in the opposite direction.

"Looks like we're the party," says Al.

"B-B-B-B-B," says Sebastian.

"I can't believe we're lost in the Gobi Desert!" I whine. "I don't want to die!"

"At least we haven't run out of gas!" says Sebastian.

"God missed her cue," I say. "She must be busy making an earthquake in Iraq or giving AIDS to children in Africa. Otherwise the engine would stop right now."

"There is no God," says Sebastian.

"Let's find a *ger* and ask," says Al.

"Brilliant!" I say.

"There are no *gers*," finishes Bishbataar. "No one lives in the open in the middle of the Gobi."

"Yeah," says Al, "who would be dumb enough to be in the middle of the Gobi?" Wiseguy.

The sun is setting. With the clouds, it's impossible to tell exactly where, but we keep the redness to our left.

In the faint night light, we see the outlines of two large mountain ridges. One is ahead to the left, one to the right.

As we approach, all of us stick our heads out the windows to look for the white flash of a *ger*.

"I see one!" says Sebastian, "Over there!"

"I see nothing," says Bishbataar, "but I go."

So go we do, now in near total darkness. It takes us half an hour to reach the mountains. When we get there, there's nothing.

"I'm sure I saw it," says Sebastian. "Keep driving."

"I see nothing," says Bishbataar, "but I go."

Bishbataar drives, hugging the perimeter of the mountain. We peer at the dark outline, looking for any sign of life. A herd of something, sheep or goats, runs along side of us. A good sign. And finally, tucked into a curve, almost hidden from view, is a single *ger*.

Bishbataar pulls up to it and shouts: "Lord Haw Haw a railroad!"

The *ger* door opens and a middle-aged woman, thin, with a worn but beautiful face, comes out and looks at us. She wears a dull blue *deel*. A kerchief covers her head.

Bishbataar talks with her. She smiles, motioning for us to come inside.

Inside, a dozen people are gathered on our right. There is the woman, and what looks like her mother and father. Then there is a woman in her thirties, a single boy about ten, two girls somewhere between eight and ten, and one girl about fifteen with a thin face and just-budding breasts, wearing very short denim shorts. Her legs, we all notice, extend the entire distance from the shorts to her bare feet on the wooden floor.

"She wants me," whispers Sebastian.

Bishbataar talks with the middle-aged woman, I'll call her mom. Of course, none of them know a word of English.

While they talk, the two girls go out to fetch water. When they bring it back, mom pours it into a kettle to prepare tea for us. Then she mixes a little water with some flour to begin the kneading and flattening necessary to make noodles for our mutton, sand, and noodle dinners.

Al runs out to the car to get the little candy that remains. We offer it to the children, who shyly come up and take a piece. I take one out and offer it to the fifteen year old.

"A little candy?" I say. "Consider it advance payment."

Sebastian kicks me.

After dinner, Bishbataar asks if we can set up our tents near the *ger.* The woman tells him it'd be no problem and asks when we want tea in the morning.

"They're so nice," I say in English, with an innocent smile on my face. "It's unbelievable. I guess we shouldn't torture them, but just quickly slit their throats before we kidnap that girl." Al, trying to hold in a laugh, sprays snot out his nose and coughs. Works every time.

Sebastian and I look at him as if he's a poor epileptic falling into a sudden seizure. I look at the woman and tap my index finger against the side of my head. She nods in understanding.

Later in the tents, puffing our Bayatov Gold, we talk about the trip, the Gobi and the family we're staying with.

"I didn't ask her," says Bishbataar, "but I think she has not husband. The father is a herdsman who left for the city, I think."

"It must be a hard life here in the Gobi." says Al.

"They don't know it's a hard life," says Bishbataar. "It how they live. They have animals. They can walk to water. There is boy in the family. They are happy. The only problem is no rain for so long. It strange, even in the desert."

"Did you ask how to get out of here?" asks Sebastian.

"No problem," answers Bishbataar, "I right, we go right way."

Eventually, we're tired enough to sleep. The dry air, open land and Bayatov Gold rock us to peaceful slumber.

We're awakened at ten by the little boy. He sticks his head into our tent; "*Tsai!*" (tea!) he says.

We go into the *ger* and are greeted with smiling faces and "*sain bain yy.*" For some reason, the milk tea aggravates my just-beginning cough — a legacy of the carbon monoxide filled car. I shake my head and shrug my shoulders in assurance that I'm not sick, but merely poisoned.

We leave the *ger,* looking back on the beautifully sad family. I think of the dryness, the harsh desert life, the people whose struggle is not their jobs but their lives.

Leaving the *ger*, my mind is deep in the consideration of philosophical problems. My lower body is deep in consideration of the shorts-wearing young woman.

A shout from Sebastian interrupts my thoughts.

"Look!" he says, pointing toward the car.

I look. It looks the same as it did yesterday.

"There," he says, "underneath!"

I look lower. There's a black puddle underneath the engine. Gradually, it's getting bigger as drop by drop oil drips from the crankcase.

Bishbataar runs into the *ger* and then runs out and behind it. He returns with an old innertube, obviously from a truck. Taking his knife from his pocket, he slices a chunk off that innertube. Then he opens the trunk and retrieves some of the wire left over from an earlier tragedy.

"Help me!" says Bishbataar.

Al gets in the car and sits heavily on the back seat. I don't make a move. Sebastian, lickety split, is on his back under the car.

One of the little girls sees there is a problem. She runs back into the *ger*. The entire family comes out, making a semi-circle, intently watching us.

Using the wire, Sebastian and Bishbataar try to tie the rubber to the bottom, against where the oil is leaking. The sky darkens while they're working. Thunder cracks. It rains. Pours.

The driest summer in the driest desert in the world — and it rains on us. More than that, it rains on us when we can't get out of it, but have to work to stop our precious oil from disappearing. And Sebastian says there is no God!

The family runs back into the *ger*. Only the little boy stays in the rain, wide eyed, watching us.

We're drenched through, our thin clothes pasted to our body. My scalp, pink and shiny glistens through my once carefully combed hair. Goats and sheep near the *ger* bleat as they huddle together. The dusty sand that Bishbataar and Sebastian lie on is now mud.

Al huddles inside the car. Feeling guilty, I stand near the working pair, asking if there's anything I can do, glad when the answer is no.

Bishbataar and Sebastian slide out from under the car. Their backs are uniformly brown.

"We can no fix it," says Bishbataar. "We drive. Maybe we make it."

I go into the trunk to get the oil. We've got about four liters. Bishbataar fills the crankcase, starts the car, and we head off into the rain. Bishbataar tells us the directions the woman gave him.

"We just head that way," he says, pointing to a large mountain in the distance. "That easy."

So we leave. Lost, leaking oil, in a rainstorm in the middle of the desert. There's nothing left to go wrong.

"Hey look over there, to the left!" says Al, somewhat alarmed.

In the distance is a tornado. A twister. Kicking up sand and dust from the ground to the funnel in the sky. Filled with the desert, it whirls, whipping it's tail back and forth along the ground. It's hard to tell how far away it is, but it's heading toward us.

Rain pounds on the car, big drops mixed with desert mud, squishing against the windshield. Through the water sheet on the windows, we see the twister on our left, a huge black funnel tapering down to a short hose.

We're driving at right angles to it.

"Go! Go!" I shout at Bishbataar.

"I go go," he says.

We drive straight ahead, fast as we can move with our dying Russian luxury car. It'd make a better story if we got caught up in the twister. Tossed in the air like a toy. Spun round, then flung to who-knows-where. Maybe Oz.

It doesn't happen. We just pass it by. It doesn't come close. Aren't we in Oz anyway?

After pulling out of the storm, Bishbataar stops the car.

"It too hot. We rest," says Bishbataar.

From that time forward, every five kilometers, we rest. It's hot and dry now. Spidery lines run through the sandy ground. It's cracked, like our lips, in the heat. No rain here, just wind and dust. My cough is back — and bad! I feel like my lungs are going to spill out through my mouth. I'm spitting blood.

Today is Saturday. Next Wednesday, I've got another adventure. I'm going with my students to Lake Hovsgul in the North. Me and a buncha girls! All alone on a lake AND they're not my students anymore. Mmmm boy, nothing is sexier than an old man spitting blood, huh?

But Wednesday is a lifetime away. The car is on its last wheels with three hundred kilometers to go. None of us say it, but we know. There's no way we can make it. This is the end.

Tiny things begin to irritate us, although the REAL source of our irritation is our impending doom.

Sebastian's cold sore, now grown to fist-size proportions, begins to take my attention away from the inevitable tragedy. I've kept my Daffy Duck water bottle separate from the ones shared by the others. It sits in the front on the floor between my feet. Weeks ago, I promised the Daffy to Sebastian, but he doesn't get it till I leave the country. That may be never. Right now, it marks MY water bottle.

The other bottles are nearly drained. Sebastian asks me for a drink.

"Not with your herpes!" I tell him.

"I don't 'ave 'erpes!" he screams. "It's a spot! Get it? Just a spot!"

"That's what the horse..." I start.

Sebastian punches me in the back of this head.

"Stop it!" yells Al. "Look over there."

To our right, clumped together about two hundred yards from the "road," are camels, sheep, horses and a few people. They're huddled together in a semi-circle. In the desert, that means one thing: a well.

Bishbataar turns and heads for the group. The mufferless car scatters the animals as we get closer. Parking about twenty yards away, we get out. What's left of the water in the radiator bubbles loudly. We gather the water bottles in the car.

I go to the trunk to get the five gallon milkcan we've been using for radiator water. I reach in and pull my hand out immediately. It's covered with sludge — black and sticky. Our reserve oil has leaked over everything we own.

By this time our car and its strange inhabitants have gathered a little crowd. Men on camels, barefoot children, women in *deels* all crowd around. As we pull everything out of the trunk and pile it in the sand, the crowd grows, smiling and talking loudly to one another.

Bishbataar talks with some of the bystanders and they head for the car. He raises the hood while half a dozen guys look under, poking here and there,

jabbering away in Mongolian. Meanwhile Al, Sebastian and I clear out the trunk, clean up the oil (we've lost about a quarter of our reserve) and repack the trunk. Then we walk to the well.

Taking turns hauling up the water, we refill the bottles. When it's my turn to haul, I hand Sebastian the Daffy Duck bottle.

"Here," I say, "hold on to the disease-free bottle."

"I DON'T 'AVE 'ERPES!" he says. He opens the bottle and licks the rim. He drools on the Daffy Duck cap, sucking the part that fits in the bottleneck.

"Here's your SAFE BOTTLE," he says, handing it back to me.

I grab the bottle and throw it as far as I can. Into the desert. Away from the well. It's lost in the scrub.

"My duck!" yells Sebastian. "You threw away my duck!"

He runs in the direction I threw it. In the distance he lowers himself to his hands and knees and sifts through the scrub. Going from clump to clump in an ever-widening circle, he eventually returns, cradling the bottle in his arms.

"That's gonna be my duck!" he says. "How could you do that??"

I don't say anything, planning further revenge. Planning how, next stop, I'll slip that duck under the car wheels and giggle as it gets crushed to a thousand black and tan pieces. Nyahaha!

My obsession with Daffy gets me through the next couple of hours. Then the car stops. It just quits — nothing. We get out. Push. The car coughs, starts, then stops again. We push some more, panting as the big car lumbers forward on foreign legpower, then stops.

Bishbataar gets out and opens the hood.

"I see nothing," he says. "Engine not more bad."

Then it hits me. Not the master mechanic, I'm suddenly blessed with inspiration as to the cause of our difficulty.

"Get me a long piece of wire," I say.

"You're gonna hang Bishbataar," says Sebastian.

"Wake me when it's over," says Al.

I go myself. Into the trunk, rummaging through the oil-stained everything. I find a long piece of stiff wire. Then I go around to the gas tank, open it and stick the wire in.

"Watch this!" I tell my comrades who're amazed at my sudden mechanical ability.

I swish the wire around the gas tank and pull it out.

"See this wire?" I say. "It's completely dry. We're out of gas."

We have twenty liters in a can in the trunk. We take it out and pour it into the tank. Bishbataar touches the ignition wires together and before we can say, "We're the party," The car purrs like a (tubercular) kitten.

"The only thing left is to be stopped by a cop," says Al. "That would do it, to be busted in the middle of the Gobi!"

[Note: We DON'T get stopped by a cop in the middle of the Gobi.]

"How far to the next town?" I ask Bishbataar. "We're gonna have to get some gas."

"It's only fifty kilometers," he says. "We have enough petrol to get there."

"If we don't get lost," says Sebastian, taking a drink from the Daffy Duck bottle. I no longer care.

Slowly, we chug along, stopping every ten kilometers or so to let the car cool. We crawl into town. Since the gas gauge doesn't work we don't know how much is left.

This town is the same sinister one we passed through on the way to South Gobi. The same drunks are at the gate. The same silent, hostile looks from the inhabitants missing the same teeth.

At the gas station, where a week ago, we argued about the cost, the same people sit on the same pipe in front. The door is closed and there's a sign, in Mongolian, hanging on it.

The same young man, wearing the same dirty *deel* comes up to the car. A tense line of muscle forms on the sides of his face as he suppresses a smirk.

He speaks to Bishbataar. Bishbataar turns to us to translate.

"He says the station is closed now. It opens again on Monday."

"I've got to be at work on Monday," says Sebastian. "We can't just wait here."

"I'm going to Hovsgul with a buncha girls!" I say. "We can't just wait here."

"Wake me when it's over," says Al.

By now, we no longer need to say any of the THREE QUOTES. Overuse has reduced them to a single word "IARN" (pronounced "yarn," it means "Insert Appropriate Remark Now"). So, instead of the horse and the bishop...

"Iarn!" I say.

Al groans, closes his eyes and rests his head against the door jam.

"What'll we do?" asks Sebastian.

"We still have gas. Next city only fifty kilometers," says Bishbataar.

"Fifty kilometers in a normal car going the right way," I yell. "How much is that for us?"

"Then we wait," says Bishbataar, folding his arms and sitting back down in the driver's seat.

The number of sinister looking guys in front of the garage starts to grow. Now there is a fat guy with an even fatter, nearly toothless girlfriend. She approaches the car with a map.

Bishbataar gets out to talk to her. She spreads the map on the trunk and begins gesturing to various points on it.

Bishbataar shakes his head.

She becomes more vehement, stabbing at the map with her finger, raising her voice, then stabbing her finger into Bishbataar's chest. Her words are lubricated with vodka.

"Ok," I say, "lets go."

Bishbataar excuses us to the group. The woman continues to shout. The gap where her front teeth should be is a black hole, pulling us back. We must escape!

When Bishbataar gets back in the car the men sitting on the pipe get up. They begin to approach us. We're off, into the desert, heading toward the next town. Yeah, right.

"Isn't the next town even smaller than this one?" asks Sebastian.

"It smaller," says Bishbataar.

"Well, if THIS gas station is closed for the weekend, don't you think one in a smaller town would also be closed," I say, completing Sebastian's thought.

"This is Mongolia," answers Bishbataar.

How can I answer that?

Except for a battery cable that regularly pops off and stalls the car, for the next fifty kilometers NOTHING BAD HAPPENS. We even see our first tree. A gnarly but green tree, alone in the sand. A tree! That means we're slowly leaving the desert.

We get to the next town and Bishbataar is right. The gas station is open and ready for us to pump. I turn the crank to fill the gas tank and our twenty liter can. Folks are friendlier here. Bishbataar asks for and gets clear directions back to *Ulaanbaatar*. Al pays and we're off.

A few miles out of town the car stops. We're on a small hill that starts the mountains separating the Gobi from the rest of Mongolia. The car tries the hill, coughs, and stalls. Bishbataar checks the battery. The duct-taped cable still holds. I try the wire-in-the-gas tank trick. It comes out wet.

While Bishbataar pokes around under the hood, a truck passes. As always, we hail it. As always, it stops. The driver and his passenger get out. The driver is a fat old man, with a round face and very rosy cheeks. He has a birthmark on the tip of his nose. A stare of recognition crosses his face.

"Where we know him from?" asks Bishbataar. "He knows us."

"I don't know," I say. "All you guys look the same."

Sebastian kicks me.

"I remember him," Al says. "He was at the first *guansa* we stopped at. He was going to drive to South Gobi at night."

Bishbataar translates for the guy. He nods.

"Nice work," I tell Al.

The guy joins Bishbataar under the hood of the car, and before long the engine struggles before turning over. Then it stops again. We push the car around so it's headed downhill. Then we push some more. It starts with Bishbataar inside. Then it stops.

We get behind the car and push uphill this time. I'm afraid that it might slide backwards and run us over. Upwards we push, me, Al, Sebastian, and the old truck driver. When we get up some speed, Bishbataar touches the ignition wires. The engine turns over. Al, Sebastian and I back away, afraid of being run over. The old man keeps right on pushing, all the way to the top of the hill...where the car stalls again.

Bishbataar slams open the door and walks down the hill toward us.

"Why you stop pushing?" he yells. "See that old man! He push. He old, but he push. You? You like women, like little girls. You push and stop!"

"We didn't want to get hit," I try explaining.

"Little girls no get hit," says Bishbataar. "You like little girls."

Actually it doesn't matter, because the car just won't start.

The truck driver agrees to tow us to the top of the next hill. We can then use the slope to build up momentum. Using the rope from one of our borrowed tents, we tie the car to the back of the truck.

"They go back to *Ulaanbaatar*," says Bishbataar. "We go first. Then they come. They come after us. Follow."

So towed to the top of the hill we are. Then the truck driver comes out, unties the rope and waves good-bye. Sebastian, Al and I push the car so it starts rolling downhill. Then we chase it as it picks up speed, getting in just as it starts.

We're off! Barely making it up the next hill, we coast easily down the other side. After a while things flatten out a bit. The road branches in all directions.

Bishbataar constantly looks over his shoulder.

"Do you see the truck?" he asks. "Is the truck behind us?"

"Why are you so worried about that truck?" I ask.

"What's the matter? You no like them? Because they Mongolian? You Americans are so high. We're so low..."

"Just shut up," says Al, curling into his corner.

"Are you sure we're going the right way?" I ask.

"OF COURSE WE'RE GOING THE RIGHT WAY!" he screams. "SOMEONE IS FOLLOWING US!"

There's a moment of silence as the unintentional humor sinks into our desert-boiled brains. Then I laugh. The tension bubble bursts. The three foreigners in the car break into unstoppable tornados of laughter. Belly-holding, teeth-jiggling, side-hurting laughter. Guffaws like we never thought possible. At first, Bishbataar grits his teeth against it. Before long, he too is caught up in the hilarity.

Together we're banging the doors, dripping snot, farting, crying, gasping for breath with our laughter. We've let loose and there's no stopping us. The laughter is out of control. It's an entire week's worth. All the anger, fear and tension, all the hate, pain and frustration, coming out now in one moment of pure glee.

Then, the car dies.

We all know it, though none of us will say the words. There's no sputter. No fade to black. There's simply a kerCHUNK. The car stops like Bishbataar hit the brakes. That's it.

Bishbataar tries to start the engine. Nothing. He looks under the hood. Nothing. This is it. The jig is up. The die is cast. The *buz* is cooked.

We still have a small mountain range and a flat plain to go before we reach *Ulaanbaatar*, eighty kilometers — if we're going in the right direction.

We get out of the car and sit in a somewhat clear place among the roadside scrub. We've taken out the rest of the food, some hard bread, jam, water, and some Lemonheads mom sent me from New York.

I break the bread into four pieces and spread jam on them. A truck passes. It's our friends from back there, the ones who've been following us.

They get out when they see we're in trouble. Again we tie our car to theirs. Again they drag us to the top of the next hill. Again they let us loose and wave good-bye.

We make it to the bottom of the hill and stay there. Stone cold still. It's half an hour before another car passes, an old black Mercedes. Bishbataar hails it. It stops. He talks with the driver, a balding man of about forty in a dark green leisure suit and sun-glasses.

They hook up some cable between the Mercedes rear bumper and our car's front bumper. Then Bishbataar gets back in the car.

"No worry," says Bishbataar. "We must pay him, but it ok. Take it from my pay."

"We're gonna take a lot more..." starts Sebastian, but I elbow him in the ribs.

"Shut up!" I say, "eee-way eed-nay im-hay ow-nay...Ater-lay, ok?"

Fortunately, Bishbataar is too busy concentrating on the problems of driving in tow, to pay any attention to our Pig Latin. Unfortunately, the Mercedes stalls halfway up the next hill. Then it starts again. In fact, it stalls and stops dozens of times during our limp back to *Ulaanbaatar*. Coming over the last hill, the city appears just on the other side of the flat plain.

It's not under water at all. It's perfect, just what I dreamed of, a beautiful sight: the electric company smoke stacks belching black into the sky, the gray brick buildings falling apart in slow motion, the empty lots filled with garbage, BEAUTIFUL!

Turning the corner onto the first main street of the city we hear a whistle. Stopped by a cop! (I said it wasn't in the middle of the Gobi!)

"You! Pull over!" is what I guess he says.

"YES!" I shout, giving Al a high five. "Stopped by the cops! EVERYTHING has happened to us! We've done it all!"

"NO!" shouts Sebastian with a look of disgusted horror.

He gets out of the car and walks behind it. He opens the trunk and fishes for his belongings. Putting his pack on his back, he carries the Daffy Duck bottle in his left hand. Then he reaches into the back seat, on the ledge.

"That's The Gold!" I say, "You're taking The Gold."

"Yep!" he says. "I'm also taking the bus."

And he's off.

The cop doesn't even look at Sebastian as he stomps off to the nearest bus stop. He barely notices Al or me either. Bishbataar hands him his license and the papers for the car. He's got a letter from the cop who owns the car.

The officer looks at the letter, then he looks at the car, now tethered to the Mercedes. He nods and says something to Bishbataar.

"*Bayerlalaa*," says Bishbataar. And we get back in.

"What'd he say?" I ask.

"He say, 'Good luck. I hope you make it,'" he answers.

So it's me, Al and Bishbataar. We're attached by the cable to the back of the old Mercedes. Bishbataar has given him directions to the garage we're supposed to bring the car to. As we approach it, Bishbataar motions:

"It's right there. Just follow that road..."

There is no road. What was once a paved street is now a series of holes, deep holes, with people working in them with pick axes.

The garage is at the end of a blind alley. This is the only entrance.

Bishbataar, Al and I get out. Bishbataar unhooks the cable and we get behind the car and push. Bishbataar pushes and steers, trying to make sure at least three wheels are on solid ground at all times.

After we "park" the car, the Mercedes takes us home. While driving in the city, a rock catches under the wheel and hits the underside. Nothing happens.

◎ ◎ ◎

As I read again this Gobi adventure, I think of all that I left out: The generosity of the locals. The awesome beauty of the empty desert. The patter of four people whose lives were utterly changed. I worry that I didn't stress the magnificence and mystery of the desert. I'm concerned you'll get a bad picture of the Mongols, who were more open and generous than any people in the world. There was a sadness in returning from the Gobi. That sadness was increased by the knowledge that I'd soon be leaving Mongolia. One more trip, and it would all be over.

NINETEEN

We're just back from the Gobi. I'm sick with a cough and lack of sleep. Today is the day of reckoning. Bishbataar comes for his money. Al, Sebastian and I have agreed to deduct a day's pay. He'll still get more than he deserves for getting a bad car when he promised a jeep. That car cost us time, and because of leaking exhaust, got me sick.

Bishbataar arrives just after Sebastian. Al never shows up.

Sebastian and I each give Bishbataar our share of the pared-down pay. When he discovers the deduction, he smiles sinisterly and says, "I'll get my money."

Then he flies into a rage, threatening Sebastian and I with his connections to "the organization." We threaten back with the police and extortion charges. It's ugly. Finally, he takes the money and stalks out of my apartment.

Shaken by visions of an "accident" on a yak or unidentified human bones picked clean by the local dogs, Sebastian and I decide to tell the world about the threat. Then we'll let Bishbataar know through Al when he pays his share. If anything happens to us, the world will know who's responsible. Bishbataar has to keep us healthy.

The problem is that Al never tells him. He pays the (reduced) money, friendly as la-de-da. Not a harsh word exchanged. He wimps out, leaving Sebastian and I stranded in the heat of the threat.

Ah well, if I let little things like a mob hit worry me, I wouldn't have come to Mongolia in the first place, right? Besides, the teachers are throwing me a celebration. It's

MYKEL'S FAREWELL PARTY

At 4PM I arrive to applause. Almost all the teachers are there. There's Sumiya, the wizened old department head. Erdenbataar, a tough man in his sixties, sits to his right. Namjil, the spunky teacher with a biting sense of humor, waits with open arms. Next to her is Tuulzul, a fragile lady whose constant smile shows her missing molars. Then there's Doytseg, the slender middle-aged woman who ditched her husband.

There's also Gutalmaa, a short woman and great English teacher, but with a temper that'd cow Godzilla. Even Ichibat, the gray crewcut ever-calm problem solving daddy of the school is here. He's stopped in to pay his respects. He doesn't stay long, though. The only ones missing are Sonya, the Russian expat who dumped her students, and Siirtbat, the nice guy/belligerent drunk, who is the youngest full professor and worst English speaker in the department.

Speeches about my greatness sprinkle their way through the "salad," sprigs of lettuce covered with mayonnaise. A bottle of "champagne" and two bottles of Vodka give the table a more Mongolian flair. I'm working on bringing out the tears for a fitting farewell soliloquy. As I'm being toasted by the department head, Al's off in a corner with Gutalmaa discussing teaching methodology.

Professors from other departments walk in and out as the daylight dims. At about 7:30, in staggers Siirtbat — drunker than a Mongolian. Barely nodding hello to me, he takes a chair and moves it to a corner of the room. The other male teachers gather around him in that corner. Al, the female teachers and I are left on the other side.

The voices on the men's side start to get louder. Siirtbat is yelling.

"How do I get home?" He shouts, "Somebody tell me where I live!"

We laugh.

He leans forward to brace himself against a desk. It's preparation for the Herculean task of rising to his feet.

By this time Erdenbataar has left the men's group. He's been speaking to me about the Jews he met in France and what scholars they were.

"Jews are very serious people," he says. "Very serious." The Jew whose party this is has just managed to wet his tearducts when Siirtbat wobbles to his feet. He staggers to our table.

"I leave now," he says.

"If you can find your way home," I say.

Erdenbataar touches me gently on the back and shakes his head. I quickly shut up.

Siirtbat says something to Erdenbatar. There is some shouting. One to the other, and back. Erdenbataar jumps up from behind the desk, then jumps clear over it. He reaches out and grabs Siirtbat by the collar. He pulls the younger man toward him. Smash! He punches him straight on the top of the head. Pow! Again. Siirtbat raises his arms to defend himself. Erdenbataar kicks at his legs and catches them. Siirtbat's on the floor.

Tuulzul wraps her arms around the man on the floor. She rocks him back and forth like a mother holding a baby.

"Siirtbat Siirtbat Siirtbat," she says.

Doytseg tries to hold back the older teacher, now standing over the supine man. STOMP! Erdenbataar kicks Siirtbat in the face. Heel-to-nose. CRACK! Blood everywhere. Spewing like a fountain. From the nostrils. From between his eyes. From his mouth.

By this time, even I'm on my feet, trying to hold Erdenbataar back. All the teachers are covered in blood: our hands, clothes, faces, like butchers or extras from a slasher movie.

"I know that kind of blood," says Al, "It's from the bridge. His nose is broken. I once broke someone's nose. I know."

I look at Siirtbat and see that Al's right. Most of the blood is coming from the top of his nose, not from inside.

Right then, Ichibat, ever the great dignified peacemaker, returns. He kneels next to the fallen Siirtbat. Gently, he consoles the man. Helps him to his feet. Puts his arm around him. Together they walk out and things calm down.

One of the teachers fishes out some soap and one by one we clean up.

The excitement, booze and mayonnaise have aggravated my cough to the puking point. I'm trying to clean up and hold down my farewell meal. Some of the teachers have left. Others want to continue the party.

Erdenbataar comes over to me to explain his actions.

"He called me a fascist," He says, "I'm not a fascist. Maybe I'm a nationalist, but I'm not a fascist."

"Sure," I tell him, "I understand."

Then Erdenbataar leaves with a few other teachers. Now it's Al, me and two of the female teachers. Siirtbat comes back.

His nose streams blood worse than ever. Ichibat is walking with him like a father. Al suggest they go to a hospital, or at least try to clean up.

Siirtbat says something.

Ichibat stares at him incredulously. Siirtbat shouts. Ichibat shouts back. They're yelling. Siirtbat throws a punch, just missing Ichibat's chin. Ichibat throws a punch. SBLAM! right the center of Siirtbat's chest. The force pushes all the air from Siirtbat's lungs and through his nose, spraying a fresh layer of blood over everything.

Al separates Siirtbat and Ichibat. Furious, Ichibat walks out. Al pulls out a handkerchief to help Siirtbat clean his face.

"Al, you're gonna get slugged," I say. But he continues.

The other teachers and I walk out. We go downstairs to the next floor. I'm impressed at Al's bravery, yet annoyed that it's so public now, when he was so cowardly with Bishbataar in private. The other teachers and I wait a few minutes on the next floor. Nothing happens. Then we go home.

I don't sleep that night. The booze and blood have aggravated my lung so much that I can do nothing but cough, puke and cough again.

I'm awake until 6AM. Time to start the next adventure, the trip to Hovsgul, the most beautiful and fire-ridden place in Mongolia.

Moron: a hapless name for a town — especially one in a country already associated with mental retardation. But who am I to argue with reality?

It's the evening of June 23, longest day of the year. The entire town loses electricity at 11PM. There's cold running water (hopefully potable, because I pote it), but no shower. At least five degrees colder inside than out, I'm wearing my jacket as I write.

This town is the capital of Hovsgul Aimag in Northern Mongolia. The guidebooks call this provence "Mongolia's Switzerland." Lake Hovsgul is the country's biggest fresh water lake and the world's most pristine. It's the only place in Mongolia where more people live in wooden houses than in gers. I usually like to write as I travel, but the first place I can scribble my thoughts is in a dank room in

THE BEST HOTEL IN MORON

Before this adventure, I need to explain my University bookkeeping system. As a memory aid, I make little notations next to the students' names in my attendance book. Someone who wears glasses is 4I'S. I'll note a plump student as CHB, an attractive one QT, an unattractive one UG. An intelligent student earns a SMRT, an unintelligent one a MRN.

Just because I notice students' personal characteristics doesn't mean I'll try for the nook. The power to grade is an authority position that makes it morally, as well as legally, a bad idea. Still, I have my fantasies. And after school's out, I'm no longer the teacher!

One of my classes was mostly filled with young women from the country-side. Less sophisticated than the city girls, they had a rosy-cheeked charm and innocence missing from the sophisticated urbanites used to electricity and indoor plumbing. Two of them, Khatzul (CHB) and Nortuya (QT) live in Hovsgul *Aimag*. After the Gobi, it's where I want most to visit. And with student natives, it should be a perfect trip. I suggest we make a class expedition of it. We'll meet at the bus station on July 21 at 8:00AM. Anyone can go.

July 21 is two days after my Gobi trip. I'm drained, with a horrific cough due to my continual exposure to carbon monoxide and desert dust. My allergy and general lack of health add a runny nose and occasional sneezing. All-in-all, I'm a wreck. Still, on the 21st, I pack my Mongolian cough syrup, ten packages of Fisherman's Friend, a poncho in case it rains, a dozen condoms just in case, a flashlight and a change of underwear. I also take along my sleeping bag and a tent. Though it's warm here in *Ulaanbaatar*, I wear a jacket. We're going north and this is Mongolia.

I'm at the bus station at 7:45. At 8:15 I hear a voice call to me. It's a young woman in a long dress. She wears sun glasses and is made up like she's going to dinner with her parents. It's Tuula (CHB UG).

"Mykel-*baksh*! Mykel-*baksh*," she says, "Why you so late?"

"I was here," I tell her. "I just didn't see you."

"I go find Gazagas. Be right back." She leaves.

Gazagas is one of the few students with no mark next to her name. No notation. She's not a good student, but not the worst. She's thin, but not skinny. With typical Mongolian high cheekbones and rosy cheeks, I often confuse her with the few other non-descript girls in the class. I can't think of one memorable incident — positive or negative — during the year she's been my student.

The two girls return. I expected more.

I cough heavily.

"Are you sick?" asks Tuula.

"No," I say, "it's just an allergy and the Gobi."

"The Gobi make you cough?"

I smile and change the subject.

"Only three of us?" I ask. "What about Khatzul and Nortuya? They live in Hovsgul."

"Khatzul is there. She will meet us," says Gazagas, "Nortuya should meet us here, but she isn't."

"Besides," says Tuula, "I cannot go. I have to meet my sister. It too bad." So Gazagas and I head for the trucks. They've lined up in the parking lot at the far end of the bus station, blue trucks with stenciled white license numbers peeling off the sides. They're old and look unsteady with closed-in backs.

"Look," she tells me pointing to a truck. "See if it is okay."

I look in. There are half a dozen other people already inside. Surrounding them are boxes, burlap bags and cloth suitcases. The sun shines through a few shuttered windows sawed irregularly through the side panels. Although it's crowded, there's enough room to sit down.

"It's okay," I tell her, "at least we can sit."

We pay our money and climb in, bringing our bags. It's really not bad. There's enough room for four or five comfortably, so seven isn't awful.

The truck doesn't move for an hour. By then, twenty-five people cramp, cram, jam, curl up into unchangeable fetal positions, like in the tiger cages the South Vietnamese used for POWs. It's a collection of some of the least attractive people I've ever seen, pock-marked, teeth missing, and warts in places I've never seen warts before.

I'm installed on a hard wooden box. The corner of another container is a knife against my back. A little flap of testicle skin catches between my underpants and the box where I sit.

Then we're off, all twenty-five of us and the driver. Before long someone lights up a cigarette. Then another. The compartment fills with tobacco smoke. My next adventure begins.

As we travel, the pain in my back grows along with a lust for Gazagas. I never noticed how thin and athletic her body was. Her high cheekbones push her face into a heart-shape, making her mouth the soft central ventricle, pulsing blood through my veins.

As the box corner pushes harder into my back, I use the pain as an excuse to shift position, pressing my left leg tightly against Gazagas's right. I glance up at her. She smiles! I cough, right in her face.

The increasingly pretty young woman squints against the spraying droplets. Subtly, like a person trying to sniff her own armpits, she turns her face to her shoulder to wipe off the saliva.

A loud BANG! interrupts the embarrassing moment. Then a thump. Finally a stop. The driver gets out to inspect the flat tire, the first of the trip. The truck has ten tires. Two on the front (cab) axle, four on each of the rear axles. During the rest of our journey, every one of the tires will blow out — several more than once. In all, there will be seventeen flats during the 600 kilometer expedition.

During the third flat I test the waters. I get out of the truck and walk to a spot in a field about twenty feet away. The male Mongols involve themselves with the tire. The females rummage through the field, gathering wild rhubarb.

I stretch out, belly against the rough grass. Gazagas walks over toward me. From my low perspective I marvel at those smooth muscular legs beneath her flimsy skirt. How come I never noticed them before?

She lies next to me, picking at the grass in front of her. I pick too.

"It's a beautiful afternoon," I say, looking directly into her dark eyes. I whisper the word 'beautiful' so she knows I'm not only talking about the weather. She looks back at me, then stares into the grass.

"Yes," she says, "It beautiful. But it too bad about the wheels."

As we talk, I casually rock back and forth. A millimeter away, two millimeters toward. One away, Two toward. My throat begins to tickle as the afternoon pollen increases my cough's severity. I puff out my chest and press my tongue against the back of my throat to prevent it.

Then comes another sensation. This one lower and more centrally located. As my arm brushes Gazagas, my blood rushes south. Suddenly, the sniffles, the lung tightness, the cough, all disappear. I discover that arousal controls my upper respiratory system. When the arousal limpens, the cough returns, even worse. I'm going to have to keep as close to Gazagas as possible — and as far away from everyone else on the bus.

We're back on the road by eight o'clock. Four young herdsmen, in dirty *deels*, play cards in the far corner. They've spread out, taking that much space from the rest of us.

The few windows in the sides of the truck let in the end of the daylight hours. I sit pressed up against Gazagas. I've managed to drape my hand over her leg. When those leg muscles don't tighten or move away, I let my hand relax and touch.

Before long, her fingertips nestle on the back of my hand. I turn it over, slipping my fingers between hers. So smooth and slender, tiny fingers, like an angel's. I wonder why I never noticed that before. My cough disappears.

The fifth tire blows about 11 o'clock. We're far enough north to make it cold outside. The driver and his helpers jack up the truck to get at the wheel. Then the jack breaks.

Mongolians are the world's most resourceful people. They'd never let a thing like a broken jack hold them back.

A middle-aged man, a few scrawny whiskers dangling from his chin, scrounges the nearby ground. He finds a thick piece of tree limb about a foot high. Putting one end under the front axle, he digs the other into the ground. The truck backs up, ever so slightly. Its weight forces the one end of the log into the dirt. That lifts the other end with the axle and entire front of the truck.

Different, older, men dig around the tire making a hole deep enough to remove the wheel. About now it occurs to me that the people helping with the tire changing are NOT employees of the trucking company. There is no trucking company. These are just my fellow (male) passengers. Only the foreigner doesn't work. I feel guilty and immediately get my flashlight. I shine it on the wheel, using Western technology to make their lives easier.

Since I broke contact with Gazagas, my cough returns. I'm gagging and spewing sputum trying to keep the light focused on the wheel while the Mongols do the more physical work. A big guy wrenches off the lugnuts and joins with another to yank the wheel off the axle. It thumps to the ground. Then the driver, a short plump man, uses a piece of pipe to separate the tire from the rim. He pulls out the tube and examines it, trying to find the leak. It's a hole big enough to put his head through.

Next comes the patching, hacked from old inner tubes too tattered to repair. After the driver cuts the patch, an old man in a frayed business suit uses a rock to scrape the back of it and around the tube hole. Once it's rough enough, the scraper spreads contact cement on the patch and the hole. The driver has a four liter bucket of the noxious glue. It barely makes it through the trip.

In twenty minutes the glue dries enough to give everyone a headache. The big guy who loosened the lugnuts puts the patch over the hole and pounds it with his hammer-and-sickle style hammer. After spit-testing the seal, he puts the tube back into the tire and slips the tire into the wheel rim. Using a pump built into the truck, they pump it up. The flat is fixed — until the next one.

We're on the road again. I'm one of the last to get back in and I have to sit squished against Gazagas. What a shame.

It's late now, dark. As we settle, I again dangle my hand casually over hers. Then comes a piercing smell, a whoosh over the whole truck. A sudden sickly,

disease-ridden foot smell, like a thousand sneakers in a thousand lockerrooms, bunched up and held to my nose. I gag. I nearly throw up. The woman next to me fans away the air in front of her. This is not normal, even for Mongolia.

I take a slug of the Mongolian cough syrup and it calms me a bit. Some one else has opened the small windows as wide as they'll go. Eventually, either the offender puts on his shoes, or as happens with everything else, we adjust.

Gazagas and I hold hands. My cough goes silent. Through my half closed lids, I see this big goofy Mongol shift position. It's the lugnut turner, an ugly guy with a thick square jaw and a big red birthmark that goes from the corner of his right eye to just below his cheek. I watch him checking out Gazagas. He's stationed himself right in front of us, lying curled up, facing her and I. He casually drapes his arm around her leg.

I squeeze Gazagas's right hand. She brings up her left hand to hold my hand in BOTH of hers. Reassured, I slowly drift toward sleep.

In a half-sleep, in the darkness, I reach out my left hand and she grabs it. I caress that hand, rubbing my thumb against her thumb, lightly touching the fingertips. I'm pleased to see she's responding, caressing me back, teasing the inside of my palm with her ring finger. So wonderful, one of my hands held in her two hands. My other hand, being caressed...?

If she's got two hands around my right hand, how could my left hand caress her OTHER hand? She didn't have three hands when we met. That means...I'm holding hands with the big ugly guy...and he must think...I start coughing again. Severely.

The next morning, an hour after our first flat of the day, we stop for breakfast at a *guansa*. This one offers our choice of lamb, noodles and tea or lamb noodle soup and tea, all for the fixed price of 500 *tugriks*. While we're eating, some other folks decide to repack the truck. That means, of course, less room for everyone except those who repacked. My sliver of space has turned into a micron. Gazagas has to sit on the floor, squeezed into the guy with the birthmark. I'm sitting on four inches of protruding wood, with my back against something hard and irregularly shaped.

As the next day wears on, Gazagas grows increasingly hostile, annoyed and frightened by my worsening cough. Once I casually throw my arm around her waist, as if I'm adjusting my body to a more comfortable position. Pow! She throws it off her and throws a jacket over my head. At the next flat she stomps out of the truck with my flashlight, holding it for the tire changers while I stay inside with the women.

The first chance to really get laid here and I'm a spewing consumptive. Tell me it's coincidence, chance. Yeah right. God has it in for me. There's no two ways about it. Alone with a beautiful girl and I spray saliva. It's the monkey's paw. Even if you get your wish, you don't REALLY get it.

It's 3:30PM on the second day. Almost twelve hours after we should've arrived.

"We're nearly halfway there," Gazagas says.

By the 8PM flat, we seem a lot closer. Some people have left; gotten out of the truck and gone home with their baggage. The way the truck was packed, some bags held others braced against the wall. With no bracing, the loose packages fall toward the center and take up more sitting room. That means, although there are fewer people, we have even less space than before. We're almost standing now.

Gazagas picks up a book. I look over her shoulder and see it's a Russian/ Mongolian/English Dictionary. I can't read the Mongolian or Russian, but the

English word is PERIOD. Is she explaining her pimples or why "not tonight," or is she talking about English punctuation? I never find out.

Whatever it is, the hand-holding stops and the cough worsens. Everyone in the truck subtly presses themselves away from me.

◎ ◎ ◎

We pull into Moron around 3PM on Sunday, fifty-six hours late. One of the men gets out of the truck to help Gazagas down. I throw my pack to her and climb out. We wave good-bye and start walking. Gazagas has never been here before, but she has directions.

The town is bleak. One-story small wooden houses, with nothing but empty dirt between them. There's a statue of a big guy who looks like a cross between Charles Atlas and Stalin. That must be THE LANDMARK. When Gazagas sees it she faces it. She looks at the name on its base, Naraanbataar. Then she turns around. Naraanbataar now stonily stares at her tight buttocks.

Like a pirate following a treasure map, she counts the steps in a forward direction: NEG. HOYER. GURAV. DORUV. *ONOO*! (One, Two, Three, Four, Now!) An abrupt left turn and we march. Through a small housing development, past a long white building. Then past a pink building with a steeple and a picture of a cow and a carrot painted on the front.

We reach an unpainted split-log fence and follow it to a gap. At that gap, we turn left. Then another left. Now we're in a little fenced-in area with three small houses. The natural fragrance of the fly-attracting outhouse greets us along with Khatzul, in jeans, a red and white kerchief tied around her head.

When she sees us she runs up to Gazagas and gives her a big hug. She shakes my hand. I cough.

"You sick?" she asks.

"Oh no," I tell her, "it's just a cough. Like an allergy. It's nothing serious. Don't worry."

Khatzul invites us into her one-room house. Mom is a small woman, slim and pretty, in stark contrast to Khatzul's rotundness. Her six year old sister is a QT in the making. Thin, her long body mostly legs, she's got the kind of smiling oval face and flirty walk that makes it easier to understand pedophilia.

Her brother is a handsome young man around twelve years old. He wears a t-shirt that says "Fun Fatry" on it and a Chicago Bulls baseball hat. In his hand is a wooden game, a Mongolian version of Mah Jong.

Dad is short and fat. He's got a crewcut on a big round head, like astroturf on a bowling ball.

"People say I look like my father," says Khatzul. "What do you think?"

"You have his eyes," I tell her.

Mom gives us bread and begins to prepare soup. Khatzul, Gazagas and I play the Mongolian tile game with bro. He wins most of the time.

I scan the house while we're playing. There's one room with three large beds and one small one. One for Mom and Dad, one for Khatzul (and bro?), the small one for sis, leaving only one for Gazagas and me. My kind of set-up!

"We've arranged a hotel room for you," says Khatzul. "You'll like it. It's in the best hotel in Moron. There's even toilet in the room. You can also eat there. We know you'll be more comfortable than in this house."

OK, Gazagas and I in a hotelroom. That's not so bad.

I look at her. "When do we check in?" I ask.

"Gazagas sleep here," says Khatzul. "Hotel room for you. You teacher."

"We want you be comfortable," she continues. "Here is not so comfortable."

The girls help me carry my stuff to the hotel. We go through a gate and pass a big white building. Some unsavory-looking folks sit at a table outside.

"What's that big white building next to the hotel?" I ask.

"Oh that hospital," says Khatzul, "a special one for skin disease."

"I see," I answer, "you mean I'm next to a leper colony."

Khatzul looks puzzled. "No," she says, "there are no leopards here. This is a people hospital. Leopards are in the mountains."

It's 10AM the next day: I've just finished an awful breakfast, soup with raw potatoes added at the last minute. They have a bitter metallic taste. Hideous. I wonder what the girls ate for breakfast.

They were here earlier, very briefly. Now I realize that I'm just an excuse for their parents. They want to hang out and do what girls do. I'm the sick old fogy in tow.

◎ ◎ ◎

It's 4:30PM: The girls left to find a car at 9 this morning. Since the trip takes four hours (yeah, right), we won't arrive until very late. More likely, they'll come back saying they couldn't get a car, so we have to spend another night here. A conspiracy to further their fun and force the sick old man to rest up for the hardships ahead.

◎ ◎ ◎

It's 11:00PM: What a surprise! They couldn't find a car for today, but they did make a deal. Margash, margash. (Tomorrow, tomorrow.)

"It cost more," says Khatzul, "two times. Not tourist season. Driver must return with nobody. We must pay." Why do I feel that besides being taken to the lake by the driver, I'm being taken for a ride by my students?

This evening, instead of going to the lake we go to the movies. There's one moviehouse in town, a ramshackle wooden building with white peeling paint. A hand-written poster in front says which movies are playing and when. The last movie starts at 9. We arrive at 8:45.

The place is shut, closed. No lights inside, no one around. Khatzul is not discouraged. She lives here and knows the system. Walking up to the front door, she bangs on it. Her chubby fists BLAM! BLAM! BLAM! against the wood. Nothing happens.

Again: BLAM! BLAM! BLAM!

A shuffling comes from inside. The door opens a crack. A thin bespectacled face peers around at Khatzul.

"*Khinbe?*" (Who is it?)

Khatzul explains that we're here to see the movie.

Clucking her tongue, the woman opens the door to let us into a waiting room. The musty room hints at old class. The walls, paneled with once-polished wood, are now scratched and pitted. Around the room hang framed black and white pictures of famous Mongolian actors and actresses. The men are all dressed in plain business suits. The older women wear western style dresses.

The younger ones wear *deels*, signs of a return to pre-commie culture.

As we wait, about a dozen more people join us: a nuzzling young couple obviously out on a date, a few older women, babushkas around their heads, a mom with two kids. The rest are male and female teenagers who are probably here because there's nothing else to do. There's no popcorn. I don't think there's popcorn in all of Mongolia. Admission is 220 *tugriks*, about fifty cents. I pay for the three of us.

The movie turns out to be a 1970s Chuck Norris/Lee Van Cleef film. It's been cut to shreds by censors, age, or both. The projectionist shows the reels in the wrong order. The whole thing is badly overdubbed into Russian. You can still hear the "original language" in the background: German.

A Russian dubbed version of a German dubbed American karate movie. It's frequently punctuated by my relentless cough.

After the movie, the girls walk me to my hotel and say good night.

"We will come early tomorrow." they say, "maybe eight or nine. Please ready and wait us."

Now it's 11:30 at night. I finish these notes by candlelight. I set my alarm for 7 tomorrow morning. If the girls aren't here by 9:30, I'll go get them. Right now, it's time to get some sleep.

It's 7AM. I can't sleep. The cold damp room brings out the worst of my cough. Mucus and blood have colored my only white handkerchief. I tried to wash it out in the hotel sink last night. There was no water.

I'm sick of being left alone in my cold little room. Those two are off on who-knows-what orgy with who-knows-how many attractive Mongols making fun of the poor sick *baksh* who needs to rest up in the hotel.

It's 8:30. They're a half hour late. I've had it.

I put a 1000 *tugrik* bill on the table and lay my room key on top of it. Then I pick up my pack, hoist it onto my back and walk out of my room.

A short hall leads to the heavy front door. Turning the knob, I push on it. It sticks. Whack. I hit it with my shoulder. Still stuck. WHACK! I hit it harder. The padlock rattles outside in the hasp. It's not stuck. It's locked from the outside.

Back in my room, I open the long thin window and climb onto the inside sill. A whoosh of cold air blows past me. About seven feet below is the hard dirt ground. I take off the pack and throw it out the window. A small dustcloud puffs in the air around it. I jump, standing like Chuck Norris would. Only he would've landed on his feet. I brush the dust from my jeans and the pain from my gluteus. The noise awakens the dog.

It's brown and black, about the size of my knapsack. His fur is thin, standing away from his body at odd angles. As it runs toward me, barking, I can see the yellows of its eyes. The mutt skids to a halt about ten feet away. There it sits, alternating a bark with a growl. GRRRRRRRR.....RRRRALF! GRRRRRRRRR-RRR...RRRRALF! GRRRRR...RRRRALF!

I put finger to my lips, motioning it to be quiet. That brings it to its feet.

"RRRALF! RRRALF! RRRALF!" it barks, forgetting the growls.

A light goes on on the ground floor of the leper colony next door. A short man, with hair as wild as the dog's, runs out, buttoning up his shirt. He looks at me walking in the yard.

Rubbing his thumb against the other fingers, he makes the universal sign for "where's the dough?"

I point toward the open window of my room.

"It's on the table," I say in English, drawing a table in the air with the index fingers on both hands. This makes the dog bark even more viciously. The man understands though. Then, he touches his thumb to his middle and index finger, twisting his wrist. I get it, "where's the room key?" I point to the room again, clapping one hand on top of the other. The man nods and heads toward the building, unlocking the padlock on the outside.

"Oi! Oi!" I shout to him. (This is the way you get attention in Mongolia.)

He looks at me. I point to the dog. He looks at the growling animal and shrugs. Then he enters the hotel.

Moving V-E-R-Y S-L-O-W-L-Y, I make my way around the dog and out of the yard. In five minutes I'm at Khatzul's house. The door is unlocked. Khatzul and Gazagas are still in their pajamas.

Khatzul's mother stands over the stove, tending to a pot of boiling sheep's entrails. I'm just in time for breakfast.

"Did I miss the orgy?" I say, then cough heavily.

"Mykel!" says Khatzul. "Why you here?"

"I said meet me at eight. It's eight thirty."

The girls look at each other like you or I might look at the ceiling. Mom scoops some intestines and a heart into a plate and hands it to me.

"Here is breakfast," says Gazagas.

"My father killed sheep last night," says Khatzul, "so we have plenty."

I'm sorry I missed that. The Mongolian sheep-killing ritual is something I want to see in person before I leave, but it's too early for entrails.

"Do you have any bread and butter?" I ask.

We pack up after breakfast. I ask Khatzul if I should bring the tent and extra food.

"What you want," she says. "I think we find food there."

Liking the idea of the three of us in my snug little tent, I decide to take it. I don't have room for food.

After packing, we walk to the same big dirtpatch where the truck let us off on the trip from *Ulaanbaatar*.

A few jeeps and some worn blue and white Russian-built trucks are parked there. All the vehicles have open driver's doors with drivers standing besides them. Khatzul goes from jeep to jeep speaking with them. Less than half an hour later, nearly eleven o'clock, she finds one she likes.

"We go this one," she says. "Gazagas and me sit in back. You sit in front. It more comfortable."

I get in next to the driver. He's a swarthy country man. The calluses on his hands cover years of ground-in dirt. He nods at me as if I weren't strange and lights up a cigarette. The girls get in the back and sit jabbering, probably about what a millstone around their necks I am.

The jeep sits there. Inside, there is space for four. Since there are four of us, I figure we must be waiting for more people. I figure right.

"We wait for doctor," says Khatzul. "You need doctor, no?"

I try to laugh at the joke, but I cough.

At noon we leave. No doctors, no one else. What a pleasant surprise! We're off on the road to Hovsgul Lake. In the city, the road is already bumpier than a gravel pit. The windows don't open. It's hot. We've stopped, not yet out of town.

"What are we doing?" I ask the backseaters. "Are we waiting for someone?"

"We wait for two ones," says Gazagas.

At 1PM, I'm in front and the girls are in back with a guy in a *deel*. Another man has joined us. He's in the back too. That's 5 back there in a seat made for 3. Not bad. At least it's comfy up here. The girls were right.

We stop again, this time for a young man — and his daughter. They sit in the front, sharing the single bucket seat with me.

It takes only five hours for the four hour drive to the lake. The girls and I are the last to get out.

We're in front of a tourist camp. Except for a parked old truck, it's empty. No wonder, it's freezing, much colder than in Moron. A biting wind comes off the lake. It heads directly for my lungs, stirring the phlegm. I pull my jacket tighter around me.

A wooden fence surrounds the camp. Inside is one *ger*, a large single-story building and two smaller ones. We're met at the gate by a well-tapered woman in her early thirties. She leads us into the *ger*. There are three beds around the periphery and a metal stove in the center. Three beds, and three of us. Looks like we're going to be mighty intimate. Mmmm boy.

"We sleep in big building," says Gazagas. "You sleep in *ger*. It more comfortable. It cost only thirty dollar."

"Thirty dollars?" I yell, correcting the plural formation. "I'm not going to pay thirty dollars to sleep by myself in a *ger*."

"It cheaper," says Khatzul, "if you no eat."

"I'll stay in the tent, outside," I say. "That's free."

Their faces squinch with reluctance as they translate for the caretaker. Khatzul tilts her head toward me as she speaks. I hear the word *"uchlarai"* ("excuse me"). I embarrass her.

The caretaker looks grim, shakes her head, and says something to them.

"She say it dangerous," says Khatzul. "Police come and make you pay."

"I won't pay thirty dollars to stay by myself in a *ger*," I say before breaking into a coughing fit. "Why can't I stay with you in the main building?"

Khatzul looks at Gazagas. Her face reddens slightly. They're silent.

"Tell her what I said," I say.

"You make us ashamed," says Khatzul. "This woman nice."

"I don't care if she's Mother Theresa," I say smashing my fist against my open palm, "I'm not paying thirty dollars."

My sudden anger scares them. Khatzul speaks to the woman glancing sideways toward me as if she's in charge of an escaped convict.

These are Mongol women: tough country girls. How can they be so meek not even to bargain? I know Mongols hate to talk about money, but $30?

Eventually we bargain to $20 a night, if I take a room in the main building. I agree.

We're put in a two room suite, the girls in one room, me in the other. In a closet in the small atrium, a large white sink drips cold water. The only toilet is an outhouse outside the compound fence. After we set up house, I need a nap. I want to rest up before embarking on this series of adventures. I have a lot planned.

First is the Mongolian Navy. This entire armed force is two small boats parked on Lake Hovsgul. I want to see them. How many foreigners can say they've seen the Mongolian Navy?

Also, there are yaks. Herds of 'em, all over the area near the lake. I've never seen a yak up close — within petting distance. I don't want to miss that either.

Then there are the hills, forests, nearby herdsmen, carvers and craftsmen — and THE REINDEER PEOPLE.

These tribesmen have their pictures in all the Mongolian museums. Closely related to Eskimos, their lives in the North are based around reindeer. They herd them, eat them, wear them, and ride them. I don't mean ride like on a sled with presents, but bareback like an Indian on a palomino.

My students tell me there are only fifty reindeer people left. They all live in Hovsgul *Aimag*. I've ridden my camel — but every Jewish tourist in Israel has done that. Riding a reindeer, though, they'll have to go pretty far to top that.

By now my cough is almost continuous. It worsens when I lie down. I stumble from bed to chair where I manage to nod off, sitting up.

An hour later, when I awaken, the girls are nowhere — or at least not in their room. I hope they've been working on travel plans while I slept.

I walk outside to find them. Even colder out here, I huddle in my thin jacket. Behind the building, on a concrete patch, is a stake and a bunch of Mongols, among them Gazagas and Khatzul. They're playing horseshoes with some young folks from Erdinet.

"Mykel-*baksh*!" shouts Gazagas. I wish she wouldn't call me that. '*baksh*' has the ring of 'professor' to it, along with the Mongolian equivalent of a straight pipe, tweed jacket and elbow patches.

"Hi Gazagas," I cough. "I got a great sleep and I'm ready to go off."

"Where do you want?" asks Gazagas. Behind her, Khatzul tosses a horseshoe and stamps her foot when it sails past the stake.

"Well, how about seeing the navy today?" I suggest.

"Navy no good. We need car. No car. Navy tomorrow."

"Let's go out by the lake and look at the yaks," I try.

"Yaks not nice," she answers. "Yaks mean. Go like this."

She puts a finger up on each side of her head. Then she puts her head down and charges me. I dodge, barely avoiding being gored. The adrenaline brings on a coughing fit.

"You still sick?" she asks.

"I'm not SICK!" I reply. "It's an allergy."

"You need rest from allergy. Forget yaks," she says.

The sweat, now glistening on her skin gives her a sunlight-catching glow. Her normally red cheeks radiate. Suddenly, I'm warm in the cold lake air.

"Well," I say, "how about if we just go for a walk in the woods? It's a beautiful day and there are lots of trees to look at. There aren't many trees in other parts of Mongolia."

Gazagas looks into my face. Her eyes move in little jerks, focusing on my chin, my forehead, my nose, my eyes. I return the gaze with as much innocence as I can muster.

"We walk later," she says. "I promise to play pool with girls. We play now."

Coughing my anger, I spin on my heel and stomp away, out of the camp, into the woods...alone.

Having no sense of direction, I pick one path and stick to it. It's safer. A dirt path runs parallel(ish) to a dried riverbed. I'll follow it, trying to stay away long enough for Gazagas to get worried and come running after me. She'll stream tears of apologies and confess her love for me and how worried she was and how I should never go off alone again. Dinner isn't for another three hours. That's plenty of time to create a panic.

The woods are empty of visible wildlife. The faint whirring chirp of an unseen bird is all the fauna I get. Although it's June, many of the trees are just budding, some are completely bare. Dried twigs litter the jeep path, sometimes obscuring it completely.

For the first kilometer, I can see the camp. It's vaguely behind me, slightly to the right or the left depending on the wind of the path. As I walk, I begin to lose my obsession with Gazagas. I simply enjoy the land — especially the smell. Not a suburban "country smell" sprayed into the park for weekend walkers. Not a farm smell, like in Wisconsin, or even the outskirts of *Ulaanbaatar*.

The smell here is different. It's a pungent green smell, almost minty in the way it enters my nostrils and opens them straight to the sinuses. As I lose sight of the camp, the smell makes me feel heady, absolutely free, like the only man in the world. Time disappears. Have I been gone an hour? Two?

I stop in the middle of the path. I spin on my toes. Turning and turning, making myself dizzy. I fall. I lay there in the dirt, among the dried twigs and small stones. On my back, drunk with the solitude. The smell of the country — so strong I can taste it. The breeze of the country washes over me. Me, alone, in the forest in Outer Fuckin' Mongolia. Absolute solitude in the most isolated place on earth.

I don't know how long I spend there, just lying, not thinking these things, but feeling them in complete bliss. That feeling slowly turns to sadness as I realize I'll probably never feel this again. With that feeling, comes the realization that the girls must be worried about me. It's time to trek back.

Since, I hate going back the same way I come. I decide to return via the riverbed rather than the trail. I climb down the almost perpendicular slope to the gravel bottom. The stones are big, rougher than I'd expect--not like the fine sand beds in the Gobi.

All that air and smell and joy that I've been breathing now reek havoc on my immune system. My eyes tear. My nose runs. And my cough gets REAL BAD. It forces me to sit down, bending over my arms, now clasped to my stomach. My throat feels like it's being torn out. I cough again, hard. My stomach tightens, forcing its contents upwards. I cough more. Some potatoes, a little lamb, some blood spew out onto the gravel. I'm dizzy again, this time without spinning.

I try to stand. To walk. It's as if I'm swimming through Jello. Each step is in slow motion as I follow the riverbed toward what I hope is the camp.

The sickness heightens my awareness of the world around me. The air seems cleaner than any air I've breathed before. The gravel under my feet crunches louder than any gravel has crunched before. The solitude of the place makes me feel more alone than I have ever felt before.

Plod by slow plod, I make my way toward the camp. Piece by piece, it comes into view: the fence, the wooden main building, the *ger*. I wonder how long I've been gone. By now they'll have called the cops. The entire navy will be searching for me. An eternity later, I reach the gate.

Walking to my room, I pull on the door. It's locked.

I stagger outside, meeting Khatzul on her way out of the central building.

"Mykel-*baksh*," she says, "I was just inside learning pool. I never play it before."

"Key," I say. "I need the room key. Where do you think I've been?"

"Were you someplace?" she says. "I don't see that you go away."

"What do you mean!" I say, bursting into a coughing fit "I was in the jungle. I almost died. You didn't even notice I was away?"

"I play pool," she says. "It too bad. You very sick man. You sleep. It be good later."

I take the key from her hand, stumble to the dorm building, go in the room and collapse on the bed.

I feel better when I wake up. I also feel very hungry. Luckily, it's close to dinner time. We arrive late to the large dining hall. Others are already eating plates full of noodles and lamb. They sit at the two front tables. Everyone knows each other.

At the very front of the room is a counter. On the other side of the counter is the kitchen — actually one huge pot sitting on a wood-burning stove. Next to the stove is a steel sink.

The hubbub of the crowd quiets as we enter through the back door. We take our seats at another table. Hour d'oeuvres are already laid out — three paper thin slices of cucumber with an equal amount of tomato. Oh yeah, there's also a thermos full of milk-tea.

Khatzul pours tea for all of us and slowly picks at the slices in front of her. Gazagas stares intently at the other table. I follow her gaze to a young man with dark sunglasses and a blue polyester shirt more suitable for Bermuda than Mongolia. He's leaning forward, talking intently with an older woman.

We've finished our hors d'oeuvres and sit waiting for the main course. One by one the people from the other table get up and leave.

"Why don't we tell the kitchen we're here?" I suggest to the girls,

"We be fed," says Khatzul. "We shy. It better to wait."

The sunglasses man and the woman he was talking to are the last to leave. Now it's just us waiting at the table. The sky gradually darkens into dusk.

"This is ridiculous," I say, "I'm asking for food."

The girls look at each other in horror, but say nothing. I walk to the kitchen counter. A serious young woman, her hair tied back, loads dishes into the sink. An old man stirs the large pot on the stove. I clear my throat.

The man looks at me, raising his eyebrows.

"Batsteseg?" he calls to the woman. She looks at him. He nods toward me.

She motions me to sit down, then walks out of the kitchen and asks the girls which of the leftovers they would prefer. We take the lamb and noodles.

We eat in silence. I can feel the girls' anger at my embarrassing them by asking for food.

After dinner I suggest a short nap and then a walk by the lake. A herd of yak was grazing there earlier and I want to take a close look at them. Maybe I can ride one.

"You need nap," says Gazagas. The concern in her eyes is not quite as touching as the slimness of her hips and her pert breasts against the cashmere of her sweater. "You sick. Maybe you should stay in. Lake too wet tonight. And we need to make ready."

"Ready?" I ask, choking back a cough. "Ready for what?"

"Ready for disco," she continues. "Big disco tonight. Everybody in camp. But you need sleep. You should stay in. It more comfortable for you."

"No!" I shout. "If you go to a disco, I go to a disco. Right now, I'll just go for a walk by the lake and come back later. What time is the disco?"

"It start at nine," says Khatzul, "but it ok if you come late."

"Yeah," I say, "I'll bet it is."

I storm off toward the lake, considering the possibility of throwing myself into it.

To my far left is the yak herd, grazing near a small wooded area. Directly in front of me, about half a mile away is the lake. The ground between is pure mud. Little mud hills with tufts of grass at the top, one after the other. My feet go ankle deep with each step.

I head for the yaks, about twenty of them, grazing peacefully. A few lay down like contented cows. Others lazily chew the sparse grass, enjoying the remaining few hours of sunshine. I trudge through the mud toward the peaceful animals. I have no way of knowing the males from the females. Their long hair skirts make it impossible to count the hangings. I don't care. I only want to pet them.

Before Mongolia, I thought yaks were black, buffalo-ish animals. Up close, they come in as many colors as cows. Gray, black, brown, with horns, without them. The Mongols told me that the ones with horns are "Yows," half yak, half cow. I suspect they were pulling my leg.

I'm now close enough to realize that yaks smell a lot like cows. Close enough for them to realize I'm not from around here. A big gray yak raises his head from the ground and stares straight at me. His nostrils widen as if stifling a yawn. As I get closer, the yaks lying lazily in the wet earth suddenly stand up. One, two, then the lot of them. Their attention focuses on me!

I stand ankle deep in the mud. Lifting each foot, the goo sucks it back again. Loud farting sounds rise as the air beneath my foot bubbles through the ooze. As I walk, I cough.

A few seconds ago, the yaks were lazing in the mud, chewing the grass, or just sunning themselves. Now, they're all on their feet. The one closest to me, large, brown and white, with horns, nods its head up and down, as if dovening at shul. I stop when it snorts. A ripple of tension passed down its left side, leaving in a quick flick of the tail.

I change my angle, approaching in a more gentle, circular way. It doesn't work. They know I'm coming. The brown and white one hasn't taken its eyes off me. Now a large gray animal moves to prepare...for what?

Its muscles tense. The skirt of hair between its belly and the ground twitches in nervous apprehension. I'm committed. I can't run if I want to because of the mud.

Slowly I continue my approach, speaking softly, trying to gain their confidence.

"Nice yaky, yaky. < cough > Nice yaky, yaky," I say, still slowly walking forward. "I'm your friend. < cough > I just want to make nice." The gray yak shakes its head like a wet dog, answering my offer of friendship with a big "NO!"

When I get about twenty yards away, things change. The formerly independent animals become a herd. The brown and white and the gray yak lead the phalanx. The others huddle behind them. They're tense, muscles tight beneath their fur.

I step forward slowly, silently. They run. Away. 100% away. Full speed, in the opposite direction. Toward the woods and a *ger* camp far in the distance. Instant view of two dozen yak butts wiggling in terror.

The ability to frighten such powerful animals gives me no joy. This is Mongolia. I LOVE Mongolia, but in my final weeks here, it's rejecting me. First the girls, now even the yaks.

Shunned, I turn and trudge toward the lake. The only sound is the farting mud around my ankles and the heavy cough coming from my chest. Smooth gravel covers the shore. Large pieces of waterworn driftwood, bleached by the sun, blink like diamonds in the fading light. It's nine o'clock. The sun is two hours from the horizon. I lay down in the gravel to look over the expansive lake and wallow in my misery like the yaks wallowed in the mud.

Before long, my misery leaves and the joy of absolute solitude and beauty takes over. The infinite waves caress the shore. A long-neck crane glides overhead like a silent Concorde. It swoops after something in the lake, touching lightly, and taking off again.

I pick up a piece of driftwood and daydream about its life, its travel through the distance, its winding up on this shore, just like me.

Despite the cold, I feel the peaceful comfort of being 'away'. How much more away can you be than at the biggest lake in Outer Mongolia?

From behind me comes the bitta bitta, bitta bitta of a car engine. A blue van pulls up about twenty yards away. It stops. The rear doors open. Out jump a boy of about eight and a slightly older girl, in bathing suits.

The girl runs toward the lake. The boy gives chase, grabbing her, pulling her hair, "Mommy! Mommy!" (actually, the Mongolian equivalent) screams the girl. The boy lets go. They run straight toward where I am. When they see me, they stop.

The boy points to me and says something. The girl looks. They both run over to me and start babbling.

"Bi *olgakhgui!*" (I don't understand) I say, shrugging my shoulders.

They find this hilarious. Still giggling, they run past me toward the lake and pick up driftwood on the way, including the recent object of my meditation. When they reach the lake, they throw the driftwood back in, wading out a bit to make sure it doesn't flow back to shore.

I figure it's time to leave. The disco must've started by now.

By the time I get back the sun has begun to set. Even my cold and depression can't ruin the beauty of it. I stop for a few seconds just to feel the colors and shooting rays of light over the lake. Like dying leaves, the beauty of the dying sun is greater than life.

Enough morbidity...I'm off to the disco. First, a brief stop in my room to change out of my muddy boots. Then a quick look in the mirror. Yuck! I run a comb over the baldspot and head to the front building, already blasting with music.

It's not disco, but a kind of polka music. An Oriental melody twists through it, like a worm hidden in an apple. It's fast, accordianless, and ear-splittingly loud. Fifteen years in a punkrock band cost me a good chunk of my hearing. Looks like the rest goes tonight.

The disco is in a large room in the building closest to the lake. The stereo and huge speakers are at one end. Around the perimeter are wooden benches. On the benches are the crew from Erdinet. Loud, friendly Mongols, they gesture and touch each other like people who've grown up together. They wear clean slacks and shirts. A few wear blue jeans. Except for the lack of cowboy hats, it's the kind of clothes you might see on city dudes at a square dance.

There are also some locals, young men, in dirty *deels*, their eyes darting at the strange city folks. Fresh from the nearby *gers*, their faces and hands show the muck and cold of the countryside.

The Erdinet people speak quietly as the Polka-ish music plays in the foreground. The locals stand near the doorway, like hawks ready to swoop down on the tourists.

A young man, filthy face with a shadow of a mustache, stands next to the door. He leans ominously against on the wall. One hand plays with a fresh scab under his lower lip. The other drums against the wall, out of time with the music.

In the middle, on the dancefloor, is no one.

I sit next to a tall man with broad shoulders and a head shaped like a deck of cards, flat in front and back, and completely square at the sides. He starts the conversation.

"You Merican?" he asks.

"Yes," I say, "my name is Mykel."

"I Tochtchaluun," he says.

We shake hands.

"Speak you Mongolian?" he asks me.

"Neg, hoyer, gurav" (one, two, three), I say.

He laughs.

Then he starts talking, on and on, mixing Russian and Mongolian with a few English words. I understand 'dance,' 'Mongolian girls,' 'animals' and that's about it. I smile at the steady lexical stream, nodding as if I understand what he's saying.

"Khoroshoo!" ("Good," in Russian), he says, slapping me on the back.

By now, the place is crowded, though there's still no one on the dancefloor. Gazagas and Khatzul come in. They see me on the bench and walk over, squeezing in on either side of me.

On the other side of Gazagas sits the sleazebag with the sunglasses and the polyester shirt. He crosses his legs at the knee. The top leg points toward her.

The music stops. Gazagas leans away from the creep, toward me, as if to kiss me. Instead, she whispers in my ear.

"We now have entertainment," she says.

"Great!" I say. "This is local culture. I came here for it. It's better than disco."

Gazagas smiles and nods. The entertainers sit on chairs in the front of the hall. They're all part of the Erdinet group. The M.C., a short fat man, half bald, with bushy eyebrows, takes the microphone. He makes an introduction and a lithe young man stands to take over.

He's a comedian. Throwing out non-stop patter, he shrugs his shoulders, gestures toward the ground, then toward the ceiling. He mimes pouring a drink. With each sentence, peals of laughter come from the audience. The big guy next to me slaps me on the back after each joke. Trying to keep a constant smile on my face, I hope the natives will mistake it for understanding. They don't even notice.

After the comedian, while the Mongols wipe laugh tears out of their eyes, the M.C. returns to the mic. He introduces a man in his early thirties, who wears a conservative suit that would fit better on a Chinese party bureaucrat than a relaxing Mongol.

Khatzul turns to me. "This interesting for you," she says. "This Mongolian long song. It only here."

Prepared to listen to a twenty minute a capella polka, I'm not particularly enthusiastic. Then the man begins to sing.

The 'long' part of long songs is NOT the song itself, but each note. The singer somehow manages to take a very Oriental sounding melody, and play it at the wrong speed.

"Biiiiiiiiiiiiii mmmmmmmmiiiiiiiiiiiiiiiiiinnnnnnnnnnnnniiiiii taaaaaaaaaaaaaannnn-nnnnnniiiiiiiiiii..."

Eyes closed, he sways back and forth. The audience relaxes on their benches. The too-friendly man next to me leans back against the wall. His eyes half-closed, an almost post-coital smile fixes itself to his lips.

The singer is in a trance, letting the sssssssslllllooooooowwwwwwww sounds come from his mouth without a vocal waver. His eyes close completely. He reaches forward, toward the audience, like a blind man begging for help. It is one of those moments, like being alone in the woods, that I want never to end. A pure moment of experience.

The dancehall disappears. The scary guys in grubby *deels* disappear. My cough disappears. There's nothing except this man in front of me, these incredible sounds coming out of his mouth, this NOW.

When it's over, the audience applauds politely. I'm stunned.

"Did you not like it?" asks Khatzul.

"It was great," I say to her.

Then, I notice the sleazebag next to Gazagas has pressed his knee against hers. While the next act sets up, the guy pretends to be intrigued by the moving of the podium and chairs in front of the room.

As he talks to the woman on his left, he presses his leg tighter into Gazagas's. He lets his right hand dangle, so the fingers just touch her knee.

Righteous hatred tenses my stomach like vomit. It forces its way upwards until I can taste it. That asshole! Taking advantage of a situation like that. What a masher! A creep. I wouldn't blame her if she elbowed him, hard! Hah! I'd do it. Just let her complain to me and I'll take care of him.

I cough in fury.

Back in front, preparation continues. The leader of the little Erdinet tourist group makes a speech. A few more people do the same. Then the music starts again.

Sleazebag asks Gazagas to dance. She shakes her head no. My heart lifts. Gazagas asks me to dance, my heart lifts and falls. I can't, so I decline. She looks genuinely disappointed as she goes off with the older man who sung the long song.

As I watch the dancers, I realize I made the right decision. I'm uncoordinated as it is, but this dance is brutal. The partners put their hands around each other's waists. They spin, like the wrestlers I saw in *UB*. Completely disregarding the music, the object seems to be to create as much centrifugal force as possible.

In order not to fly off and smash into a wall, the partners have to cling ever more tightly to each other as they step carefully in their dizziness. Twenty couples, twirling like gears in a demon machine. Faster, faster. Gazagas's normally red cheeks are drained of blood, now spun to the back of her neck.

When the music stops, people stagger like drunks to their seats. Gazagas now sits on the other side of me, away from the scumbag.

In a few seconds, the stereo cranks out another Mongol polka. The scumbag stands up and walks past me, standing directly in front of Gazagas. Again he asks her to dance.

What's the matter, asshole? Can't you take no for an answer?

Gazagas nods her head and the two of them get up and start spinning. She looks so happy I could puke. A women in a bright red *deel*, walks over to me.

"You dancing?" she asks.

A fantasy flashes: whirling her around, smashing into the joyful new couple, like a *buzz* saw into a log. But I shake my head.

"I don't dance," I say.

"You please dance," she says. "You nice man."

I cough.

"You sick man?" she asks.

"I'm not sick..." I start, but catch myself.

"Yes," I say. "I'm a sick old man. I need sleep."

With that, I get up and walk out of the place. I go into my freezing room, take a hefty slug of Mongolian cough syrup and shuffle to the chair. I drift in and out of sleep until I hear the fumbling on the outside door.

Then there's laughter. Two laughing girls' voices. Two more laughing boys' voices. There's the sound of the inner door, the door to the girls' room, opening and closing. Then, more laughter.

I choke back a cough.

I think of my own college days, my own chance to get away from my parents, my own youthful lust. Don't these young Mongols also deserve a chance? Fair thoughts. Altruistic thoughts. They don't work.

What about my PRESENT lust? Doesn't that count for anything? The coughs slip out. Fast, loud and hard. The talking and loud laughing on the other side of the wall don't change.

I don't know what happened that night. In and out of a fitful, cough-ridden sleep, I awaken to silence, broken only by my wheezing.

After breakfast, the girls say they've met some people and promised to do 'things' with them. They'd like to go with me, but they can't. Besides, "You go alone, see anything," says Gazagas. "It more comfortable for you."

Maybe they're right. My experience in

the woods was transcendent. A long walk by the lake might be the same. I could ignore the yaks and just walk north, toward the reindeer people. There are a few *gers* about a mile up the coast.

I head out, the cough worse, but my spirits better than the night before. Soon, it's just me and the trees and the yaks and the cows.

I turn left and walk. Before long it returns: the nirvana of knowing the same liquid in the lake also runs through my veins and the veins of that big yak across the mudflat. We are one, water and carbon join us together in a glorious universe. One with that world. This is true peace. Me and the whole wide wonderful Mongolian universe. Then comes the forest ranger — and the rain.

The first few drops begin to hit when a Russian-made jeep passes me about twenty yards to my left. If a car could stop, do a double take, and come back for a closer look, that's what that jeep did.

Pulling up right next to me, the door opens. A tall man with a boxer's jaw gets out. His steel gray temples reek of officialdom. He looks at me.

"*Sain bain yy,*" he says.

"*Sain bain yy,*" I reply.

"You stay here?" he asks.

"I stay there," I answer, pointing toward the tourist camp.

"You permit?" he asks.

"I'm not camping," I say, "I'm staying in the tourist camp."

"You need permit," he says. "I forest ranger. You buy permit from me."

I shrug, look skyward and cough a bit.

"You wait here," he says. "I come back."

He gets back in his jeep and heads north, toward those reindeer folk. Within ten minutes the trickle becomes a downpour.

Still no sign of the guy, I turn back. By now, the mud of yesterday has become a bog. Shloooop. Shloooop. Shloooop. It sloshes to my calf with each step.

My clothes stick to my body. Soaked through four layers, the cold rides piggyback on the wetness. No jeep passes me on the way back. Although I'm miserable, I have a bit of solace in escaping the fine.

It's when I enter the camp gate, that I hear the engine behind me. I don't have to turn around to know its Soviet origin.

"*Sain bain yy*" comes the official voice behind me. "We go your room now, and talk."

When we get there, he sits on the bed. I take the only chair in the room.

"You like Hovsgul?" he asks, more enthusiastically than menacingly.

"It's great," I say.

"Beautiful nature, lake, nice places," he says, nodding in agreement with himself.

"Sure," I answer.

"You help. Please write and mail," He gives me a sheaf of paper.

I glance at the top "Survey on Mongolian Recreational Land Use, prepared by The University of Idaho in Cooperation with..."

"Sure," I say, "I'd be glad to. Nice talking with you..."

"You also pay," he says.

"I do," I tell him, "and often."

He doesn't get it.

"We need money for nature. We need to keep it beauty."

I nod a resigned, "How much?" and cough.

"You sick?" he asks.

"Yes," I tell him, "I need to change out of these wet clothes."

"You nice man," he says like a Mongolian tells a lamb 'you nice sheep,' before he prepares it for dinner. "You pay only two thousand *tugriks*."

That's about four dollars, not bad, really. I reach in my pocket. Too quickly.

"How long you stay?" he asks.

"I'm leaving tomorrow," I tell him.

"How long you here by now?" he asks.

"I came yesterday," I say, figuring I'll get off easier with a short stay. For once, I figure right.

I pay my 2000 *tugriks*. He shakes my hand and leaves. I strip off my wet clothes, get under the flimsy bed covers and cough into a fitful sleep.

◎ ◎ ◎

A little past midnight there's a knock on my door. It's Khatzul.

"Mykel," she says. "Everything good. We go with Erdinet people. They want us."

"Yeah, I'll bet they do," I answer.

"Yes!" she says. "We leave tomorrow, after breakfast. They take me to Moron. You and Gazagas go to Erdinet. You get train from there."

Hmmm, me and Gazagas, together in a sleeper car for fifteen hours. Not a bad prospect.

"Great," I say, with a cough. "Where's Gazagas now?"

"She with one Erdinet boy," says Khatzul. "He very nice."

"Yeah, I'll bet he is." I answer.

Khatzul nods and goes off to her room. I take a slug of cough syrup and fall back into a fitful sleep.

The next morning, much after breakfast, we pile into the truck to Erdinet. Gazagas sits near the cab with her friendly sleazebag in sunglasses. I sit in back and cough. She looks so happy I could shit.

The truck ride through the muddy hills is rough enough to make me sicker. Leaping and kicking like an angry yak, each vertebra rattles in a different direction.

Every few kilometers, the Erdineters stop and take pictures of each other. This is Altanbaatar in front of a swan on the lake. This is Batzul next to a wooden house. This is Uyantuul with a tree.

The truck stops near the top of a hill. We pile out and take our familiar picnic positions. This time I wander off to look at the countryside and cough in peace. When I get back they're putting a just-bought sheep into a burlap bag.

In front, a wiry man with very long nosehair has hammerlocked the sheep around the neck. In back, a stocky man wearing a jet-black *deel* holds a burlap bag. A middle-aged man, with a shock of silver hair, hugs the animal's rump.

"Maaaaaaa Maaaaaaaaaaaaa!" brays the sheep.

The stocky guy holds open the burlap bag. The rumpman lifts the sheep off the ground and pulls it toward the bag. The sheep shits — loose and green. It spills down its legs, over the ground, onto the rim of the bag and inside.

The wiry guy at the head pushes like you might stuff a jack back in a jack-in-the-box. The animals eyes are opened wide, bulging in terror.

"Maaaaaaaaaa! Maaaaaaaaaaaaaaa! Maaaaaaaaaaaaaaaaaa!"

The stocky guy pulls the bag over the sheep's rump, forcing its hind legs up under it. The shit drops with a soft muddy sound in the bag.

The middle-aged man now grabs the top of the bag, pulling it up to the animal's forelegs. The original bagman gives a boost from behind. Then the middle-aged man leans around the sheep's neck, coming very close to the wiry man holding the head. He leans forward. He grabs both of the sheep's front legs and pulls them back and up. The sheep rests a second in mid air before slamming chest first onto the ground. Thunk! A small dustcloud rises around the quartet. The rear man, in control of the bag, yanks it over those front legs, pulling it up to the animal's neck.

"Maaaaaaaaaaaaaaaaaaaaaaaa! Maaaaaaaaaaaaaaaaaaaaaaaaaaaaaaaaaaaa! Maaa-aaaaaaaaaaaaaaa!"

They tie the bag tightly around the animals neck. Then the front man and the bag man grab the burlap and lift the now-bagged sheep off the ground. Together, they stumble toward the back of our truck.

"Neg, hoyer, gurav!" they count, then throw the bundle into the truck. BLAM! It lands hard on the metal floor. The rest of us pile in after it.

Gazagas takes her place at the front end. I sit as far away as possible at the back end — right next to the sheep.

The truck bounces off, on its way to the barbecue. Avoiding Gazagas means I look at the sheep. Its big dark eyes are moist with fear. I close my own eyes, pretending to sleep. The big man next to me gets the same idea. He's tired too. Lying across the truck floor, his body forces me to huddle back closer to the sheep.

Sitting with my legs in lotus position, my knee brushes the burlap bag. The sheep looks up at me and rests its head on my lap like a dog begging to be scratched behind the ears.

It's silent now, shaking in the sack. Every time the truck bounces, those moist big eyes become even bigger as they look up into my face. Unable to re-sist any longer, I pet the animal, scratching it behind the ears, stroking its head.

"This is my test," I think. "If I can eat an animal I've been this close to, then I am a moral person."

It's so easy for civilized people to divorce themselves from their food. Someone else does the killing. We eat what looks like meat, not like animals. We're responsible for the killing, but we won't take the responsibility. That's wrong. If you're going to eat meat, then you'd better be able to first look it in the eye and pet it behind the ears.

"Ok, Lambchops," I say in a low voice, "soon this will all be over. You'll join your shepherd in His kingdom where there is no mutton."

An hour later, we're in a small town. The truck parks in front of a weathered wooden fence. A squat man with a puckered face and tiny ears gets out. He bangs on the green gate.

The gate creaks open. From behind, an old lady, weathered as the fence, peers out. When she sees the squat man, she hugs him. Then she waves to the truck driver and opens the gate wide. Two big men shoulder open the truck's back doors. Leaping over Lambchops and me, they jump to the ground.

Two women, built like the men on the ground, set themselves behind the sheep.

"Neg! Hoyer! Gurav!"

They push the sheep out of the truck. The men below break its fall. The rest of us jump down.

We enter the woman's house. It's a log cabin, built around one room. A pretty young woman, wearing a dirty *deel*, stokes the central stove. To the right of us is a bed, covered with a wool blanket. Two boys, about six and eight years old, sit on that blanket. They're watching a Mongolian movie on an old black and white TV. When I walk in, they immediately sit up and squeeze together.

A crinkle-faced man smokes a long pipe with a silver bowl and mouthpiece. Tiny red capillaries crisscross his face. With his pipe, he motions me to sit on the bed. I nod, smile, and take my place next to the kids. Khatzul sits next to me. I've lost track of Gazagas.

Suddenly, I begin to cough furiously, spraying saliva over the green-painted floor. The old man speaks to me in Mongolian.

"No," I answer, without understanding a word, "it's only an allergy."

The young woman, pants-popping cheekbones and heart-melting eyes, offers us milk tea.

Khatzul points to the squat man who first got out of the truck.

"He old people's nephew," she explains. "They not see for long time."

After tea and catching up on old times, we go outside for the barbecue.

The sheep is on its back, still alive. Two young men, each on one end, hold her hooves. They pull them up and back, away from the body. Using a small sharp knife, the squat man with the small ears makes an earlength cut in the lamb's belly, just like in the movie I saw before I came to Mongolia. The knife slides in smoothly, to the hilt.

A thin red line forms as the man pulls the knife southward, stretching the slit to about ten inches long. After rolling up his right sleeve, he presses his fingers at the edge of that slit. Slowly those fingers enter the body cavity. He fumbles momentarily, feeling for the large artery that leads to the heart. The muscles on his forearm tighten when he finds it, grabs it and squeezes.

The men at either end of the sheep fight harder as the sheep jerks, trying to pull its legs together as if to cover the wound. Those dying eyes stare at me, "Et tu Mykel?" before they half close into permanent sleep.

Working with longer knives, three of the younger men slice under each leg and pull the skin away from the muscle underneath.

The animal jerks as its skin separates from its body. They're spasmatic jerks — like the frog muscles in a high school science experiment. Or else they're the jerks of horrible pain from being skinned while not quite dead.

The men pull the woolly skin away from the muscle underneath. Occasionally, they cut gossamer tissues of fat to help the separation. Bit by bit, an obscene nakedness reveals itself. The roadmap of veins and arteries crisscrossing the newly exposed muscle mirrors our host's veined face.

A tap to my shoulder. It's Gazagas, the first time she's spoken to me since we left the lake.

"We need water. They go. You go help. It nice. I stay here."

So I'm back in the truck with the two boys from the house and two very large men. They watch me warily as I cough and wheeze. We're going to a nearby river to fetch water for the house. We've got a pair of metal barrels, their seals repaired with layers of innertube.

The yaks bathing in the river turn toward our arriving truck. Jumping out, the Mongols pick up small stones and throw them at the hairy animals. Taking the hint, they lazily climb up the far bank and wait, ready to resume their bath when these pests leave.

The large men take the barrels down from the truck and bring them to the river. The boys and I ladle the yak bathwater into the barrels. When they're filled, it's one two heave ho back into the truck.

Returning to the log cabin, the smell of barbecued lamb greets us at the gate. Khatzul is inside, wiping off her mouth. Others, too, seem in their last stages of dinner.

I feel too sick to eat, but I also realize I must — to prove myself. The old woman sees me. Saying something in Mongolian, she calls to the beautiful young woman now stirring a large pot on a makeshift fire.

She spoons something into a metal bowl and hands it to the wiry man with the long nosehair. Steam rises from it as he walks carefully toward me. I roll down my sleeves to receive the special treat.

Lamb chops? Not exactly. But Lambchops' brain, stomach and a foot each of large and small intestines. All for me. My own guest-of-honor special treat.

Forcing a smile, I take the bowl from the man. He also hands me a small sharp knife — the murder weapon. I nod my head in thanks and go for the small intestines.

I slice a thumb-sized chunk and thrust the knife into it. Rubbery, it slips away from the point, sloshing lamb lipids onto my pants.

I try again, this time successfully spearing the organ slice. I bring it to my mouth and take a bite. The knife slips out, and the entire tube section hangs from between my teeth.

Grabbing the end with my hand, I mean to pull off a piece. Instead I squeeze it, like a toothpaste tube, forcing the contents directly down my throat. I gag, spit up, covering my pants and the ground near me with a fine brown spray. I cough until I can't breathe.

In trans-cultural stupidity (why do people everywhere do this?) the thin guy hits me on the back. It only makes it worse.

By now everyone is watching me. The old woman has fetched me a cup of tea. She watches as I sip it.

A woman missing both her front teeth believes she knows the cause of my problem. I'm a Westerner, and Westerners eat with forks. I'm choking on that piece of sheep gut. Why? I was eating with a knife. She disappears into the log cabin and returns with a fork. Smiling in triumph, she presents it to me as you might present a glass of 20 year old scotch to a visiting dignitary. I accept it as graciously as I can.

With everyone watching, I slice into a hunk of liver. I poke a forkful and gingerly put it into my mouth. Choking back a gag, I smile and say, "*amtatai*," delicious!

They nearly applaud.

I eat slowly, waiting for the Mongols to become involved with each other again, so I can subtly leave the bowl of innards in an inconspicuous place. An entire liver and part of a brain later, I get the chance.

After the meal, we give our thanks and good byes to our hosts and pile back in the truck. Gazagas takes her seat in front with the evil seducer. I sit in back, and a few stops later again find myself accompanied by a live sheep.

During the trip I become sicker and sicker. The combination of Lambchops' innards, the lingering Gobi disease, and the increasing friendliness of Gazagas with the sleazebag drive me further and further into my corner next to the sheep. When not glaring at Gazagas's non-stop conversation with the sun-glassed sharpie, I write on my yellow notepad avoiding all contact with those around me.

A woman offers me a cookie from a bag she has with her. I thank her but am too sick to eat it. Her face shows the insult of my rejection. I take one. I bite off a piece and chew until it's liquid. Somehow, I force it down. I smile and nod my thanks. She offers another cookie to someone else. I quickly slip the remainder of mine under my right thigh.

Sometime later, the master of ceremonies at the Erdinet party looks directly at me and says something in Mongolian.

"I don't understand," I shrug.

It's as if I farted at a cubscout camp. Laughter breaks out from the entire truckload of occupants. The wiry man, the hefty guys, the lady with no front teeth, the small eared-guy, Khatzul, Gazagas, beautiful Gazagas, all laughing at me, showing their gums, jiggling their bellies.

Hate like I've never known it before rises from my ankles to my knees to my stomach. It washes over me. My skin tingles and glows from it. It spurts out my eyes like warm coke from a shaken can. I don't say a word, but the laughter stops. Immediately.

It's nightfall, nine or ten o'clock. In the distance, faint forms of wooden buildings silhouette themselves against the dusk sky.

Khatzul shuffles in her seat. We must be coming to Moron. Soon: Drop Khatzul off, continue to Erdinet with the crew, then Gazagas and I, finally, alone together. I cough in anticipation.

The truck stops. The wiry guy stands up and moves toward the corner where my bag is stored. Crushed behind a box, he struggles to remove it.

"I sorry. I sorry," he says.

"It's ok," I say. "I'm staying on. You don't have to do that."

"We get off now," says Khatzul.

"What?" I say. "This is Moron. This isn't Erdinet. They said they'd take us to Erdinet. YOU get off here."

"I sorry. I sorry," says the Erdinet guy.

"They refuse," says Khatzul. "We must get off here."

I'm seething. My last chance. The fantasy that kept me going. The intimate train ride. The chance to talk alone. No more cramped trucks. No more smelly feet. They promised, and now they take it away.

Betrayed! How long have they known this but not told me? Furious, I push the Erdineter away and take the bag myself. I jump off the truck and don't look back. Behind me comes the double thump of the two girls, as they land on the ground and say their good byes.

Tha! Tha! Tha! Tha! Their footsteps quicken in the wet dirt as they catch up with me.

"I want to leave now!" I say.

"It too late," says Gazagas, frightened by my anger. "Why you want to leave?"

"I hate this place. I've had enough."

"It too late! It too late!" cries the girl, a waver of tears in her voice.

"We're going to that field," I shout, "the place where the trucks go. I'll sleep outside if I have to." I begin coughing so hard, I curl up on the wet ground, my arms wrapped around my stomach.

The girls panic. "Please, Mykel-*baksh*, you cannot. You must stay. Early, tomorrow, we go. Early. I promise."

They pick me up, one girl under each arm pit. We walk in a direction all too familiar.

◎ ◎ ◎

It's 11PM. I'm alone in my room in the best hotel in Moron. Cold, wet, sick and full of hate, I write these words by candlelight on one of the few scraps of paper I didn't leave in the truck.

The girls have dropped me here, and gone to Khatzul's house for the evening. They'll be here at seven o'clock tomorrow morning. Sure they will.

Right now I'll bathe in my own bile and phlegm, coughing and shivering as I write these words. Anger shakes me as much as the cold.

◎ ◎ ◎

At 8AM, there's a light tap on my door. Khatzul is there, asking if she wants me to have the hotel get breakfast. I shake my head.

"I only want to leave," I tell her.

We go to her house where I nod hello to her family and say not a word to Gazagas.

"Do you want some breakfast here?" asks Khatzul.

"I only want to leave," I repeat.

"Gazagas stay here," says Khatzul. "She go by plane, later."

Together, Khatzul and I go to the giant parking place. She finds me a seat in a jeep. Eight of us, including a very fat woman, will ride to *Ulaanbaatar*.

"Good bye Mykel-*baksh*," she says, "I write you."

I say nothing.

The trip back is more fun than the trip there. My fellow passengers adopt me, buy me meals, treat me to candy, refuse to take money. I hum along to their Mongolian songs, while the fat woman keeps offering me tea and tries to tell me how I should care for my cough.

One time, we stop to watch a children's horse race on the plains. Another time, it's some wild stallions fighting over a mare.

Between my scant Mongolian and their non-existent English, there's not much conversation. But these are fine people.

I arrive back in *Ulaanbataar* with only a week until I leave for good.

My new friends have renewed my love of Mongols — as long as they're not from Erdinet or haven't stuck me in the best hotel in Moron.

THIRTY ONE

Flashback: St. Patrick's day 1996. I'm at a US Government sponsored party. Party-goers had to buy their tickets from the American Embassy in advance. Few Mongolians know about it and that's the way the embassy likes it.

The party is in the old Russian cultural hall. This stone gray building has become just another disco since the fall of communism. Though I don't know its official name, I call it the Puke House, because the Russian letters PUHK blaze in neon from the roof.

I've come to the party with Bishbataar and Tsetsesseg. They have no tickets. Leaving them just outside the door, I enter. My students watch for their cue.

"I have my ticket here somewhere," I say loudly, fumbling through my wallet.

As I continue to fumble, I approach the ticket taker, standing at a small white desk near the food table. She's an American, about 50, with red hair and freckled white skin.

"Look," I say to the redhead, pointing over her shoulder to a spot on the ground, "did my tickets blow over there?"

The woman swings around to look at the spot. The Mongolians immediately slide past while her back is turned. They quickly lose themselves in the crowded main room.

The woman turns back to me. "I don't see anything there," she says.

"I must need new glasses," I tell her.

She looks at me strangely, perhaps noticing that I'm not wearing glasses in the first place.

"Anyway, I found the ticket," I say, handing it to her. "Happy St. Patrick's day."

She smiles, takes my ticket and I walk in. Middle-aged couples crowd the room. They dance to music that would embarrass even my parents in its quadrilateraltude: Mel Torme, Dean Martin, I don't know. All those guys sound the same to me. But there's free food and somebody is bound to be buying drinks.

The Mongols are off in another room where they found a karaoke machine. Bishbataar is at the microphone singing Yesterday. I find myself seated at a table with the new set of VSO volunteers. My future friends Al, Sebastian, James and Hannah are there. I introduce myself.

"Hi," I say, "my name's Mykel."

I sit myself between Sebastian and Hannah.

"A Yank!" says Sebastian. "Just when we're getting comfortable."

"St. Patrick was a Yank," I say.

"A wiseguy Yank," says Sebastian.

An intruder arrives. He's a squat Mongolian with a ten o'clock shadow and breath that could strip paint. He leans over the table and puts his arms around Sebastian and me, giving us more of a headlock than a hug. He calls us his "droogs."

"Hello, my droogs," he says. "I Mongolian. You American."

"We're not American," says Sebastian. "We're English."

"American. English. Same thing!" says the Mongol, laughing at humor beyond my comprehension.

The next part of his speech consists of foreign words, some German, some English, mostly Russian, dropped into a string of Mongolian. We have no idea what he's talking about. We only know that he is causing an extreme pain in our necks.

"Why you in Mongolia?" he finally asks, still hanging on us. "You tourists? Come to see beautiful Chinggis Khan land?"

"No," I tell him, trying to be as civil as possible, "we're English teachers. We work at the university. What do you do?"

"Me?" says the drunk. "My job Mongolian Airlines." He slaps his chest. "I pilot."

◎ ◎ ◎

That was many months ago. It seems like a different time, and it was. I think about the story now because in two weeks I'll be on the way to China. I'm flying MIAT, Mongolian Airlines — a free trip, paid for by the travel agent I teach. I wonder if "free" is too heavy a price.

In the meantime, it's the end of my life in Mongolia. A winding down time. A time to say,

GOOD-BYE MONGOLIA, HELLO ALICE OR NAADAM THE TORPEDOES, FULL SPEED ASTERN

It's July Fourth. Back in the US there would be fireworks, hotdogs and who-knows-what-else. Here, it's another day in a too short summer. The US Embassy is having a small party, but you've got to bring your own food. Budget cuts, they say. Do Americans have to bring their own food for the celebration at the Embassy in France? Yeah, right.

Well, it doesn't matter. I'm leaving. I've paid my $24, US cash only, for an exit visa. I got my plane ticket to China. It didn't cost me a *tugrik*.

Ulaanzul, the woman who took me on the *buz* adventure, runs a travel agency. In exchange for English lessons, she gets me tickets. She set up my train-ride to Korea. She also arranged for this last trip out of the country.

"I'll book you on *MIAT*," she says. "That way you won't have to deal with train smugglers."

"*MIAT*?" I ask. "Don't they fall out of the sky?"

"*MIAT* is very good," she says.

I tell her the story about the drunken pilot at the Puke House.

"I'm sure he doesn't fly internationally," she says. "All the international pilots have to pass a test."

I want to spend as much time in Mongolia as possible. The plane is the only way. The only other airline that flies to Beijing is Air China. They have an even worse reputation.

"OK," I tell her, "book the flight." I give her the dates.

"Great!" she says. "You'll be around for *Naadam*, the most important holiday in Mongolia. The stadium show will be pretty special this year."

"This isn't another one of those visit-relatives-and-eat days, is it?" I ask. "I don't think I could take another one."

"Oh no," she answers, "this one celebrates the three manly sports."

"Booze, sex, and brawling?" I ask.

"Mykel," she says, "this is Mongolia..."

I don't answer.

"Wrestling, horseracing and archery," she continues. "You've been here long enough to know that."

"I haven't been here long enough to know anything," I say, succumbing to momentary maudlinism. "You got any connections to get me into the festivities?"

She shakes her head. "Sorry," she says, "things are tight this year. They're charging foreigners $12 to get in."

"Twelve dollars?" I say, "How much is it for natives?"

"A hundred *tugrik*," she replies.

"That's twenty cents!" I say, "Don't you think that's a little unfair."

She shakes her head again. "Foreigners can afford it," she says. "We can't."

I have to agree with her. That's the reality of the situation. Kind of like affirmative action, first it looks unfair, but if you get behind it...I don't know. I don't know anything except that the best year of my life is coming to a close. I try to avoid the depression, the clichéd leaving feelings. But I can't.

The year passed like a dream. It's almost over. The dream, dreamed out. The couple days in China mean nothing. For me, it's good-bye Mongolia, hello New York.

I'll be going from the land where nothing is like anywhere else to the land that decides what anywhere else is. I'll be going from a place where my students ask, "What's McDonald's?" to one that IS McDonald's. I'll be going from a place where they'll kill a sheep in your honor to one where I might be killed for someone else's honor. I'll be leaving the greatest people on earth, the most pristine land in the world, a place where every day is NOTHING like the day before. And going back to...what?

Only a year. I still haven't been to Hovd, that far away mystery city in the East. I haven't killed a sheep myself, or had horizontal sex with a Mongol. And I haven't seen the navy. The ultimate irony, visiting the navy in a land-locked country, that dream smashed by two girls more interested in discos than navies.

My depression feeds on itself and I begin to treat people unpleasantly. My humor turns sardonic, cynical. Every cloud becomes a hurricane. I'm getting grouchy.

◎ ◎ ◎

Naadam comes sooner than I want. I'm meeting my friends at nine at Sukhbataar Square, where the festivities start. First there's an assembly, then a parade to the sports grounds outside of town.

On July 11, I'm at Sukhbataar Square by 9AM. The schedule in the English language paper says "assembly at 10AM." Al, James, Hannah and Sebastian said they'd meet me at 9:30. Right now there are very few people in the square. Among them are the usual photographers taking pictures of the country folk in front of the equestrian statue. A man and woman, in freshly cleaned *deels*, pose in front of Sukhbataar himself. The man hooks his thumbs under his yellow sash and the woman stands stiff, her arms at her sides.

There are a few foreign tourists, cameras strapped around their necks, jabbering away in German, French, Japanese. Occasionally, I hear some dialect of English.

Yesterday, when I went through the square, a large flatbed truck was parked at the north end, in front of the parliament building. Today there's a stage, about five feet off the ground. On either end of the stage are two large loudspeakers. There's a microphone on a stand in the center.

Figuring that's where things are going to happen, I station myself directly in front. At exactly ten o'clock, things begin. Yeah, right. At ten thirty the Brits show up. At eleven, a John Phillips Sousa march blasts from the stage speakers: BE KIND TO YOUR FINE FEATHERED FRIENDS...

From behind us comes the clomping of hooves on cement, two double rows of men on horses. One row enters the square from the east, the other from the west. They turn on opposite corners, going up either side toward the stage.

The riders are dressed in chainmail over heavy leather. Each wears a leather helmet. They maneuver the horses with one hand and hold a long bow in the other. The four lead horsemen, young men with very stern faces, carry bows made out of entire buck antlers, as long as I am tall. Slung over their backs are quivers full of arrows.

The two rows join in the back of the stage. Following the horses comes the infantry. The music plays on. An occasional crackle or pop only gives authenticity to the recording — obviously taken from a real vinyl record. There's nothing digital about Mongolia.

While our backs are turned to the stage we hear the shuffle of people climbing up to it. When we turn back, we see about a dozen men and half that many women crowded together. Some wear *deels*, some business suits. All of them wear medals. A late middle-aged man wears his on a sash, strung from one shoulder like Miss America. Most are pinned directly to the front lapel. A frail old man stands right behind the microphone. His shoulder droops under the weight of the metal on his chest. He starts to speak, the first of many.

During the third or fourth speech, I feel a tap on my shoulder. It's Sebastian. Al is behind him. Both are grinning like a Gobi mountain lion who just ate a tourist.

"James and Hannah are going to meet us at the stadium," says Sebastian.

"Sorry we're late," he continues, "you should've come with us last night. Al and I picked these girls up at The Motorrock and brought them home. Woweeee! That's why we're so late."

"Great," I say to him, "I hope you caught something."

He laughs.

About this time, the speeches finish and the politicians leave the stage. The march music starts again, as does the thump of horses and foot soldiers. They parade out in two directions and converge on the street outside the square. From here begins the long march to the fairgrounds.

"Let's follow them," says Al, "it'll be fun hiking to the stadium."

"It's miles to the fairgrounds," I whine. "I'm not going to follow horses. These are clean shoes!"

"OK," he says, with more than a little disgust, "we'll take the bus."

As usual, we have to squeeze on to a bus. Not as usual, it's filled with white people. This is tourist season in Mongolia. Here they are, these yahoos who want to brag about how they've seen it all. Two days in Outer Mongolia. Something to tell the grandkids. Yessireebob. You should see the natives in their little costumes with their turned-up shoes. And those round tents they live in. Boy, you ain't seen nothing like it. A real adventure in a nice stopping off place between Beijing and Moscow. I want to kill them.

Sebastian and I find ourselves crushed together near the door. Sitting on the seat we're crushed into are a couple who would look more at home playing golf in Century Village than riding a bus in *Ulaanbaatar*.

The woman wears one of those white Gilligan hats. She's about 65, with a head of thick gray hair. Bright pink flowers impregnate a regular pattern on her white dress. Next to her sits a man, slightly older, with a tight face around a large angular nose. They both smile in a way that makes me wonder if their twin facelifts were pulled too tight. After Sebastian and I bang into the seat in front of them, the woman talks to us.

"Hello," she says in an annoying sing-songy voice that makes me want to sic the wolves on her.

I nod.

"Do you speak English?" she asks.

"Yeah," I tell her, "dat's my job. I tawk English and den get paid faw it."

"Oh," she answers, "you're an English teacher! How wonderful! My husband and I are English teachers."

The man nods, broadening his smile.

"We've been teaching in Mongolia for two whole months." She continues, "How long have you been here?"

"I been here a year," I tell her, "and dat ain't long enough."

"Oh my," she says, "You really must like it here. We find it...interesting. Don't we, Sam?"

The man nods again.

"We're with the Church of Jesus," says the woman.

"This is my stop," I say.

"Aren't you going to the *Naadam* festivities?" she asks, "All those children riding horses? It's priceless."

"Nope," I say as the bus pulls to a halt, "We gotta get out here."

When the doors open I grab Sebastian by the collar and pull him out of the bus. Al jumps out behind us.

"It's a long way to the stadium," says Al. "Why'd you leave that bus?"

"They're Christians!" I say.

He shakes his head.

It's a mile walk over muddy hills to the fairground. The sky is clear overhead, but some ominous-looking clouds are gathering in the North.

We start walking. Once over a few rolling hills, the land becomes less green. Dust fills the air. The ground is hard clay. A few Mongols on horseback pass us as we walk.

A little further on we see some men playing cards, using a large rock as a table. A little boy on horseback is dressed in a racing costume. His blue silk shirt and pants flap in the wind has he rides proudly back and forth between the tents. His horse, too, is specially groomed, dressed with a silk ribbon hanging on its forehead.

There are some old cars, trucks, laundry hanging on tent strings. These are not *gers*, but army tents or thrown together scraps of cloth. Ulanzuul told me that people from the countryside set them up for the three days of *Naadam*. For most, this is a trip to the big city. *Ulaanbaatar*, where they have buildings made out of concrete, where the shops sell jewelry, candy, flashlights and American cigarettes. The whole family comes for this, mom, dad, all ten sisters and brothers.

A few campfires cook lamb on wooden spits. The sound of a long song rises over the crackling wood. Empty vodka bottles litter the area. A guy in his early twenties, dressed in a dirty black *deel*, with a dirtier face, calls out to us as we pass his tent.

"Hello! Hello!" he says. "You English?"

"Yes we are," says Sebastian.

"I'm not," I say. "I'm American."

"English, American, same thing," he says. "Come drink with us."

He waves us to join him around a table set up in front of his tent. Some people peek out from inside.

"They my family," he says, gesturing to them.

A woman about my age smiles at us. I figure she's the grandmother. The gaps between her teeth don't detract from her generous beauty. There's also a very pretty young woman, probably his wife, and four young children, two of each gender.

"Hello, hello, hello, hello," say the children one at a time.

The wife brings some bread from inside the tent and sets it on the table for us. The man brings a bottle of vodka and pours a glassful. He hands it to me first.

This is Mongolia, right here in front of me. People doing things for me for no reason. People sharing because its fun to share. A toast to me because I'm different from him. Where else in the world...? I'm afraid I'm going to cry. Instead, I drink. Quickly.

"You drink like Mongol," says the man putting his hand on my shoulder.

"So I've been told," I answer, smiling.

He refills our glasses. We offer some firewater to the gods and down the rest. Then another. Sebastian stands up.

"*Bayerlalaa*," he says for all of us.

I stand too, slightly wobbly. I look at this man, his *deel*, his tent, the wife and kids. I realize this will be the last time I'm ever in a situation like this. I walk up to him and face him. Our noses are just a few inches away. I grab both his shoulders. I feel like kissing him on the mouth. Hugging him to my breast. Crying "hold me and never let me go." But I don't do any of that.

"Thank you," I whisper, "thank you very much."

"Mykel, you're losing it!" says Sebastian, grabbing me by the shoulder. "Let's go."

"*Bayartai*!" I shout, waving as Sebastian pulls me by the sleeve toward the arena.

When we come to a large open field we pass a lot of men in uniform, or rather part uniform. All of them are in various stages of getting dressed. There's a man putting on his uniform top over a yellow-stained t-shirt. Another tries to suck in his stomach enough to button his pants. Still another is almost dressed.

He's just fixing a green hat to precisely the right tilt. As far as I can see in any direction, there are soldiers, or police, or something else putting on a uniform.

"Look," I say, pointing to our left. "There's James and Hannah."

"And behind them," says Al, "a tank."

Sure enough. It's made of metal, with a big fat gun poking through the front. It's got caterpillar treads, too. Only it's closer to station wagon size than tank size.

"It's probably the tank," I say.

We call to our friends and join up with them, walking the last hundred yards together.

Just outside the stadium, the grounds are crowded with tourists. Besides them, peddlers, hucksters and showmen are everywhere. It's like a carnival. Throw the hoop over the stick. Use a BB to knock out a bottle cap (one BB, used again and again). Fresh grilled lamb on a stick. They're even selling bottled water for the tourists. Nobody in Mongolia drinks bottled water. The local stuff is cleaner than the bottles. But even the Mongols have learned there's one born every minute.

We pass a long strip of grass roped off to form the archery pit. Half a dozen women in new *deels* shoot at targets about ten yards away. The set-up is different from what it would be in the West. The targets lie on the ground. In order to hit them, the archers have to shoot the arrows into the air. They come down on the bullseye, rather than hit it directly.

A chunky woman with a worn country face carefully places the arrow against the bowstring. She pulls back, aiming at a spot halfway between the sun and the horizon. She lets go.

TWINNNNNG! Right through the redspot.

"Women?" I say "I thought this was supposed to be a manly sport."

"Maybe they're manly women," answers Sebastian.

They sure are good.

We continue our walk to the stadium. I hear a familiar masculine voice behind me.

"Mykel-*baksh*! Mykel-*baksh*!" says the voice.

All of us turn. It's Bishbataar, the first time Sebastian and I have seen him since he threatened to call the Mongolian mafia on us. I guess he and Al have been palsy walsy, but we've avoided him. Now, here he is, all smiley and wavy, acting like we're best friends.

"Mykel," whispers Al, "be nice."

By now the alcohol has worn off and I'm back to my old grouchiness. Besides, the last person in the world I'd want to be nice to is Bishbataar.

"What the fuck..." I start, but am quickly silenced by a hard kick to the back of the knee. I nearly collapse.

"Stop it!" says Al. "You're leaving. I might have him as a student. I can't function if he's the enemy."

"Besides," says Sebastian, "we might need to use his car after you're gone."

We walk over to the guy and exchange pleasantries. He introduces us to a family of tall blondes.

"Please to meet you," says the man. His camera swings from his neck as he leans forward to shake hands.

"Bishy here told us about studying English. It must be an adventure for an American to live here."

"It sure is," I say. "Bishy?"

"They're tourists from Sweden," says Bishbataar. "I'm taking them for a ride."

"I bet you are," I answer, then flinch in fear of the kick that doesn't come.

"I want to go inside," says Al.

"Me too!" says Sebastian.

"Yo," I say, "it's gonna cost us twelve dollars each. We've already seen the parade. It's all out here on the field. Soldiers, a machine gun, even the tank, for God's sake. What else do you want?"

"Look over there on the grass," says Al, pointing to an old man and a boy. Both wear gray button-down shirts and jeans. They sit behind a large leather pouch. People are lined up in front.

"I bet he's selling tickets," Al continues.

"He's selling Mongol tickets," I say. "You think we could pass? You smear on lambfat. I'll drink a bottle of vodka. Hannah will squat and pop half a dozen sexy Oriental kids. That'll convince them."

"Let's try," says James. "The worst that can happen is they say no. They're not going to chain us to horses and drag us through the mud."

"This is Mongolia," I say. "Anything can happen."

I finally agree to check out the old guy. We bid farewell to Bishbataar and head toward the ticket sellers. Ticket scalpers would be more exact.

"*En jamar enteve*?" I ask.

"Guran *zuu*," he says.

"That's three hundred *tugriks*!" I whine, "triple the price."

"Mykel," says James, "that's sixty cents."

"Okay," I say, opening my wallet and counting out the bills.

Sebastian collects the money from each of us. We take the tickets and head for the nearest gate. I hold mine up to the sun, looking through it.

"I bet its counterfeit," I tell him.

"What's wrong with you?" says Sebastian. "These last couple weeks you've been such a whiner. You trying to make us glad you're leaving?"

That shuts me up.

There's a line at the gate. We're the only occidentals in it. The ticket taker is a stocky, heavily bearded man. He wears a shiny black *deel* and a wide-rimmed black hat. He takes each ticket and carefully looks at it before tearing it in half. It's like going through customs. There's no way we can pull this off, but here we are, and I've been shut up.

As we approach the door I begin to sweat. My palms feel clammy. It's my last week here. I don't want to be arrested for impersonating a Mongolian. I don't want to end up in chains, in the middle of a desert, having birds peck at my liver, while I'm raped by hordes of wrestlers with Gobi sand in the KY. KY? They don't have KY in Mongolia.

"Calm down, Mykel," says Al. "You look like we're robbing a bank. They can only turn us away and we lose sixty cents. They're not going to arrest us."

"This is Mongolia!" I tell him.

The ticket taker looms over us. His hard face breaks into a smile, widening to show double tin teeth right in the Bugs Bunny slot. As he collects our tickets he looks squarely at us, tears the tickets in half and hands the halves to me.

"I say you welcome," he says.

In we walk, taking our places along the benches that make up the stadium bleachers. Across the field from us is the shaded area of the arena. There's a grandstand with VIPs on it. Around the grandstand are a lot of white faces. The $12 seats. There's Bishbataar and his Swedes sharing some food out of a plastic bag.

Now I get it. Race doesn't matter. What matters is only if you're a sucker or not. I wonder how much Bishbataar charged them for their seats.

March music signals the start of activities. A door opens to our right. The costumed *Chinggis Khan* horse riders enter and circle the field. Then come the costumed foot soldiers. Then the modern day military, with infantry and jeeps. Then comes the airforce, in khaki jumpsuits, wearing Red Baron hats and goggles. What a display of military might!

Then I see the uniforms. Black, with white kerchiefs and hats. Tight little pants with flares on the bottom. It's the Navy! Yes! The Mongolian Navy that I missed in Hovsgul. Here they are. All ten of them. The whole fleet. Here together. Yes! Yes! Yes! I've seen the Mongolian Navy.

"Ahoy mates!" I stand and shout, "Full speed ahead! I'm glad somebody is going ahead. I'm going back!"

Sebastian tugs at my arm.

"Take it easy, Mykel," he says. "It isn't nice to make fun of these people."

"Make fun?" I shout. "Who's making fun? It's the fucking Mongolian Navy. I've seen the Navy. My life is complete. I can really die now — or go back to New York."

Sebastian shakes his head like you might if you saw a man beating his dog.

The arrival of the tank diverts our attention. It joins in the parade, circling the arena. Following that is another group of men in uniform. As more and more of the parade enters the arena, more and more spectators enter our tiny section of the stadium. There is no place for the newcomers to sit, so they don't. They just stand where they are, in front of us. I stand on the bench to look over them. The people behind me stand to look over me.

The military has cleared the field. Now come the girls — tall ones, short ones, thin ones, plump ones. They all wear orange t-shirts with pleated blue dresses. Some of them carry batons. Some carry pompoms.

They arrange themselves into nice orderly rows of blue and orange. Holding the formation, they stand at attention until the march music ends — and the disco begins. It's not "The Skatman," but it is Eurodisco.

As the music plays, the girls dance. First one leg up, then the other. Batons up, pompoms down. Pompoms up, batons down. Everything in perfect synch, working without a hitch. Not very Mongolian.

A whirring comes from above.

"Over there," says Sebastian, pointing to the right. A helicopter approaches, flying low over the stadium wall.

"Over there," says Al, pointing to the left. Another helicopter approaches from that direction.

I say nothing as a third helicopter comes from directly in front of us. Hoping that these are not *MIAT* domestic flights, I watch them converge overhead. When they reach the center of the stadium, they hover just a few dozen yards away from each other. Suddenly the door on the right helicopter opens. A man in a yellow jumpsuit appears. He looks down from the great height and jumps. A parachute pulls out from his back. Below, hanging from his foot is a Mongolian flag.

The girls shift on the stadium floor. Like a drop of penicillin in a bacterial petri dish, the crowd makes a wide circle just under the drifting man. A sudden wind gust shifts him. The circle shifts too, making space for the sky diver. Lifting one leg up, he plucks the flag from his cuff just before he lands. Fffft! Right in the middle. The flag now in his hand, he runs to the grandstand. There he presents it to a man in a black business suit with lots of medals on his chest. There's brief applause. Then, the doors open on the other two helicopters. Two parachutists this time, one in a bright blue jumpsuit, the other in red. They jump simultaneously.

There's chaos on the field below. Costumed girls with their pompoms run back and forth, shifting, trying to avoid both falling men, yet unsure of where they'll land.

The chutes open. This time attached to their legs is *Chinggis Khan*. A picture of the great one himself, blue on a yellow flag.

Down they drift. The wind catches the blue man. It pulls his chute up and back, like God jerked on a string. His body shakes. He rises, directly toward the helicopter's spinning blades.

The girls on the ground scream. The audience gasps. Before he can be diced by the propeller, the wind lets him loose. The propeller pushes him down, and he drifts gently toward the field again.

Meanwhile, the first jumper is halfway to earth. He's heading directly for the crowd of cheerleaders. Waving wildly, it looks as if he's shouting a warning, but its impossible to hear. A woman in the crowd points up. Others do the same. Screams comes from the frightened girls as they back up. Pushing and squeezing one another, they force themselves to the arena periphery. A circle of field clears itself.

Along the sides, scores of Mongolian cheerleaders press against each other, batons and pompoms held high to make more room. A teenage girl, her face contorted in pain, screams as the crowd presses her, face first, into the wall in front of us. There's another scream. And another. The girls crush against the sides of the stadium.

The two chutists reach land, missing the crowd squeezed to the perimeter. Immediately the crowd releases, spreading out throughout the arena floor, breathing freely.

The jumpers squeeze through to present their flags to the officials. The girls arrange themselves as if nothing happened.

A few more speeches, then half-naked men come out on the field to begin the wrestling.

"I can't sit through this again," I tell my friends, "two wrestling stories are enough."

"OK," says Al, "we'll stay for a bit, then meet you at the horse racing."

I leave the stadium and wander off to the racing area. There is a large open area near the tents. Right now, it's more like a mutant picnic. White tourists have come and spread beach towels on the dirt. Lazing in the disappearing sun, they've brought bread, kiosk cheese, and vodka.

Around them prance Mongols on horses. There are even a few camels. Luxury ships of the desert, sailed into town for the big festival. I'm used to horses and even goats in the city, but camels? God, do I love Mongolia!

The horses and camels roam among the picnickers. More serious race lovers crowd toward the sidelines. These are the families of the racers. Most of the tourists don't bother.

There is no track. The horses race from somewhere, over some hills, and end up at a specific spot. Family, friends, and spectators, all with their horses, wait on the sidelines.

I am on foot behind the mostly unmounted audience. They stand with their horses waiting for junior to finish the big race. Besides horses, there are camels, wagons, Russian jeeps, everything. I cram my way through the metal and hairy animal flesh to get toward the front. Angry-sounding Mongolian epithets follow me as I push my way through.

I've made it. Right to the front. A perfect view of dirt. That's it. Just a big patch of dirt between two sides of people on animals.

Some dust in the distance. Here they come. A few horses run in the dirt about half a mile away. They tell me the riders are all children, none older than ten. They've grown up in the countryside and could ride before they could spit. They're all like that little boy we saw earlier, only they're farther away. I can't see a thing. It's a blur and over before I can pick the dust out of my nose. Not very manly — or exciting.

By this time the sky is an ominous black with jagged gray lines marking the cloud edges. The first few drops hit my cheeks. I push my way back toward the open field.

"Yo Mykel!" I hear from behind me.

It's my friends, finally showing up at the races. Actually, they've been there for awhile, having quickly had enough of the wrestling.

"This is boring," I tell Al. "I'm going. Besides, it looks like it's going to rain."

"You're right this time," says Al. "Once it starts, we'll never get on a bus."

A camel, annoyed at the crowd, the drizzle and the tourists, decides to take matters into his own hooves. The animal lowers its head like a bull. The driver, a teenager in a dusty black *deel*, pulls back on the reins. They're attached to a piece of wood that runs through the animal's nose. The animal is not pleased by the pulling.

It brings its neck up sharply, as if it wants to strike the rider with the back of its head. The young man loses his balance and nearly falls to the ground. Then the camel paws the ground and runs directly into the foreign tourists picnicking on the field.

They spring to their feet as camel hooves land on their beach towels. Baskets of fruit and bottles of vodka are strewn forward and backward as the driver wrestles with the angry beast. A dark-haired man with a pencil-thin mustache picks up his little girl and pulls his wife to her feet.

"Mon dieu!" screams the man, as he and his family run toward the Mongol tents, leaving behind what might be the only wine bottle on the field.

Then the rain starts in earnest. The skies open up. God pukes his bad *hoosher* on the crowd below. The rampaging camel has never seen rain like this. It freezes. It tries to shake like a wet dog. The poor rider nearly breaks a leg as he, again, just barely holds on to the smelly brown animal.

We don't stand and watch the conclusion. We're off toward the buses with a thousand other tourists also running for cover.

At the busstop, hundreds of bedraggled people stand in the downpour. The puddles gradually rise around us. The crowd grows as does the anger of the people in it. As a bus nears, it slows. The driver peers through the front window at the teaming masses. His eyes widen in fear. Blam! It speeds up and passes us, sloshing the entire crowd in its wake.

Another bus slowly approaches. This one stops a hundred feet before the busstop. The crowd shifts. People push each other to reach the bus. The doors open. The crowd surges forward. Those in the bus who want to get out, can't. There's no way they can fight the people forcing their way inside. The conductor tries to get some order among the ever-wetter passengers. It's hopeless.

Sebastian makes it to the first step of the bus. I'm right behind him. He forces his way in. The doors shut. I'm on the outside. I kick at the bus as it pulls away.

Twenty wet minutes pass. Another bus comes and I squeeze in with Al, Hannah, James and another two score of muddy angry passengers. I get home soaked and filthy and mad.

It's time to take a bath. There is no water.

◎ ◎ ◎

So ends my last adventure in Mongolia. A fizzle of dirt, a mud bath, an ignoble ending to an amazing year. Ah well, at least I've seen the navy.

My friends have promised to meet me when I leave for Beijing. We'll have a farewell contingent to the airport. Then, it's really good bye.

◎ ◎ ◎

I'm in my apartment waiting for the entourage. Packed, I'm leaving more than

I'm taking. Let the vultures pick through it all. I don't need it.

I asked everyone to meet me at 8. I have to leave at 10. That means they can't be more than two hours late. I bet they'll never get here in time. I'm wrong. They're all here by nine o'clock. Al, Sebastian, Sainamdrar, James, Sarah and Odortuya, the teacher who first met me in Sumiya's office — back when this adventure began.

More than that, there's even Dorj, the gate keeper from the US embassy. He's brought me a bottle of *Chinggis Khan* Vodka as a going away present. I think I'm going to cry.

No time for that, we're off to the Flower, the nearby hotel with a working phone. Our safari sets off down the hill. Each person carries a piece of luggage. Despite what I gave away, I have plenty more than I came with: a jar of Gobi sand, a blue *hatakh*, books, a camel hair sweater, two snuff bottles, maps, and other reminders of the greatest year of my life. I'm going to have to pay a fortune in overweight charges.

At the hotel, the desk clerk calls a cab. It'll be the first real cab I've taken here. And my last. The clerk must have told them how many of us there are, because the cab is a van. We pile in the luggage, then pile ourselves on top of it. Sainamdrar says something to the driver, and we're off.

We arrive at the airport four hours early. Leaving the taxi, we head into a large white building, still under construction.

There are two entrances to the building. One is through a freshly painted white door. Over that door, in very permanent-looking paint is INTERNATIONAL FLIGHTS, with Mongolian cyrillic underneath. At the other end of the building is an unpainted door with a Mongolian sign and DOMESTIC written in what looks like magic marker.

Just inside the door, a woman sells sandwiches: lettuce, tomato and lamb-meat on a hard roll, $2 each, payable in dollars only. Al treats us all. That's the least he can do after Sainamdrar moved in with him, completely ditching my more sincere and mature love overtures.

We take our sandwiches inside to the main waiting room. I check my two giant bags at the counter. Nobody cares about the weight. Besides us, the only other person in the room is a young blonde woman. Thin, with a classically pretty-though-wholesome face, I stare at her as we enter.

"Mykel," whispers Sebastian, "she's white!"

"I know," I whisper back, "sometimes you just lower your standards."

During our mindless bantering and good-time recalling, my gaze keeps returning to the young woman. She's so engrossed in a book that she doesn't notice.

"Go talk to her, Mykel," says Al. "Go on. You're too shy."

"I don't know what to say to white people anymore," I tell him. "This is all new to me."

"Just go," he says, "you'll think of something."

So, in front of my own private audience, I walk around the chairs and stand in front of the girl.

"Excuse me," I say, "are you going to Beijing?"

A stupid question. Planes leaving from here don't go anywhere else. Sainamdrar giggles. The girl pretends it's a perfectly normal thing to ask.

"Yes," she answers.

"Oh good," I say, "me too. I don't know where I'll be staying though. I have no idea about hotels in China."

"Well," answers the blonde, looking better every minute, "I'm meeting my sister in Beijing and we're staying in this cheap place recommended in the Lonely Planet guide."

"Wow," I say, "would you mind if I came along? I wouldn't know what to do otherwise."

"Sure," she answers, "I'm sure there'll be room."

"My name's Mykel," I tell her.

"I'm Alice," she says.

By this time, the audience noise is becoming unbearable. I have to acknowledge them.

"I've been in Mongolia for a year," I tell her. "I'm going back home today. These are my friends who've come to say goodbye. Why don't you join us?"

Alice walks over to the group. We talk about *Naadam*, Mongolian weather, life as a teacher, the usual.

She's been a teacher here for two years, with the Peace Corps. Lately, she's been training other teachers based on her experience in the countryside. She's traveled more than I have.

With her addition, the farewell becomes easier. I can lighten up a bit. Before, it had been a good bye trip. Now there's something to look forward to. A stay in China with a pretty girl who might even be smart and fun to talk to. I begin to fantasize about a quickie on the Great Wall. My spirits lighten.

"And then he said, it doesn't matter how many Mongolians it takes to change a lightbulb. The new one won't work either."

There's laughter. James was speaking and it brings me back to the conversation.

"You with us there, Mykel?" he says. "You look like you're already back in New York."

"Sorry," I answer, "I was just daydreaming."

"Well you better wake up," says Sebastian. "They just opened the airport tax office. You can go in now." He points to a little alcove.

Not only do you have to buy an exit visa to leave Mongolia, but you have to pay an extra eight dollars to use the plane. I grab my bag and head for the tax office, eight dollars in hand.

"Sorry, no good. Mongolian money only," says the woman. "New law. We only take Mongolian money."

"But I've spent all my Mongolian money," I tell her, "and your sign says eight DOLLARS. Mongolian money isn't dollars."

"That old sign," she says. Then she points to a little booth a few steps away; "There is bank."

At the CHANGE booth I pull out my eight dollars. "I need eight dollars worth of *tugriks*," I tell the young woman in the booth.

"It cost nine dollars," she says.

Suddenly, I laugh. Hard. I haven't laughed so hard since the Gobi madness. Like the beautiful Mongols sharing vodka and bread at the *Naadam* tent, this too is Mongolia. This is the madness I'll miss. This is the unpredictable frustration and illogic that I've come to love in Mongolia. Eight dollars worth of *tugrik* costs nine dollars. Yes! Yes! Yes!

"You ok Mykel?" asks Alice when I finally catch my breath.

"Yes," I tell her, "I'm sorry about that. It was just so...so Mongolian, I couldn't help myself."

Leaving my friends is not as hard as I thought. There are hugs, pecks on the cheeks, promises to write, and that's it. I'm surprised I'm not crying.

Once we're through the gate, I have Alice to myself. We stop for a bite to eat at the canteen/souvenir shop. I pick up a few carved camels for my friends back in New York. Alice turns out to be funny, bright, with enough sense of humor to triple sexiness that was already pretty high by the time we walked through the gate.

On the plane I offer Alice the window seat. I'm glad when she doesn't take it. Suddenly, I feel as if life is just ordinary. It's an ordinary Boeing 727, with ordinary stewardesses in ordinary stewardess costumes. There are no extra rattles or air drafts. The doors look solid. The wings seem to have a good grip on the plane body. The peanuts and coffee taste like peanuts and coffee on real planes from real countries. Mongolia is behind me.

After takeoff, I watch the land pass under us. We're over a rolling brown landscape, cracked earth, from horizon to horizon. My lungs cramp. My chest grows very heavy. The back of my throat tightens. And I cry.

It's not an anguished cry, with painful gushing sobs. It's a small quiet cry. A few tears edge over the lids. A drop, maybe two or three, run down my cheek. Either Alice doesn't notice or she's tactful enough to ignore it.

◎ ◎ ◎

Alice's sister meets her at the Beijing Airport. Alice introduces me as a "friend from Mongolia." Her sister is a slightly older, slightly larger, copy of her. Blonde, she's got a more fully-developed build than her sibling.

The girls help me with my massive baggage, dragging it out to a taxi. After price-bargaining and map-looking, we're off.

We arrive at the hotel tired and worn out. Behind the counter is an attractive young Chinese guy. Completely ignoring me, he speaks to Alice.

"Are you American?" he asks.

"Yes, we are." says Alice. "We have a reservation for two, but we have another one."

The guy glances at me, smiles politely and says, "Sorry, single room all fill up. All fill up."

I think about having to get a taxi and go back to that Mongolian hotel. I think about being tired, hot. I think about leaving these two beautiful girls behind while I eat Beijing-style *buz*, alone. I'm just about ready to burst into tears in earnest.

"Sorry, sorry," says the man. "You no want dorm?"

"I can't stay in a dorm," I tell the girls. "I have my computer with me."

"How many people are there in a dorm room?" asks Alice.

"Only four. Only four," says the desk man. "Now, no four. It only you." He looks at me. "Only you and two girls. That all."

Alice looks at me and shrugs. "Well, it'll be just you, my sister and I in a room. I don't mind if you don't mind."

"No," I say, "I don't mind at all."

"Yes!" I think. "Yes!"

EPILOGUE

Nothing happened in China. At least nothing sexual. I climbed the capital-G capital-W Great Wall with the two girls. The greater wall was never mounted. Still, they were fine partners during my last days in Asia.

The plane ride back to New York is a complete blank. I know I had to transfer twice in Canada. I know I went through customs, both US and Canadian, in Vancouver. The rest, no matter how hard I concentrate, was nothing.

Returning to New York, however, is not a blank. It is hell. I walk through the city, looking at the buildings, the people, the streets. It's not the city I left.

A new mayor who'd fit better in Des Moines is destroying this place. The peep show heaven of Times Square is now Disneyland, with a Disney Theater and a little Warner Brothers Store. Welcome to New York.

The former Lower East Side drug and punk scumpit is now filled with expensive restaurants, sushi bars and — God-help-me — K-mart! Welcome to New York.

On every corner is a *Staples, MacDonalds or Barnes* and *Nobles*. There are enough *Starbucks Coffee Houses* to gag on a different bad flavor seven days a week. Welcome to New York.

Even the people look bad. Too many white people. Too many neckties and serious looks. It's all so sterile. A mother pushes a stroller in front of her, gazing down at the curly-haired blond angel. It makes me retch.

The Yankees have traded their best pitcher and now struggle for third place. Welcome to New York. There's been a campaign against green places. The new mayor is changing public gardens into housing projects for rich people. Welcome to New York.

Things work here. The subway runs regularly. The lights turn on when I flip the switch. People enter buses one-by-one, never touching one another. Traffic lights turn from red to yellow to green — and back again.

My friends? What friends? I never see my new neighbors. The others are workers, stuck in day jobs that leave them too dead to do anything but watch television during the weekends.

My parents are both sick. My father had a stroke. My mother has alzheimer's. My sister hates me because I didn't come home earlier. My girlfriend, Jean, left me because of my sex adventure at The Hollywood. One transgression in a year and I'm out the door.

I'm alone and depressed in a sterile, increasingly ordinary place.

Here I sit typing these last words, a blue *hatakh* draped over the computer. A just-emptied glass of *Chinggis Khan* vodka reflects the light from my single apartment window.

I've been to Mongolia. But I've still got another thirty years — or at least twenty — to go. I can't just sit around and watch New York become America, or my friends become serious adults.

Maybe I'll go to Africa. Hannah and James worked in Senegal. It sounds like an interesting place: sand and seafood. I'll go anywhere free of McDonalds and Walt Disney.

No place will be as ferociously awesome and wonderfully awful as Mongolia. But even a daughter is better than nothing.

GLOSSARY

[The following are mostly Mongolian words and phrases used in this book. All spelling is idiosyncratic to the author.]

Amtatai	That was delicious!
Angli	English.
Anglikhun	Englishman or English woman.
Amerikhun	American.
Aimag	A political division of Mongolia, roughly equivalent to a state in the U.S.
Airag	Fermented mare's milk; next to vodka, the most popular drink in Mongolia.
Baksh, Bakshaa	Teacher or professor. *Baksh* is used as a suffix, added to the first name as a sign of respect. For example, *Mykel-baksh* is something like "Professor Mykel." *Bakshaa* is used by itself, when addressing or calling to a professor or teacher without using a proper name.
Bakhgui	No/not/none.
Bayerlalaa	Thank you.
Bayartai	Good bye.
Bid	I/Me.
Bish	No/not/without, also used as an expression of disbelief, similar to the English, "Aw, come on!"

Buz	A Mongolian dumpling, usually steamed, filled with lamb.
Chinggis Khan	You know him as "Genghis Khan." He's the most famous Mongol of all time. The Washington Post named him "man of the millennium." He's a source of pride to the Mongols.
Chyoo	"Giddyup," said to horses while striking them in the rump.
Coffee King	Served in restaurants or sold in little packets from kiosks. This is what passes for coffee in Mongolia. Mostly sugar and dried milk, you get 10% coffee, if you're lucky.
Deel	The traditional Mongolian dress. Kind of like a Kimono, it's heavier and worn by both men and women.
En jamar enteve	"How much is it?"
Ger	A large round white tent-like structure. Mongolians have lived in these for thousands of years. Most still do.
Guansa	A *ger* or wagon along a well-traveled path through the countryside. Its owner sells simple meals to travelers.

Hatakh	A long strip of blue silk. It is a Mongolian symbol of welcome, and is part of most holiday celebrations.
Hiid	Mongolian Buddhist temple.
Hoosher	A deep-fried meat patty.
Inner Mongolia	Currently, an "autonomous" province of China. The people there speak an older form of Mongolian with fewer borrowings than those in Outer Mongolia. Often, the citizens of Inner Mongolia are looked upon as hicks by their Outer siblings.
Khaana	Where?
Khinbe	Who is it?
MIAT	Mongolian International Air Transportation, the national airline of Mongolia.
Naadam	The summer celebration of the "three manly sports:" horse racing, archery and wrestling.
(Bid) Olgakhgui	(I) don't understand.
Onoo	Now.
Ovoo	A large pile of rocks, often with animal heads and crutches, topped by a flag. It is a good-luck charm and a remnant of ancient Mongolian animism.

Outer Mongolia	Common western name for the actual country of Mongolia. Until 1990 it was The Mongolian People's Republic, a satellite of Russia.
Sain bain yy	Traditional Mongolian greeting, sort of like "how's it going?"
Shess	Urine, an important part of traditional Mongolian medicine.
Sukhbaatar	The hero of the Mongolian revolution and next to Chinngis Khan, the most important man in Mongolian history. His name means "Axe Hero."
Tsagansar	The Mongolian New Year celebration. The name means "White Month." It starts the first day of the lunar new year.
Tsak	"Hour" or "o'clock."
Tsai	Mongolian tea, usually made in a large pot with water, milk, salt, and just a hint of Russian tea.
Tugrik	The official currency of Mongolia. When I first arrived about 400 tugrik equalled a dollar. By the time I left, it was 600.
UB	A foreigner term referring to *Ulaanbaatar*. Mongols never use it.

Uchlarai	Excuse me.
Ulaanbaatar	The capital city of Mongolia. With about 600,000 people, it's more than three times the size of Darkhan, the number two city. It's name means Red (Ulaan) Hero (Baatar). Baatar (or Bataar, depending on the transcription) is a common part of boys' names.
Urgaa	A knotted rope loop at the end of a long stick. It's used by the Mongols to lasso cattle.
VSO	The Volunteer Service Organization. A British volunteer network, similar to the US Peace Corps.
Zhuulchin	The Mongolian national (government sponsored) tourist agency. Up until 1990, this was the only one.
Zogcox	Enough!
Zuu	Hundred.

ACKNOWLEDGEMENTS

This book is for my parents. I couldn't have written it without them. It's also for Alicia Campi, who made the trip possible, for Marlin and Rose at the US Embassy, who made a lot of people's lives a lot easier, and especially for the people of Mongolia, the greatest people on earth. (Except for Mongols from Erdinet, who are assholes.)

I want to thank Berry Myers, who collected my email messages from Mongolia. They provided the raw material for these chapters. Thanks also to Andrew Avery, Simon Asker, Namjil and Dr. Sumiya who helped in Mongolia both with this book and with my life.

In the US, Shirley LaMere, Julien Nitzberg, Elena Glasberg and Paul Harrington came to the rescue with the red pencil. Anna Jardin, Ben Foster and Caitlan have been helpful in getting this to press.

Then there's Maximum Rock'n'Roll, Transitions Abroad, Jersey Beat, and Batteries Not Included, who have previously published some of this material and let me reuse and rewrite it for inclusion here. Also Pressure Drop Press's Martin Sprouse led me in the right direction. There have been many others, all of whom I'll remember just after it's too late to change these notes.

Within the book, some names have been changed to legally protect my ass. All events recorded here are within the literary licensed parameters of truth.

MYKEL BOARD

ABOUT THE AUTHOR

Mykel Board has written dozens of freelance articles and seventeen novels under pseudonyms. *Maximum Rock'n'Roll* has been printing his column for more than 20 years. *I, A Me-ist,* a book of those columns, is scheduled for publication in 2005. His essays have appeared in several anthologies including *Bisexual Politics,* Hayworth Press 1995 and *Good Advice for Young People,* Last Gasp Press, 2005. This is Board's first book with his name on the front cover.